Hamish   September 91

In p...
our "Hi...

Love & Kisses

THE
TRAVELING
GOLFER

THE TRAVELING GOLFER

20 FIVE-STAR GOLFING VACATIONS

GLEN WAGGONER

DOUBLEDAY

NEW YORK
LONDON
TORONTO
SYDNEY
AUCKLAND

PUBLISHED BY DOUBLEDAY

a division of Bantam Doubleday Dell Publishing Group, Inc.
666 Fifth Avenue, New York, NY 10103

DOUBLEDAY and the portrayal of an anchor
with a dolphin are trademarks of Doubleday,
a division of Bantam Doubleday Dell
Publishing Group, Inc.

Library of Congress Cataloging-in-Publication Data

ISBN 0-385-26717-7

BOOK DESIGN BY SIGNET M DESIGN, INC.
ILLUSTRATIONS BY DEBORAH READE

ACKNOWLEDGMENTS

A lot of people helped me get this book into your hands, and they should be required to accept some responsibility for their actions.

I particularly want to thank my friend and adviser, Daniel Okrent, who directed me to the first tee; my editor, Joel Fishman, who could spot Job two a side in a patience playoff and still take his money; and my agent, Dominick Abel, who doesn't know a brassie from a bass fiddle but who does know everything else.

Traveling companions Lee Eisenberg and Michael Pollet dug divots with me in some unlikely places along the way, always with great good humor. (If you could see my swing, you'd laugh, too.) Teaching pro T. R. Reinman generously shared his astonishing knowledge of golf, course design, nineteenth holes, and Mexican food. Colleagues Kathleen Moloney and John Boghurst provided much practical guidance along with sustaining friendship. Editors Anita Leclerc at Esquire *and Tom Passavant at Diversion let me play at their clubs, while editor Robin McMillan at* Golf *gave me much-needed swing tips. Ace copy editor Estelle Laurence tried to keep my scorecard honest, while crack researchers Lynn Waggoner and Sabin Streeter pitched in with some heavy lifting at a critical moment. Buchan mon Ian Devenish gave me a guided tour of Dracula's Castle and a chance to observe firsthand how deeply and truly the Scots love their game.*

Finally, and foremost, golf widow Sharon McIntosh did everything but cure my slice: she read the manuscript with a sharp eye, provided essential moral and material support, contributed numerous astute observations, sublimated her own ideas of what a vacation should include, and laughed at all the right places, always with amazing grace.

CONTENTS

CONTENTS

CONTENTS

FOREWORD
"Have One-Iron—Will Travel"

T HAT'S THE MOTTO THAT OUGHT TO BE STEN-
ciled on the golf bag of every member of the PGA Tour.
Every year I travel close to 30,000 miles just to play golf.
That's a lot of travel. And a lot of golf. It's a good thing I love the
game. Sometimes I wonder which suffers more wear and tear,
my sand wedge or my frequent-flier card.

Even so, I envy you. The idea of visiting for the very first time
some of the great courses described here is exciting. To see and
play courses such as Pebble Beach and Harbour Town and the
Old Course at St. Andrews . . . well, all I can say is that anyone
who cares about golf would love to be in your spikes. And best
of all, you'll be on vacation!

The best golf trip I ever had? That's easy. It was in April 1982.
I went with a bunch of my buddies from the PGA Tour down to
a little town in Georgia, stayed a week, and got in a round every
day. The azaleas were in full bloom, I remember. Not only was
the golf great, but I also picked up this really nice green blazer.
Funny, I like it so much I wouldn't mind having another.

Even if you've visited some of the places described here before,
you'll benefit from the information and insights in this book.
Just as good course management is a prerequisite for scoring
well on the golf course, careful planning is critical to getting the
most out of your golf vacation. Knowing where to stay, when to
go, and what to expect won't shave any strokes off your handi-
cap, but it will clear your mind so you can focus on the business
at hand: knocking a little white ball into a hole in the ground.

One word of caution when planning your golf vacation: don't
get too carried away with the idea that you must play "champi-
onship" courses to have a good time. The trend in recent years
to design every new course so that it's meaner, tougher, and
longer than the last one has gotten way out of hand. Just be-
cause a course measures 7,200 yards from the tips, has a 75.0
rating, greens harder than your kitchen floor, and bunkers
deeper than Crater Lake doesn't necessarily make it fun to play.

And if golf isn't fun, you might as well spend your vacation butting your head against the wall: it costs less, and you never have to worry about shanking.

In the chapters that follow, you'll travel all across America, into the Caribbean, and to Scotland, the ancestral home of golf. Some of the courses and places you'll visit are household names; others are a bit off the beaten track. The common denominator? Each vacation plan outlined here provides a truly special golf experience.

The author, Glen Waggoner, has been perfecting his slice for a lot of years. His game doesn't seem to get any better, but when it comes to knowledge and appreciation of top-quality golf courses, he's a scratch shooter. A year ago he followed the PGA Tour from the Tournament of Champions in January right on through the Nabisco Championships in October, so he also knows a thing or two about travel. He's a reliable guide whom you can trust when it comes to planning your next golf vacation. Just don't ask him for any swing tips.

—CRAIG STADLER
SAN DIEGO, CALIFORNIA

INTRODUCTION

Lucky you.

Next to actually taking a golf vacation, there's nothing more satisfying to a golfer's soul than planning one. In some ways, the planning is even better, because at this stage there are no three-putt greens, chili-dips, or buried lies. All that comes later. Yet we will not be deterred. It is one of the puzzling but enduring attributes of the game that the enthusiasm with which a golfer anticipates his next round is not diminished in the least by the memory of his last one, proof positive that the human spirit is indeed indomitable.

Or maybe it's just that golfers are deeply sick masochists whose crippled imaginations can't conjure up more inventive forms of self-torture. Why else would we—I—keep on going back to the scene of the crime, always a golf course, to expose our—my—ego to another sound thrashing? Unless, of course, it's because we genuinely love the game for its inner beauty in spite of the way we play it.

Most of the time I play in the low-to-mid-90s, a few strokes better when I keep my tee shot on the fairway, a few worse on a really tough course. I take a mulligan on the first tee when I haven't had time to hit a few balls at the range (and sometimes when I have). I drive with a three-wood because I can't trust my driver. I pull-hook too many long irons and hit too many short irons fat. I putt decently. I loathe slow play. Other things being equal, I prefer to use a pull-cart and walk.

This little résumé is not intended to earn me a place in your Saturday foursome, but to give you a frame of reference for the course, hotel, and resort recommendations contained in the twenty golf vacations described in this book. If your handicap is a low single digit, you'll know to discount my occasional ravings about the toughness of a certain course and to translate my observations about a certain hole to fit your game. And if your handicap is voting age (i.e., 18 or over), you'll know that no such adjustments are needed.

The loose premise of the golf vacations charted here is that you have a couple of weeks, less a travel day or two, to devote to golf. That's why some chapters include as many as a dozen courses you might play. But you may not have two weeks, or you may not care to move around too much on a vacation, and that leads us to another loose premise—namely, that each destination described be of sufficiently high quality so that a traveling golfer could spend his entire vacation (however short or long) in one spot and never become bored with the golf.

The last part of the assignment was easy, given the number of splendid golf courses accessible to the traveling golfer. What was tough was having to leave so many terrific places out. In so doing, I'm sure to ruffle a few feathers, and I'm bound to hear from traveling golfers who want to make a case for their favorite tracks. That's great. Next to a fisherman, nobody likes to talk about his passion more than a golfer.

Now let's take a look at a few local rules.

The terms quoted for lodging accommodations are for room only, double occupancy. "Modified American Plan" means two meals (breakfast and dinner) are included. "Full American Plan" means all three meals are included. Unless otherwise noted, the resorts listed in this book accept all the usual credit cards. Most also have special golf packages for stays of two nights or longer. In some cases, duly noted, only resort guests may play at a given golf course. In most cases, however, it's possible to get a tee time on an "as available" basis, even if you're staying off-campus, particularly during low season.

For the golf courses described in these pages I have given the length from the championship tees, not because I ordinarily play from them myself—nor should any golfer whose handicap is in double digits—but because the yardage from the tips best conveys the designer's vision of the course. The year the course opened for play is included to give you a hint at what you can look forward to: a course built in 1928 is going to have a substantially different look and feel than a course constructed in 1988.

Where available, both the "course rating" and "slope rating" are given. (In instances where either is left out, it usually means the course has been recently redesigned and has not yet been rerated.) Each numerical rating represents an attempt to describe a golf course's difficulty relative to other courses. Thus a course where par is 72 and the course rating is 73.9 will play a whole lot tougher than another par 72 track with a course rating of 69.9. But course rating is based almost exclusively on course length, only one of a platoon of factors that can smash a golfer's fantasies faster than you can say "stroke and distance." Slope rating, a newer means of expressing the challenge facing you when you tee it up, takes into account such pesky items as water hazards, fairway bunkers, width of fairways, and the like. While somewhat more subjective, a course's slope is a more precise indicator of its toughness. An average slope is 115–16, so when you play Spyglass Hill at Pebble Beach with its 135 slope, you won't be shocked when it eats your lunch.

That's it. Get out your calendar and start plotting your next vacation. You should find everything you'll need for that happy task in the pages that follow. The golf, of course, is up to you, but I will pass along this one key to a lights-out round from Louie, my once and future playing partner:

"Tee 'em high, and let 'em fly."

THE NEW ENGLAND TOUR
Swinging Through New England

MAPLE SYRUP. TOWN MEETINGS. AUTUMN leaves. Church steeples. Plymouth Rock. Country stores. Scarlet letters. Red Sox. Clam chowder.

When you say the words "New England," a lot of things come to mind. But dollars to doughnuts "golf" is not one of them. And that suits New Englanders who play golf just fine.

Private and reserved by nature, New Englanders grudgingly suffer outsiders. In the fall, they endure with practiced stoicism the hordes of leaf peepers who sweep through the region to see the mountainsides explode in bursts of red, gold, and yellow. In the winter, New Englanders who don't own a piece of the ski business curse under their breath as rosy-cheeked armies of downhill party animals flood in from New York and Boston in search of the perfect *après*-ski experience. And in springtime, the locals chuckle to themselves in poorly disguised pleasure when the mud season sends visitors packing.

Come summer, knowing that vacationers cannot be held back from their borders without calling the Green Mountain Boys to arms, certain wily New Englanders—New England *golfers*, that is—fight a surprisingly effective guerrilla war against poachers from beyond their borders. They extol the pleasures of the Maine coast, sing anthems in praise of the wondrous seascapes on old Cape Cod, and wax rapturous about the *je ne c'est quoi* charms of Martha's Vineyard, anything to keep one of New England's special treasures—its golf courses—all to themselves. And you know what? It works. Otherwise, the word "golf" *would* immediately come to mind when you heard the words "New England," because there's plenty to be played there—if you know where to go.

You can't really blame New England golfers for wanting to keep their courses a secret. After all, for anyone who loves golf *and* who happens to live in New England, winter is truly a season of discontent—and a long one at that.

Like the growing season for tomatoes, the time a New Englander can spend playing golf is short. Just as he's on the verge of fixing his slice once and for all time, just as he gets *this* far from divining the ultimate secrets of the game, the elements suspend his pursuit of the dimpled pellet for five long months. Or more, depending on how close his local course is to Hudson Bay.

From the last leaf's fall every autumn until the sloppy end of the mud season every spring, all he can do is swing his two-iron in the garage, dream of birdies, and mashie his niblick. Sure, he could join the migratory hoards of golf junkies who flock to warmer climes the minute the local mercury dips below 40 degrees Fahrenheit. But inbred stubbornness and regional pride prevent him from doing so.

No, the dyed-in-the-wool New England duffer has too much grit in his craw to capitulate to the "R" months so cravenly. (Or, some would say, he's too hidebound and hardheaded.) Instead, he waits. And waits. And waits some more. Like a bear with insomnia, he waits for the long winter's night to end. He crosses the days off his calendar, one by one, like a GI short-timer counting down the minutes to his discharge, and he waits. Resolutely, even heroically, he waits, until one fine morning the robins gather outside the window, throw back their tiny heads, and warble together in glorious harmony, "Fore!"

And the wait is over.

Fortunately, the payoff for such exemplary patience is rich. Golf courses in New England garner less hype and hoopla than do the golf factories of the Sunbelt States, but they certainly deserve no less respect from the serious golfer. Indeed, New

England courses offer much more variety than you'll find in the cookie-cutter courses of, say, Myrtle Beach. Classic links courses, what the British call "parkland" tracks, and mountain courses—New England has them all.

When planning your own golf vacation there, you might want to consider the behavior of the fully credentialed, Sunbelt-hating New Englander—let's call him Winthrop Standish—when *he* goes on holiday . . . in his own backyard, of course.

Winthrop Standish on a golf vacation is a man with a mission. No medieval knight errant in pursuit of the Holy Grail displayed more single-minded dedication than a New England golfer in search of compensation for winter's travails. He crams more holes into a single week of daylight hours than mere mortals from the rest of the world might play in a whole summer. While they nap, Winthrop plays. They can afford a casual attitude; he's in a race against time. Before he knows it, Jack Frost will come nipping at his nose again, and he knows from bone-chilling experience how hard it is to concentrate on a ten-footer when the sound of chattering teeth can be heard coming from the next tee box.

A laconic, reserved man who abhors excess fifty weeks of the year, Winthrop Standish on a golf vacation plays from sunrise to sunset. For his daybreak round, he might haul one of the kids out of bed and press him (or her) into service as a forecaddy in the morning haze. As dusk settles on his last round of the day, Winthrop knows to club down (all the way to a wedge off the tee) so that he'll be able to follow the flight of the ball in the gloaming. In between he never yields to distractions such as lunch and scenery; there will be plenty of time for eating, drinking, and sight-seeing after dark.

Fortunately, you don't have to be a New Englander to follow this approach; it works for outsiders just as well. Be sure to take it with you on the New England Tour.

As described below, the New England Tour—seven courses for seven days—lets you sample the variety of golf available in the region in a single, whirlwind week. You'll play along the ocean and in the mountains. You'll tee it up at ritzy resort layouts and daily fee tracks. You won't find the courses on the New England Tour of uniform challenge or quality, any more than you'll find them of uniform feel. What you will find are a lot of different looks and a heckuva lot of fun.

WENTWORTH-BY-THE-SEA

Squeezed into barely 100 acres along the coast just northeast of Portsmouth, New Hampshire, Wentworth-by-the-Sea is an easygoing seaside frolic, part links layout and part woodlands, complete with an evocative, *extremely* British name. It's short (6,179 yards from the blue tees), simple, and a whole gang of fun. Nothing complex or heroic, mind you, but more than enough challenge for your first day. If Wentworth were a wine, it would be a Beaujolais.

WENTWORTH-BY-THE-SEA

Design: Donald Ross, Geoffrey Cornish

Year Open: 1897

6,179 Yards   67.8 Rating   123 Slope

Information: (603) 433-5010

★

The course came into being in 1896 as a six-hole complement to a posh Victorian-era resort hotel perched high on a bluff overlooking the ocean. Today the grand old place is an empty shell destined to meet the wrecker's ball, if its current owners can sidestep local preservationists and landmark designation. But it once attracted the next-to-upper-crust Bostonians—no Irish, please—who had more pretensions than ready capital and couldn't afford a cottage in the mountains or a beach house on the Cape.

Three decades later the great Donald Ross redesigned the existing six holes and added three more. Characteristically, he moved very little earth around, and accepted the linksland as he found it, molding fairway and green to conform to natural contours shaped by wind and ocean.

His best hole is the eighth, a 520-yard par 5 that bends to the right around Little Harbor and dares you to bite off more shortcut over water and beach than you can chew. Take a big enough bite and you put yourself in good shape for an eagle. Take too big a bite and you get to play beach blanket bingo.

Geoffrey Cornish added a second nine in 1964, a small miracle in itself considering how little acreage he was given to work with. There are dinosaur burial mounds smack dab in the middle of the third fairway, but Cornish didn't move any earth to achieve the effect; he just left the lumps where he found them. Even so, you begin to fear you're in for a tricked-up nightmare. That's not the case, but later on, if the wind is off the ocean, the long carry over water on the 415-yard par 4 fifteenth will leave you cursing Cornish's heart. Otherwise, the Cornish holes are straightforward, unadorned, and altogether fitting companions to the Ross layout.

(For the record, Numbers 1, 2, 6, 7, 8, 9, 10, and 18 are Ross; the rest are Cornish.)

Okay. It's 9 A.M., and you've just finished at 92 instead of the 88 you'd been counting on after your first glimpse of the numbers on the scorecard. Wentworth plays tougher than it looks, so don't fret. Or, if you're like me, and fretting is an integral part of your game, save it for I-95, because it's time to head for Maine.

SAMOSET

Piece of cake. That's what you think the first time you see the scorecard for the Samoset Resort golf course in Rockport, Maine. It's short. And it's a resort course, whose bread-and-butter business comes from the conventioneers attracted by Samoset's state-of-the-art conference center. That means wide fairways and slow greens, right? After all, they don't want vacationing hackers like you and me to get their golf egos and four-irons bent out of shape, do they? Piece of cake!

Better make that a piece of humble pie.

SAMOSET RESORT GOLF CLUB

Design: Bob Elder

Year Open: 1978

6,362 Yards   70.1 Rating   125 Slope

Information: (800) 341-1650, Extension 111

Narrow, tree-lined fairways with landing areas tiny enough to cramp a family picnic prompt better players to use an iron off the tee on half the par 4s. The rest of us numbly pull out our drivers and bang it into the woods. Or, in some cases, into

the bordering ocean. Or, if we are very naughty and lose our tempers, into first one, then the other. (Where is it written, by the way, that you can control a long iron any better than a wood? I've got to read that book some day.)

And when you finally make it to the greens, your troubles really begin. They're huge. And fast. How huge? Well, it's possible to find yourself looking at putts that are longer than an average NFL punt—150 feet, as a crow flies. Only don't count on having any putts as straight as a crow flies. How fast? Well, the greens at a typical U.S. Open register 9.5 to 10 on the Stimp Meter—and so do the greens at Samoset.

(What's a Stimp Meter? It's a meter that measures stimps, which is British Thermal Unit slang for "Eight feet past the hole and I barely touched the damned ball!")

Add a gusty breeze off the ocean and you have a course so feisty that in scores of state and regional PGA championships, club competitions, and other tournaments since its opening in 1974, only two sub-par rounds have been recorded from Samoset's blue tees. That's right, two—a 69 and a 68 recorded on the same day in 1987. As you'll discover, Samoset gives a whole new meaning to the phrase, "plays tougher than it looks."

You don't have to be a resort guest to play the course, but you might as well stay there if only for the convenience. There's something appealingly efficient about falling out of bed, grabbing a cup of courtesy coffee in the hotel lobby, and stumbling onto the first tee just as your eyes open up. Constructed in the late 1970s on the site of a grand old nineteenth-century hotel that conveniently burned to the ground a few years after it closed its doors for good, the Samoset specializes in conference business. That can be a drawback if a hundred or so high-tech wockies up from Cambridge have booked all the tee times for the three mornings you want to stay there, so be sure to reserve your tee times at the same time you reserve your room.

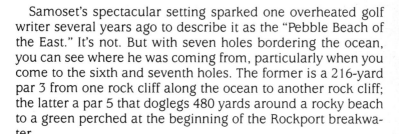

SAMOSET RESORT Rockport, Maine 04856. Just off U.S. 1, about 75 miles north of Portland, Maine. Telephone: (800) 341-1650. <u>Accommodations</u>: 150 rooms with private balconies, many with views of Penobscot Bay. <u>Amenities</u>: Tennis; indoor and outdoor pools; fitness center; fishing. Heavy-duty shopping in nearby Camden (aka "Boutiques-on-the-Sea") and fairly close Freeport, the factory-outlet capital of the universe (and home of L. L. Bean). Plus golf, of course. <u>Terms</u>: From $170 for non-ocean view to $185 for ocean view. No pets.

Samoset's spectacular setting sparked one overheated golf writer several years ago to describe it as the "Pebble Beach of the East." It's not. But with seven holes bordering the ocean, you can see where he was coming from, particularly when you come to the sixth and seventh holes. The former is a 216-yard par 3 from one rock cliff along the ocean to another rock cliff; the latter a par 5 that doglegs 480 yards around a rocky beach to a green perched at the beginning of the Rockport breakwater.

Par them both and you'll start thinking of that California course as the "Samoset of the West."

SABLE OAKS GOLF CLUB

Fine golf courses have this in common with fine wines: it's usually best to let them get a little age under their belts before sampling them. But you may want to make an exception with Sable Oaks, a Geoffrey Cornish course in South Portland that was opened for play in 1989. Cornish designs are almost invariably satisfying, because he seems genuinely committed to disturbing the natural settings of his courses as little as possible. At Sable Oaks this means that rolling hills, rocky ledges, a meandering stream, steep ravines, and a forest of birches, oaks, and pines are the primary design features.

SABLE OAKS GOLF CLUB

Design: Geoffrey Cornish
Year Open: 1989
6,359 Yards   70.2 Rating   129 Slope
Information: (207) 775-OAKS

★

The premium at Sable Oaks is on precision, not muscle. At only 6,359 yards from the blues, Sable Oaks won't intimidate the big hitters. But Jackson Brook, which comes into play on six holes, will most certainly get their balls wet.

To wit: on the thirteenth (par 3,182 yards from the blues), the brook borders the green and leaves no margin for error . . . on the fourteenth (par 5,480 yards) the brook defines target areas for both your drive and your second shot . . . and on the fifteenth (par 4,399 yards), after you fly 185 yards over the ravine in front of the tee, the brook runs alongside the left fairway all the way up to the hole.

Play Sable Oaks now. And come back again in five years to see if it develops the body to match its nose. My bet is that it will.

POLAND SPRING COUNTRY CLUB

You may know about the bubbly water that Poland Spring, Maine, is regionally famous for. You may even know about the inn, whose colorful history stretches back to a stagecoach stop built on the site 200 years ago. But you probably don't know about the golf course. And there's no good reason you should.

There's nothing special about the short wide-open layout, even though Donald Ross had a hand in its redesign and extension to eighteen holes in 1923. It's not in particularly good shape: too many harsh Maine winters, too little capital for proper drainage and preventive maintenance, too little oper-

---

POLAND SPRING COUNTRY CLUB

Design: Donald Ross
Year Open: 1923
6,196 Yards   69.5 Rating   113 Slope
Information: (207) 998-6033

★
---

ating budget for the manicuring and fine tuning found at posh courses such as Samoset and Sable Oaks.

What Poland Spring does offer is a simple, straightforward, unadorned game of golf much like what the Scots had in mind when they dreamed up the game several centuries ago. Some good, honest holes, but nothing fancy. You hit the ball, you go find it, and you hit it again. No hoopla or folderol. No call for lime green pants, range finders, designer bags, and ermine head covers. Never mind smoothing out the bumps in the ground, or trimming the grass just so, or tarting up an honest field. Just play.

Travel to the north of England or to Scotland today, and you'll discover easygoing country courses by the score, courses just like Poland Spring. Courses where playing golf is no big deal, just part of everyday life. Courses where you can go out, bang the ball around, and not worry about your handicap.

Our handicap is that there aren't enough courses like Poland Spring around, courses where you can check in on the simple, straightforward roots of the game.

THE BALSAMS

"I tell people that to play this course it helps to be a sidehill badger," says Warren Pearson, one of three managing partners who in the last two decades has pulled The Balsams in Dixville Notch, New Hampshire, back from the brink of collapse, and restored it to its former glory.

"Y'know, one leg shorter than the other," he adds for the edification of a city slicker who doesn't run into a lot of badgers, "so you can walk along the side of the hill without rolling over."

Never play golf with a guy who tells badger stories, my daddy used to say, and you'd be wise to heed his advice. Pear-

---

PANORAMA GOLF CLUB
AT THE BALSAMS

Design: Donald Ross

Year Open: 1912
6,804 Yards   74.5 Rating   142 Slope

Information: (800) 255-0600

★

---

son plays to a "five or six or seven" at The Balsams' Panorama course, a Donald Ross masterpiece that measures 6,804 yards from the back tees and carries a hefty 74.5 course rating with a monster 142 slope. But figure local knowledge is worth another "five or six or seven" here, mainly because there are only two or three flat lies on the whole course—and none of them is on the greens.

THE BALSAMS Dixville Notch, New Hampshire 03576. Take U.S. 3 north (*far* north) to Route 26; turn right (east) 13 miles until you come to a colossal white hotel in a picture postcard setting. Telephone: (800) 255-0600. Accommodations: 232 rooms, some only slightly bigger than large closets, some quite huge; many with spectacular views. The best room: Number 125, an enormous, circular room with half a dozen windows. Amenities: Tennis, outdoor pool; serious hiking and mountaineering; fly-fishing and canoeing; horseback riding—all on a 15,000-acre private estate; 2 golf courses. Terms: From $127 to $168 per person, Full American Plan (all 3 meals). Price includes greens fees at golf courses. No pets. Book at least 6 months in advance for July and August.

★

"We're near the forty-fifth parallel, y'know," explains Pearson, who assumes you know that means a mite over 210 miles north of Boston. "Ross knew you had to allow for the snow and ice to melt off in the spring. So he built everything with a lot of pitch." A *lot* of pitch, with everything rolling away from Keysar Mountain, and always faster than you reckon.

For Donald Ross to have designed as many courses in New England as he's credited with, he'd have to have been on the road more than Johnny Appleseed. Common sense and a casual look tell you that the only basis many "Ross courses" have for claiming his name is that he may have stopped off once and given a few tips to the local greenskeeper. That's not the case at The Balsams, whose historical records show that Ross himself both designed and supervised construction of the tough mountain course. And The Balsams, which has been around since 1866, is nothing if not proud and protective of its historical records.

The Balsams is the grandest of the grand old New England resort hotels, with enough verandas and reading rooms and game rooms and assorted nooks and crannies to keep you busy a week just exploring the interior. And outside, you have 15,000 acres of prime New Hampshire mountain scenery to ogle. Stay a couple of days and you may want to make coming here an annual ritual. A lot of people do: the Balsams claims that over 80 percent of its guests are repeaters. You're way to hell and gone from anywhere else; but after you're here awhile, that doesn't seem to matter.

You can play at The Balsams from mid-May until mid-September, but the best times are July and August, when the course has had a chance to dry out and the black flies have gone north for the summer. No large group meetings are booked in July and August, so you won't find the course overrun by a conventionload of frolicking proctologists. But bear in mind that The Balsams runs at nearly 100 percent occupancy in high summer, so make your reservations early.

And remember: if a guy who walks like a sidehill badger comes up to you and suggests a little two-dollar Nassau, tell him you're there for the tennis.

LAKE MOREY COUNTRY CLUB

Located no more than a driver and a four-iron (maybe a three if the wind is from the west) off I-91 at Fairlee, Vermont, the Lake Morey Country Club represents a bit of a breather after the Panorama course at The Balsams.

LAKE MOREY COUNTRY CLUB

Design: Allan Avery/Geoffrey Cornish

Year Open: 1927

6,024 Yards

Information: (802) 333-4800

★

It's not that Lake Morey is easy. No golf course is easy, at least not for me. The minute you start thinking easy, you start racking up snowmen, and nothing spoils a vacation faster than a card full of eights. So don't ever call Lake Morey, or any other golf course, easy. At least not to its face.

But if anxiety about your game is causing you to wake up in the middle of the night and ask the person next to you in bed whether you're getting enough hip turn in your stroke, Lake Morey may be just what you need. Short, flat, and well trimmed, it has wide fairways and virtually no rough. Even though it's the annual site of the Vermont Open, Lake Morey's par 70 track will never be mistaken for a championship course. On the other hand, you don't have to be a champion to play it.

But don't let yourself start thinking Lake Morey is a pushover. Sure as you do, a hole like the thirteenth—a 552-yard par 5 running down from an elevated tee to a rolling fairway and then up, up, and away to a well-trapped green nestled in a stand of tall evergreens—will turn around and bite you on your handicap.

Think of Lake Morey instead as "user-friendly." Your scorecard will be safer that way.

QUECHEE CLUB—LAKELAND COURSE

The toughest course in New England, in the opinion of Doran F. Jones, is the Lakeland Course at the Quechee Club in Quechee Lakes, Vermont. And when Doran F. Jones expresses an opinion about New England golf, people listen.

A past president of the New England Golf Association, Jones knows the region's golf courses as intimately as Jack Nicklaus knows the back nine at Augusta. He never touched a club until

LAKELAND COURSE
AT QUECHEE CLUB

Design: Geoffrey Cornish

Year Open: 1973

6,569 Yards   72.2 Rating   129 Slope

Information: Unless you're a member, you must be a guest at the Quechee Inn to play here. Call the Quechee Inn at (802) 295-3133 for information and reservations.

he was forty-six, establishing his credentials as a wise man—at least until that point in his life. He took up the game under the tutelage of Tommy Keane, longtime Dartmouth College golf coach, and eventually worked his handicap down to a six. At seventy-five, he plays to an honest twenty, which means he could spot me a quarter of a century and *still* walk away with the cash.

QUECHEE INN Quechee, Vermont 05059. On U.S. 4, just west of the intersection of Interstates 91 and 89 at the Vermont-New Hampshire border. Telephone: (802) 295-3133. <u>Accommodations</u>: 24 double rooms. <u>Amenities</u>: Hiking, bicycling, fly-fishing, canoeing; float trips on the Connecticut River; access to golf and tennis at the Quechee Club. <u>Terms</u>: From $148 to $198 for room, plus Modified American Plan (breakfast and dinner) for 2 persons.

Among New England courses accessible to vacationing hackers without reciprocal playing privileges at the region's better private clubs, Jones likes the Maplewood course in Bethlehem, New Hampshire, and the Equinox course in Manchester, Vermont (not to be confused with Ekwnok in the same town, unless you want to spend a night in the slammer for trespassing on very private property). He speaks highly of the municipal course in Springfield, Massachusetts . . . of The Orchards, a Ross course in South Hadley, Massachusetts, owned by Mount Holyoke College . . . and of Vermont country club courses open to the public in Rutland and Burlington.

But topping his list is the Lakeland Course at Quechee, which Jones says is the best Geoffrey Cornish design he's ever seen—and that's saying a lot. From the tips the par 72 stretches to almost 6,600 yards, and water comes into play on eleven holes (just in case you wondered why it's not called Desert Vista). Always in immaculate condition, Lakeland and its adjacent sister course, Highland, are part of the Quechee Club, which is Private, Members Only.

Fortunately, there's a catch. Stay at the Quechee Inn, and you acquire golf privileges at the Quechee Club. It's the only way you'll be able to play there without becoming a member. Hey, why not? You've got to sleep some place, even on the New England Tour. Don't you?

The New England Tour Redux

What's that? You say you want to spend *two* weeks in New England playing golf? No problem! Here are a half dozen other New England treasures to fill your calendar:

Big, modern resorts designed with the conference trade in mind aren't usually my cup of tea for a golf vacation, but the **New Seabury Resort** on the southern tip of Cape Cod merits an exception. Start with the **Green Course**, the friendlier of the resort's two eighteens. It's set in a forest that shelters you somewhat from the Cape's omnipresent wind. Chances are you'll remember that relative tranquility fondly when you take on the **Blue Course**, whose front nine marches you along Nantucket Sound and dares you to make the right club selection in the gusting winds off the water. The Blue's back nine invites you inland to cope with dunes, sand, and long, sloping fairways. By the time you've negotiated the full 7,175 yards (if you're good—or nuts—enough to hit from the back tees), you'll feel as if you'd just returned from a fishing trip with Captain Ahab. For reservations: (800) 222-2044.

Despite its private-sounding name, the **Lake Sunapee Country Club** is open to just plain folks. That's good, because this well-groomed, enjoyable course is fun to play. It's also long been the winter headquarters of the Country Squire himself, Gene Sarazen. For reservations: (603) 526-6440.

The **Woodstock Country Club** in Woodstock, Vermont, boasts a fine, 6,100-yard, par 69 course by Robert Trent Jones that is laid out along Kendron Brook just south of town. The stream intersects the fairway eleven times and comes into play on fourteen holes, so bring along your waders. A fine course in one of New England's most beautiful towns, one you've seen before (whether you know it or not) in movies, TV commercials, and magazine layouts. ("This is the production designer for a Bowser Doggie Chow spot. I need a perfect New England town. Get me Woodstock.") To get a tee time, you'll need to stay in the **Woodstock Inn.** That's okay, because it's a perfect New England inn. For reservations: (800) 448-7900.

Don't let the sixteenth hole at the **Maplewood Golf Course** in Bethlehem, New Hampshire, intimidate. Sure, it's 635 yards long. But par is 6. Feel better already, don't you? This is a classy Donald Ross layout that's been around forever. Stay at the **Wayside Inn.** And save your mulligan for the sixteenth. For reservations: (800) 448-9557.

An item just in from the "Omigod, Now I've Heard Everything Department": a golf course originally built as a therapeutic assignment by rest home patients with nervous disorders. Yep, that's the way the golf course at the **Bethel Inn** in Bethel, Maine, came into being during World War I. Redesigned and expanded to eighteen holes by Geoffrey Cornish, Bethel is a 6,663-yard track nestled in the White Mountains that is as exacting as it is beautiful. For reservations: (207) 824-2175.

A typical four-bedroom house in New England with a fireplace and a couple of wood-burning stoves might go through a cord of wood in an average winter. To clear ground for the **Sugarloaf Golf Club** in western Maine, construction workers removed *4,000* cords of wood from the club's stunning site in the Carrabasset Valley. The Robert Trent Jones, Jr., design takes full advantage of the extraordinary mountain scenery; Sugarloaf's seventy-four bunkers, narrow fairways, sidehill lies, and ball-grabbing trees take full advantage of your masochistic streak. Bring a compass. For reservations: (207) 237-2000.

When to Go

Cotton Mather's descendants play golf on some of the rawest November mornings and on some of the wettest March afternoons this side of Pilgrim Hell. You, on the other hand, are on vacation, not in search of punishment for your sins. July, August, and September are the best months. June can be okay, but black flies may be a menace if you stray too far north. (That's like saying the Atlantic Ocean can be wet. If you insist on playing golf in the upper reaches of New England in early June, leave your visor at home and wear a pith helmet with a mosquito net.)

OFF COURSE

If you play the New England Tour with the intensity it deserves, there won't be many daylight hours available for sight-seeing, except for what you might spot driving from one course's eighteenth green to another course's first hole. Nights are free, but New England isn't exactly the best roosting place for a night owl. Except for **Boston**, of course, and I assume you can find your way along the **Freedom Trail**, over to the U.S.S. *Constitution*, and across the **Charles River** to **Harvard Square** without my assistance. Anyway, the only part of Beantown I know really well is **Fenway Park.** If you've never been there, make sure you go—even if you hate baseball. Everything the poets say about the place is true: it's a national treasure.

The heart and soul of New England are to be found in its towns and villages, of which you will see aplenty in your golfing odyssey. All you have to do is get off the interstate every time you have a few spare minutes before your next tee time.

Lodging is a piece of cake—or, more likely, a fresh-baked muffin, the common denominator in New England's ubiquitous country inns and bed-and-breakfasts. If you're game for adventure, turn into just about any small town and start looking for signs to the nearest inn or bed-and-breakfast. It's almost impossible to go wrong.

Eating is another matter. Whenever you're within one hour's driving distance of the Maine shore in summer, you have to eat lobster. (It's a regional law dating back to the Pilgrims, I think.) You can perform this culinary ritual in a restaurant, I suppose, but you really should do it at a lobster pound, preferably while dressed in a bathing suit. Two of the best pounds in Maine: **Beal's Lobster Pier** in Southwest Harbor (not too far from Samoset); and **Chauncey Creek Lobster Pound** in Kittery (207-439-1030), up the road a bit from Wentworth-by-the-Sea.

Except for lobster, all your eating while playing the New England Tour should be confined to diners. Yep, diners. From **Moody's Diner** (Waldoboro, Maine; 207-832-7785) to the **Peterborough Diner** (Peterborough, New Hampshire; 603-924-6202) to the **Roberts' Fairlee Diner** (Fairlee, Vermont), the region has many marvelous examples of this peculiarly American eating establishment. Discover a great one I've not visited and I'll spot you two a side for the tab.

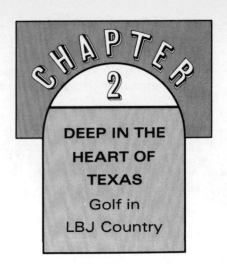

CHAPTER 2

DEEP IN THE HEART OF TEXAS

Golf in LBJ Country

WHEN NINETEENTH-CENTURY SETTLERS PUSH-ing across the dreary plains of central Texas first set eyes on the Hill Country, they saw a land of staggering beauty. Rolling hills, covered with stirrup-high grass punctuated by stands of live oak trees, stretched out before them. And when a man got to the crest of one range, there would be another, and another, on out toward the sunset. Endless fields of blue-bonnets and Indian paintbrush and buttercups and wild plum bushes infused this verdant empire with vivid color every spring, while in the fall sugar maples and wild sumac painted the hillsides red. Deer, wild turkeys, rabbits, pheasants, even bears were plentiful. Springs gurgled forth cool, clear water from subterranean limestone reservoirs to feed streams that twisted and curled through the hills. These streams emptied into a winding river that Mexican settlers who had come before called the Pedernales, which in turn fed the more muscular Colorado.

What an astounding sight this magical land south and west of Austin must have been to the hardy travelers from the pine forests of east Texas, the delta swamps of Louisiana, and the featureless flood plains of south Alabama. Little wonder that they believed that they had arrived at paradise on earth.

But one thing is surprising: how come it took a hundred years for somebody to figure out that this was a great place to build a golf course?

SHHH! IT'S A SECRET!

Flash forward to 1970, when a Texas real estate developer named Norman Hurd decides to do just that. Hurd, a land huckster who much prefers to be thought of as an artist creating an empire of beauty, buys up an area the size of a small European country about fifty miles west of Austin, clears out a mess of underbrush and mesquite trees, and looks up Robert Trent Jones's number in the telephone book. Two decades, lots of dollars, and three Jones masterpieces later, Hurd is innkeeper at the Horseshoe Bay Country Club Resort, proudly billed as "The Best Kept Secret in Texas."

HORSESHOE BAY COUNTRY CLUB RESORT Box 7766, Horseshoe Bay, Texas 78654. Just south of Marble Falls 50 miles west of Austin. From Austin take Texas Highway 71 west to Route 2147, just past U.S. 281. Turn right and drive 4 miles to resort entrance. (If you're bringing your own plane, Horseshoe Bay has a 6,000-foot runway that accommodates anything up to a DC-9.) Telephone: (800) 531-5105. <u>Accommodations</u>: 49 motel-style rooms, over 300 condo units. <u>Amenities</u>: 14 tennis courts, a 325-slip marina, riding stable, 3 pools, beach (on Lake LBJ), hiking, nature trails, 3 golf courses. <u>Terms</u>: Rates from $110 to $175.

Horseshoe Bay commands the high ground on the south shore of Lake LBJ, a twenty-three-mile-long monument to the man who did more than anyone else to make this part of the country safe for golf. Lyndon Baines Johnson didn't care a whit about the game, of course, privately dismissing it as a rich man's pastime even after he became rich. There's no record of him ever spending quality time on a golf course, except when

the exigencies of office absolutely required it (i.e., when somebody's arm had to be twisted, and the only place to twist it was between the tenth and eleventh holes).

But LBJ did know the Hill Country, and he did know the devastation that could be unleashed when the Colorado became bloated with spring rain and overran its banks. So, for two decades as a congressman and a senator, and later as a vice president and president, Johnson expended a significant amount of his enormous energy and political savvy on securing federal dollars for flood control dams along the tempestuous Colorado and its tributaries. Once tamed, the Colorado became a reliable feeder stream for a series of placid lakes, and thus it came to pass that Norman Hurd had a place to build his playground for the Texas well-to-do.

Actually, Horseshoe Bay is not "The Best Kept Secret in Texas" anymore, at least not officially. That was just the third of four slogans churned out by Horseshoe Bay public relations people over the last twenty years. The common goal of all four: to attract well-heeled buyers for the 7,000 half-acre home lots that Hurd sculpted out of the country that Lyndon Johnson's forebears had found so appealing 125 years before.

The first slogan, "Go to It," lasted from 1971 to 1978; but not enough people did, maybe because the message was a little too zen for Texas. It was like something out of *Field of Dreams*, a decade before the book was published. Then came "The Place Where You Can Have It All," which took on a certain ironical twist when the price of crude oil nosedived, and many erstwhile purchasers of vacation home sites were "taking the chapter"—Chapter 11, that is. This was followed in 1981 by "Secret," which had a certain plaintive tone to it (huge successes are rarely secrets, at least not in Texas) as well as a grain of truth. But since 1985, Horseshoe Bay has been "The Standard by Which All Others Are Compared," which begs an important question (All Other Whats?), and goes a bit overboard, even by Texas land developer standards.

But not too far overboard, because if you were measuring American golf resorts on the basis of quality *and* quantity of golf offered, then Horseshoe Bay would have to rank pretty doggone high—at least in the top ten, and maybe higher.

Take the youngest of the three Horseshoe Bay courses, Applerock, which was named by *Golf Digest* as the "Best New Resort Course of 1986." The magazine's architecture editor, Ron Whitten, called it "as natural a golf course as [Jones] has produced in many years." He saluted Jones for the subdued but effective bunkering, for greens that are generous without being behemoth, and for "an exceptional job of contouring the fairways to fit the existing land."

APPLEROCK AT HORSESHOE BAY

Design: Robert Trent Jones

Year Open: 1985

6,999 Yards   74.0 Rating   134 Slope

Information: (800) 531-5105

★

Applerock is built on high, rocky terrain with terrific views of Lake LBJ and beyond. One of your first impressions on the early holes is how generous the fairways are. But what Jones giveth in fairway breathing room, he taketh away by letting the course conform to the steep ups and downs of the site. This may be one time where you will wish he'd done a little more bulldozing. Native oaks, elms, and persimmon trees abound, as do descendants of the deer and wild turkeys that fed the early settlers.

A beautiful, demanding course, Applerock may well turn out to be the best of the three tracks at Horseshoe Bay, but we won't be able to judge for sure until it's had a chance to mature.

The middle child—Ram Rock—opened in 1981 and earned a reputation from the git-go as an ornery, pesky critter that will take a bite out of you if you don't watch out. A lot of sand (sixty-two traps), a lot of water (hazards on ten holes, dry creek beds on six holes), a lot of up and down (it's the Hill Country, remember), and plenty of length (just shy of 7,000 yards) without much width make Ram Rock one tough 71. It's far and away the least popular among members of the Horseshoe Bay Country Club, at least among those who aren't scratch shooters and/or mucho macho. That doesn't mean you won't like it. It's just that you're not likely to lower your handicap at its expense.

RAM ROCK AT HORSESHOE BAY

Design: Robert Trent Jones

Year Open: 1981

6,946 Yards   74.5 Rating   137 Slope

Information: (800) 531-5105

★

The most popular Horseshoe Bay course, among club members and resort guests alike, is Slick Rock, which opened for business during the winter of 1973–74. One trip around its varied, graceful layout and you'll see why. Compared with its younger, more rambunctious siblings, Slick Rock seems graceful, even subtle. Where they are hilly and sometimes abrupt, Slick Rock is gently rolling. While less dramatic than the other two, Slick Rock is beautiful in its own right, with stands of live oak, cedar, willow, and persimmon trees giving it strong definition.

Robert Trent Jones has long been an advocate of a rock-solid principle of golf course design: a good golf course, he has said on many occasions, should yield par grudgingly and bogey generously. It takes an imaginative, creative designer to walk that fine line between hard par-easy bogey. And at Slick Rock, Jones succeeds superbly. The fairways are wide enough to give hope to the high handicapper, but there's also plenty of trouble waiting for the better player who gets overconfident. Hard par, easy bogey.

No doubt Slick Rock's appeal has a lot to do with its relative maturity. As it has aged, small refinements, subtle adjustments, and added enhancements have built on the course's strengths. Throw in outstanding maintenance and a break or two from Mother Nature, and it all adds up to a wonderful golf course.

SLICK ROCK AT HORSESHOE BAY

Design: Robert Trent Jones

Year Open: 1973

6,839 Yards   72.6 Rating   135 Slope

Information: (800) 531-5105

★

Horseshoe Bay was conceived as a real estate development, not a resort. That means the golf courses were built to sell houses, not to attract tourists. It also means that the physical layout may seem a little odd to the vacationing golfer. The Horseshoe Bay Inn, for example, is a twenty-five-room facility of no great distinction adjacent to the building that houses the conference center. The Beach House Inn offers another twenty-four rooms nearer the Horseshoe Bay Marina. Both offer spacious, well-appointed rooms, but I have a feeling that they were built to accommodate would-be purchasers of residential lots, not vacationers. There are an additional 300 bedrooms available in condo units, but housing vacationers seems like a secondary side of Horseshoe Bay's main business, which is selling real estate.

If so, then that's a blessing in disguise for the traveling golfer. The slowdown in the Texas economy in the last five years has retarded the growth of Horseshoe Bay and other similar operations in the region, which means fewer purchasers of vacation homes, less country club traffic, and fewer golfers overall than the three courses were built to handle. Now, if you throw into that mix a resort side of the operation that was something of an afterthought, and was never fully oriented toward the tourist trade, then you have a traveler's dream—a great facility that is significantly underutilized.

Oh, you can get clobbered by a big convention now and then, and midsummer (not the best time anyway) can sometimes get pretty crowded. But one of the great, glorious virtues of Horseshoe Bay is that you can go there for a late spring or mid-fall vacation and not feel rushed. If Norman Hurd's dream had come fully true, I suspect, there wouldn't even be a resort per se at Horseshoe Bay, and the three golf courses there would be restricted to property owners and country club members. But we all know what can happen to the best-made plans of mice and men, and in this case the traveling golfer is the prime beneficiary.

Just don't tell everybody and his brother. Even though the official slogan may have changed, Horseshoe Bay is still "The Best Kept *Golf* Secret in Texas."

LAKEWAY

Back down the road a piece toward Austin is a resort *cum* second-home community whose centerpiece is a Jack Nicklaus "Signature" course. (That signature will cost you a cool $1 million in 1990 dollars, just in case you were thinking about building a new course and wanted the Golden Bear to oversee it

---

LAKEWAY RESORT AND CONFERENCE CENTER 101 Lakeway Drive, Austin, Texas 78734. About 25 minutes from downtown Austin. Take Highway 71 to Highway 620; follow signs to Lakeway. (The Lakeway airstrip is only 4,500 feet long, so you'll have to leave the DC-9 at home.) Telephone: (800) 525-3929. <u>Accommodations</u>: 138 guest rooms in the inn; another 160 or so rooms in privately owned villas and houses. <u>Amenities</u>: Boating, fishing, and swimming on Lake Travis; horseback riding, jogging, hiking; 32 tennis courts (indoor and outdoor); 3 swimming pools (the one in the tennis complex is in the shape of a tennis racket); Jack Nicklaus Academy of Golf; 3 golf courses. (Note: The Hills, the Jack Nicklaus "Signature" course, is open only to guests staying in the privately owned villas; make arrangements when you book reservations.) <u>Terms</u>: From $110 for a standard room in the low season (November 15–March 1) to $240 for a 2-room VIP suite with a kitchenette. Villas from $240 (2-bedroom) to $480 (4-bedroom).

★

personally.) It's one of his prettiest and is definitely worth a stop during your stay in the Hill Country.

The Lakeway Resort and Conference Center is located about twenty miles as the crow flies from the tower on the University of Texas campus, the one that is bathed in orange light each night after a victory by a Longhorn sports team. Situated on the edge of Lake Travis, the most easterly of the chain of lakes created as a result of LBJ's efforts to hogtie the Colorado River, Lakeway is a whopping great complex with 32 tennis courts, 3 swimming pools, a marina, its own airstrip, state-of-the-art conference facilities, and 3 golf courses.

Two of the courses, designed by Leon Howard, offer good, solid resort golf. Yaupon is hilly with wide fairways; Live Oak is tree-lined with wide fairways. I don't know about you, but I like wide fairways. The notion that every course has to be a "championship" course is fine if you play golf like a champion. I don't, and I like to have some fun on a golf course. At least sometimes.

But, like everybody else who's ever shanked one into the tall grass, I also love to walk the fairways where champions walk, even if it means five or ten more hacks than I normally need back home at Podunk C.C. That's why I like to tackle a course like The Hills at Lakeway.

If Horseshoe Bay has the best complex of courses of any golf resort in Texas, The Hills at Lakeway is the best single course in the region. In recent years Jack Nicklaus has caught a lot of heat, and deservedly so, for the newer courses he has designed, each one of which seems longer, tougher, more grandiose in scale than the last. But The Hills is relatively Early Nicklaus, and embodies more restraint, perspective, and consideration for the limitations of mere mortals than some of his more recent creations. In Nicklaus's defense, he builds the kind of course his customers ask for, and increasingly they want only the most heroic, the most difficult, the most *everything*. But this can turn golf into a bad day at the office for the likes of me, and I frankly don't need the aggravation.

The Hills is different. (I know what you're thinking, and I agree. "The Hills *is* different" doesn't sound right to me, either. Actually, it sounds exactly like something my uncle Pem would say, only he would be saying "the hills is different" instead of "The Hills." But "The Hills is different" is grammatically correct. True, too.)

Don't get me wrong now; I'm not suggesting that The Hills is a pushover. No way. It's a lot more golf course than I can handle within the constraints of my rather flexible handicap. But at least I don't end up feeling like some sub-human mass of protoplasm after it gets through whupping me. That's because, with its multiple tee boxes, it gives me a fair shot at my bogey and my occasional par. And also because it's so doggone gorgeous.

THE HILLS AT LAKEWAY

Design: Jack Nicklaus

Year Open: 1981
6,813 Yards   73.0 Rating   130 Slope

Information: (800) 525-3929

★

The seventh hole at The Hills is arguably the most beautiful golf hole in the state (which makes it, if you're a Texan, the most beautiful in the universe). On this spectacular par 3, you have to carry the sparkling clear waters of Hurst Creek to a green that is perched just above a gurgling waterfall. Please note that this limestone waterfall, draped with moss and other greenery, was designed by Mother Nature, not Jack Nicklaus. But you have to give credit to the Golden Bear for having the imagination to figure out a way to squeeze a green in between the waterfall and the hill rising to the rear, and for doing it with a gentle hand.

Warning: The standard Lakeway golf packages apply to Yaupon and Live Oak *only*. If you want to play The Hills, you have to be a guest in one of the privately owned villas for rent at the resort. There are other restrictions as well (e.g., weekday play only, no madras pants allowed, must have red hair, etc.), so be sure you sort everything out when you book your reservations. Don't come back and say I didn't warn you.

BARTON CREEK

Closer to Austin, the Barton Creek Conference Resort is another of the hybrid private club-resorts that are becoming more and more common these days. (Ditto Horseshoe Bay and Lakeway.) Play is restricted to club members, their guests, and resort guests, so you'll have to bunk in one of the complex's 148 rooms and suites. Rest assured that doing so will not bring back any memories of boot camp. The luxurious, ultramodern resort has every imaginable amenity, including a glossy European-style spa that will tempt you to give up golf and take up fitness. But if you can tear yourself away from your loofah body buff for an afternoon, you'll discover the real reason for spending a few nights at Barton Creek.

BARTON CREEK CONFERENCE RESORT 8212 Barton Club Drive, Austin, Texas 78735. About 15 minutes from downtown Austin. Take Highway 71 to Bee Caves Road (Route 2244), then left to Barton Creek (follow signs). Telephone: (800) 527-3220. Accommodations: 148 guest rooms and suites. Amenities: Tennis, swimming, golf; plus a world-class spa with every fitness whirligig you've ever seen, not to mention a battalion of masseurs and masseuses to knead away your troubles. Terms: From $90 for a standard double room during the low season to $140 during peak (February through mid-May, Labor Day through mid-November); 1-bedroom suites range from $180 to $235. Presidential suites go for $525, and you don't even have to be a president of anything to rent one. Enough special packages to give Federal Express a backache.

Designer Tom Fazio was given a couple of hundred of the prettiest acres this side of Eden to work with, and he let the land have the last word. Of course, there was never any question that he would do otherwise: not even the U.S. Army Corps of Engineers would take a bulldozer to the dramatic cliffs, limestone caves, rushing waterfalls, and rolling terrain that make Barton Creek such a treasure. It's long enough at 6,956 yards, but you'll wish it was twice that long, that's how beautiful Barton Creek is.

You'll want your round never to end. And if you hit your ap-

BARTON CREEK CLUB

Design: Tom Fazio
Year Open: 1986
6,956 Yards   72.2 Rating   136 Slope
Information: (800) 527-3220

★
---

proach into the gaping mouth of the limestone cave that guards the eighteenth green, and then insist on finding your ball and playing it where it lies, maybe it never will.

When to Go

The best time is in the spring, when the Hill Country is in full bloom. Fall is also nice, with warm days and crisp nights. It's a bit riskier in the winter, but the mean high temperature is 60.3 degrees F., so you don't need to worry about frostbite. In the summer, the mean high temperature zooms to 95.1 degrees F., and that can be pretty damned mean, even though the humidity is reasonably tolerable in these parts. The thirty inches of annual rainfall usually come as about half a dozen frog-stranglers in the early spring, so you probably won't have to break out your rain suit. Not that it would do you much good if you did—when it rains in the Hill Country, it *rains*.

OFF COURSE

LBJ Country. You're smack dab in the middle of it. Seventeen miles south of Marble Falls on U.S. 281 is Johnson City. Take a right to the **Johnson Ranch** at the **Lyndon B. Johnson National Historical Park;** take a left to a perfect place to picnic at the **Pedernales Falls.** Get lost driving aimlessly through the prettiest countryside Texas has to offer.

Bluebonnet Trail. Go in the spring to see the bluebonnets, Indian paintbrush, and other wildflowers in bloom. Stop and say "Howdy" to all the folks in **Luckenbach** (Pop. 3), made famous by "Waylon, Willie and the Boys." You'll find it on Route 1888, which shoots off U.S. 290 about halfway between Johnson City and Fredericksburg, unless you happen to blink your eyes.

Fredericksburg. After the Revolution of 1848 in Europe, a lot of German liberals and Utopian socialists migrated to, of all places, central Texas. Among the most charming of the towns they founded is Fredericksburg, whose architecture, bakeries, local sausages, and appreciation of beer make it a heckuva nice place to visit.

Big Fish Eat Little Fish. If you don't believe it, just visit **Sea World** in San Antonio. I'm not much on theme parks, but this is definitely one of the biggest and best. And if you can con someone in the party to escort the kiddies, you can sneak off and play a quick round at **Breckenridge Park,** a short, sweet A. W. Tillinghast track just north of the Alamo.

Remember the Alamo. If you're in San Antonio, which is about an hour and a half south of Horseshoe Bay, stop by and see the Alamo. Just prepare yourself for a big letdown; it's no-where near as big as John Wayne led us to believe. Next door, have a drink in the **Menger Hotel** bar (512-223-4361), where Teddy Roosevelt recruited Rough Riders for the charge up San Juan Hill. Walk along the river that runs through town. Visit the **Lone Star Brewery** (512-226-8301) and the **San Jose Mission** (512-922-2731). And don't forget to stop by **El Mirador** on Sunday morning for a couple of bowls of soup and a basket of flour tortillas. If you haven't eaten breakfast at El Mirador, you haven't visited San Antonio.

Deep in the Heart. Austin isn't quite in the geographic center of Texas, but it'll do. If you're under twenty-five and like music, you already know about the music bars and honky-tonks along **Sixth Street.** For the rest of us, there's the **University of Texas** campus, **Scholz's Beer Garden,** and the **State Capitol.** Fans of low comedy should visit a session of the **Texas State Legislature.** For authentic country music, head out to the **Broken Spoke,** where George Straight got his start. If you know somebody who knows somebody who knows **Willie Nelson,** try to get yourself invited out to the nine-hole golf course he owns just outside of town. Par is whatever Willie says it is. On a hot day (Austin has about 200 of them in August alone), head for **Barton Springs,** the best swimming hole in America.

CHAPTER 3

ROCKY
MOUNTAIN
HIGH FIVE
Gold in Them
Thar Hills

THE LONE RIDER ASTRIDE THE BIG BAY STALLION makes his way slowly down the middle of the main street, his hand never far from the Colt .45 strapped to his leg. Even though it is nearing high noon, the wooden sidewalks of the weathered Western town are empty. Faces appear in windows along the way, at the barbershop and the general store and the saloon, but the lone rider pays them no mind. His gaze is steadfastly focused ahead of him on the solitary figure waiting at the end of the street, a woman with golden hair. Suddenly a shot rings out . . . CUT!

The year is 1952, the lone rider is Robert Stack, the woman with the golden hair is Virginia Mayo, and they are making a Western movie in the old, nearly deserted silver-mining town of Durango, Colorado.

And that twelve-year-old kid standing over there behind the ropes? The one with his eyes glued to the woman with the golden hair? Well, he's just experienced a portent of the next decade of his life, his knees almost buckled by the charge of pre-teenage hormonal lust rocketing through his body. He's hopelessly, head-over-heels in love with Virginia Mayo. He's me.

This all came to mind the last time I stood on the first tee at Tamarron, the extraordinary golf course cut into a high mountain valley eighteen miles north of Durango. Try as I might, I can't remember the name of the movie being shot that day in Durango, nor a single other detail of that long-ago vacation trip with my older brother, Henry, the best golfer in my family. Robert Stack is host of some TV show about true crimes and unsolved mysteries, probably as a result of all that time spent being Elliot Ness. And Virginia Mayo, with those inviting red lips, those playful blue eyes, all that golden hair? What of her?

She hasn't changed a bit, at least not in my dreams.

First-tee jitters are bad enough without thoughts of Virginia Mayo dancing through your head, so I'm going to step back and take a couple of practice swings before taking on Tamarron, the last and best leg of a five-stop tour of Colorado. A state better known for its skiing, Colorado makes up for a painfully short golf season with some of the finest mountain golf to be found between the Urals and the Urals. Our first stop, appropriately enough, is a ranch 9,000 feet above sea level.

KEYSTONE RANCH

The first question that comes to mind when you pull up to the front entrance of the main lodge at the Keystone Resort is a pretty basic one: "Where's the golf course?"

There's ski spoor all over the place: ski shops, ski equipment sales, ski condos for rent and sale, ski-theme restaurants, ski racks on every car with a Colorado license plate. But there's no sign of golf anywhere. Maybe I've got the wrong Keystone. Maybe I should ask a cop.

Not to worry, I'm told by the bellman, clearly a ski bum temporarily making ends meet between snowfalls; the golf course is only a ten-minute drive away. Hey, I *am* worried. A ten-minute *drive*? If a resort is really serious about its golf, I'm thinking to myself, you usually don't have to drive anywhere, except from the first tee. The course is right there, just outside your front door, no more than a short par five away.

I shouldn't have worried. For one thing, the ten-minute drive takes you out into the mountains away from all traces of modern ski culture. I don't ski. Never have and never will. Probably for that reason, I don't like to be in a place filled with ski stuff.

KEYSTONE RESORT Box 38, Keystone, Colorado 80345
About 65 miles west of Denver just south of Interstate 70
off Route 6. Telephone: (800) 541-0346. <u>Accommoda-
tions</u>: 152 rooms in the hotel, over 700 condominium
units. <u>Amenities</u>: Tennis, rafting, sailing, windsurfing,
horseback riding, biking, jeep tours, fishing, hiking, swimming. <u>Terms</u>: From $95 to $165. Special golf packages
available. No pets.

It makes me feel cranky. I love mountains, but not ones that
have been scarred with ski trails and encircled with fake alpine
architecture and choked with stores selling multicolored zinc
oxide. As far as I'm concerned, the ski lift represents the greatest misuse of engineering skill since the thumbscrew.

Anyway, to get to the golf course at Keystone you drive back
into the woods, past some riding stables, and into a mountain-
guarded valley right out of *Shane*. Really, I wouldn't have been
shocked to see Jack Palance, dressed in black and menacing
as a rattlesnake, stride out of the old ranch house at the end of
the road and challenge me to slap leather.

It didn't come to that—fortunately for me, as I'd left my six-
gun in my other golf bag—because the old ranch house is now
the clubhouse of the Keystone Ranch Golf Course.

KEYSTONE RANCH GOLF COURSE

Design: Robert Trent Jones, Jr.

Year Open: 1980
7,090 Yards   72.9 Rating   135 Slope

Information: (303) 468-4250

Some ranch, you think to yourself after playing the first two
holes, which are sliced out of a thick pine forest more reminis-
cent of Pinehurst than the Ponderosa. But then, on the third
hole, the Robert Trent Jones, Jr., layout opens up and spreads

out over a picturesque little valley where cattle once roamed and lettuce once grew.

Lettuce? Yes, lettuce. It seems that some time around the turn of the century, somebody had the bright idea to dam the stream running through the Keystone Ranch and use the abundant water and warm summer sun to grow lettuce, the better to supply the burgeoning population of Denver, sixty-three miles to the east, with fresh salad. Amazingly, lettuce cultivation continued for almost twenty years before somebody else—the original somebody's first son, probably—decided that trying to grow lettuce at 9,000 feet was pretty dumb, particularly since California was only one time zone to the west.

I like salad as much as the next person, but I'm glad somebody else—the ski people the original somebody's son sold the ranch to, probably—decided to turn the secluded valley into a golf course. The site, ringed by imposing peaks, is utterly tranquil, with nary a paved roadway in view and only a handful of vacation homes scattered under the surrounding trees. It's too small an area to handle many cows, but there's plenty of room for eighteen splendid golf holes, now that the lettuce is gone.

If you're a flatlander like me, you're high enough in the Rockies to be short of breath the first few days you're there. But the course at Keystone Ranch has the look and feel of a Scottish links. That's because the terrain was sculpted by a retreating glacier in much the same way that true linksland was formed by the retreating sea. Jones had the good sense just to place a few flagsticks here and there and not to try to improve on Mother Nature with a bulldozer.

There are a lot of good holes running over the valley floor and back and forth across a winding stream, but the one that's the most fun to play is the ninth, a dogleg-right par 4 over water that's only 368 yards from the tips and 318 from the middle tees.

If you take the safe way, a medium iron to the left and another to the green, it's just a golf hole. What makes it fun is that you can drive the sucker, because the 368 yards are as the fairway zigzags, not as your ball flies if you hit in on the screws. Even if you've been playing the white tees, climb up the hill to the blues and take a whack. The carry over water to the fairway down below is 215 yards or so in a beeline toward the green, a definitely possible dream in the thin mountain air; and from there to the center of the green it's less than ninety yards, slightly downhill.

Yes, Virginia, it is possible to drive the green from the back tees, I tell you, although I can't say I quite managed to do it myself. One of the guys in my foursome did, though, and he's a hacker just like me. Rolled it onto the green while the group ahead of us was putting is what he did.

What a great thing to have to apologize for!

All we care about is the golf course, but the other members of your entourage may not be so passionate about the game. For them, Keystone offers as wide a range of resort activities as any you'll ever encounter. Mountain biking along paved paths. Horseback riding along mountain trails. Sailing, boating, and kayaking on nearby Lake Dillon. White-water rafting for beginners and advanced thrill-seekers as well. Fishing, lake and stream. Hiking. A music festival, featuring classical and pops. On and on it goes—where the activities stop, nobody knows.

And if you play your cards right, you can squeeze in thirty-six holes a day and not have to take part in *any* of them.

BRECKENRIDGE

The next stop on the Rocky Mountain High Five is a municipal course. Steady, now—I know you can play on a municipal course without leaving home, and that what you are looking for on vacation is something special. Trust me: the Breckenridge Golf Club *is* something special.

BRECKENRIDGE GOLF CLUB

Design: Jack Nicklaus

Year Open: 1985

7,279 Yards   72.3 Rating   139 Slope

Information: (303) 453-9104

★

For starters, it's the only Jack Nicklaus-designed municipal course in the world. Better still, it's one of Jack's best, and that's saying a lot.

The course winds through natural wetlands, crisscrossing beaver ponds and streams, curving around stands of pine and fir, and lifting the golfer's spirits with wide-open vistas punctuated by towering mountain peaks. The scenery is every bit as breathtaking as the course is tough. How tough is that? Well, a slope of 115 is considered average, and the slope from the back tees at Breckenridge is calibrated at 139. That's tough.

An accurate description of the rough at Breckenridge sounds like the title of a porn flick: wet and wild. Of the course's 165 acres, only about 75 are maintained. The rest consist of beaver dams, ponds, impenetrable underbrush in swampy bogs, and dark thickets that make the sod-walled fairway bunkers look inviting by comparison. The fairways are of generous width. If they weren't, I'd still be there. Everything else, though, is wet and wild.

One ancillary benefit of the Breckenridge Golf Club is that it lies just northeast of Breckenridge proper, which means that if you're approaching from Interstate 70 you'll have no need to venture into the town. Perhaps I'm just being contrary, but I think Breckenridge (the town, not the golf course) is one of the region's greater eyesores. It's typically described as "a charmingly authentic Victorian-era mining town," but I see it as a tricked-up, tacky, artsy-cutesy mess. Maybe it's all those damned ski shops.

Anyway, my advice is to stay somewhere else — Keystone is an easy half-hour drive away — when you play Breckenridge. But whatever you do, don't miss it when you're in the neighborhood. You don't run across a muni course like this very often.

About as often as Jack Nicklaus designs one, I suppose.

BEAVER CREEK

Mustn't dawdle, though: Avon is calling.

Sorry, I couldn't resist that. But it's true: Avon *is* calling. Located less than an hour's drive from Breckenridge, Avon is just ten miles west of Vail, congregating spot of the Rich and Famous. Too close for comfort, in my view, but worth enduring for the chance to play yet another precious gem from the king of Colorado golf, Robert Trent Jones, Jr.

The Hyatt Regency Beaver Creek opened its doors on December 1, 1989, to considerable fanfare. At a cost of $65 million, the spanking new resort could afford a lot of fans, among them golfer and former President Gerald Ford, who normally hangs out down the road at the Vail Country Club. But Ford will go anywhere he smells a good golf course, and he sensed that under all that snow was a pretty swell track. (Hey, he may have played too much college football without a helmet, but he does know his golf.)

HYATT REGENCY BEAVER CREEK P.O. Box 1595, Avon, Colorado 81620. About 105 miles west of Denver on Interstate 70. Telephone: (800) 233-1234; (303) 949-1234. <u>Accommodations</u>: 296 guest rooms, 6 suites, and a variety of condo units. <u>Amenities</u>: Spa and health club, hiking, backpacking, fishing, chair-lift rides, swimming, jeep tours, hot-air ballooning, horseback riding, kayaking, rafting, biking, 5 tennis courts, jet boating, windsurfing, and just about everything else that doesn't require an ocean. <u>Terms</u>: From $150 for a standard room with a valley view to $225 for an "Executive King" with a mountain view. Go for the standard valley; you'll see plenty of mountains from the course. Special golf packages available.

Open for play since 1982, Beaver Creek is one of the stars in Jones Jr.'s Colorado crown. From the championship tees, the course measures only 6,464 yards—not long by any yardstick, but particularly not for a course 8,100 feet above sea level. Par is 70, with five par 3s and only three par 5s, so you begin to think to yourself: this must be one tricky sonuvagun.

That it is, and you can blame it on the beavers. The course goes nine holes out and nine back along their creek, criss-crossing the water more than Pan Am. Only two beaver ponds along the way come into play, but the creek or one of its tributaries is a factor on all but a handful of holes. If you spray the ball, you'd better know how to swim.

BEAVER CREEK GOLF COURSE

Design: Robert Trent Jones, Jr.

Year Open: 1982

6,464 Yards   69.2 Rating   133 Slope

Information: (303) 949-7123

★

The handsome new Hyatt Regency hotel, whose exterior uses native stone offset with stucco and rough timbers, is strictly state of the art, luxury resort division. Even if all you care about when it comes to hotels is an ample supply of clean towels, you can't help but be impressed with the place's amenities and tasteful decor. The available activities include all the usual ones, plus such exotica as hot-air ballooning and jet boating, ("Boats will fly across the water at speeds of up to 50 miles per hour in Glenwood Canyon.") And for those who congregate around the fireplace, there's even a resident storyteller who proffers tall tales of the mountains.

Which reminds me, have you heard the one about the duck who goes into a drugstore after a long day on the golf course and asks for a Chap Stick? Pharmacist says, That'll be $1.98. Duck says, Just put it on my bill.

And then there's the one about the traveling salesman, the farmer's three daughters, a goat, and the golf pro . . . Oh, I see. You've heard it.

SKYLAND

For stop number four on the Rocky Mountain High, throw your sticks in the trunk and take Route 24 south just outside of Avon on the way to Vail. Better pack a lunch, because this is a long mountain haul. The road takes you above the timberline, through mountain passes that make you glad it's summer, and through Leadville, one of Colorado's boom towns a century ago. Grab a bite, take a look at the opera house (Jennie Lind sang there), and keep on chugging. On the way south toward Buena Vista, Ivy Leaguers should take note: the three big peaks on your right are Mount Harvard, Mount Yale, and Mount Princeton. (If it matters, Harvard is the tallest at 14,420 feet, Princeton is next at 14,197, and Yale is a close third at 14,196.) Everyone else, keep a sharp lookout for the turnoff at Buena Vista for Taylor Park, due west across the Continental Divide. Still with me? Okay, at Taylor Park head southwest along the Taylor River (one of Colorado's better trout streams) to Almont, where you turn north again for seventeen miles toward Crested Butte.

Crested Butte is a ghost town.

No, it's not. But it used to be, almost. At least it was doggone near deserted when I first saw it, back in 1952, the year I fell in love with Virginia Mayo. Founded in the 1880s, the town seventy years later consisted of three or four saloons, about fifty run-down houses, and a bunch of boarded-up storefronts. Hunters used the place as a jumping-off point in the fall and winter, and a few anglers stopped there while fishing the East River. But a chair-lift was what you did when you wanted to sweep the floor, and condos were something you bought in gas station restrooms.

That was then, and this is now. Crested Butte is today one of the biggest, splashiest, fanciest, hottest ski emporiums in the Rockies, its spiffed-up and decidedly quaint storefronts bulging with regional artifacts hand-crafted from Gore-Tex by Ralph Lauren himself. And, since there are times of the year

---

THE LODGE AT SKYLAND P.O. Box 1549, Crested Butte, Colorado 81224. About 28 miles north of Gunnison, 210 miles southwest of Denver. Telephone: (303) 349-7541. Accommodations: 49 rooms in the lodge, plus two 2-bedroom condo units nearby. Amenities: Tennis, swimming, racquetball in golf clubhouse across the street. Terms: $153 per day, double occupancy. Rate decreases slightly with length of stay. About 18 percent less before July 1 and after August 31. Special golf packages available.

★

when there's no snow on the ground, it's also a logical place for a golf course.

The Skyland Resort and Country Club lists a local rule on its scorecard that tells you a lot about the place: "Free Relief from Elk Tracks." Located in a river valley smack in the middle of a national forest, Skyland has a front nine that will lull you into overconfidence and a back nine that will make you fight for your golfing life. The surrounding sage, heather, and wildflowers on the back nine are quite beautiful, at least until you hit into them. And the water that comes into play on the front nine is extremely cold.

SKYLAND RESORT AND COUNTRY CLUB

Design: Robert Trent Jones, Jr.

Year Open: 1983

7,208 Yards   71.7 Rating   122 Slope

Information: (303) 349-6131

Stay at one of the condo units managed by The Lodge at Skyland right across from the golf course, and stay out of town. That way you'll be able to enjoy a truly fine course in a magnificent mountain valley setting without having to expose yourself to too much ski culture. Even in the off-season, it can be injurious to your eyes. If you want to combine work with play, attend a session of the John Jacobs/Shelby Futch Practical Golf School, which runs classes all summer.

Just be sure to remember one other local rule: "Let the Elks Play Through."

TAMARRON

The bad thing about Durango is that you can't get there from here, unless you reside at Four Corners, where the borders of Utah, Arizona, New Mexico, and Colorado intersect. Denver is 332 miles away, for example; and the drive down from Crested Butte—about 225 miles on the odometer—will take a long, long day because mountain roads don't know from straight lines.

The good thing about Durango is also that you can't get there from here. Tucked down in the left-hand corner of Colorado, Durango has maintained more of the flavor of its silver-mining past than similar towns to the north precisely because it's so isolated.

There are direct daily flights to Durango from Denver, Phoenix, and Albuquerque, however, so it's not as if you had to go looking for one of the Seven Cities of Cíbola. That's a relief, because Durango is the doorway to one of the most spectacularly beautiful resort courses in America: Tamarron.

TAMARRON RESORT P.O. Box 3131, Durango, Colorado 81301. About 18 miles north of Durango west of Highway 550. Telephone: (800) 678-1000. Accommodations: 412 units, including 140 guest rooms in the main lodge and 272 housing units in 3 clusters of nearby townhouses. Facilities: All that you would expect from a 4-star resort, including horseback riding, backpacking, swimming, tennis, fishing, horseshoes, and lots, lots more. Terms: From $116 for a guest room in the lodge (double occupancy) to $289 for a 3-bedroom condo unit.

★

Designed by architect Arthur Hills, Tamarron is a stunner. Hills later was responsible for TPC at Eagle Trace, a stop on the PGA Tour for which he can be forgiven because all he had to work with was a dreary, featureless stretch of flat Florida pasture. But at Tamarron, he started with extraordinary natural beauty, and he was wise enough not to embellish it with tricks of the designer's trade.

TAMARRON GOLF COURSE

Design: Arthur Hills
Year Open: 1975
6,885 Yards   72.5 Rating   143 Slope
Information: (303) 259-2000, Extension 1240

★

Rugged rock formations, seventy-two sand bunkers, eight water holes, stands of soaring ponderosa pine, and large, undulating bent-grass greens are framed by the towering San Juan mountains. Locals say you can see more 14,000-foot peaks from Tamarron than from any other point in Colorado, and I always say local knowledge is worth two strokes a side.

Tamarron is owned and operated by the same people who own and operate Innisbrook at Tarpon Springs, Florida. In this case, pedigree is important, because Innisbrook always ranks among the top handful of Florida resorts, and the same attention to a golfer's needs prevails in Innisbrook's sister resort up in the Rockies.

How beautiful is Tamarron? Well, consider this: if your game goes sour, you can always put your clubs away and start snapping pictures. You'll probably end up making a fortune in the postcard business.

When to Go

The mountain courses of Colorado open up in late April and close in early November, a little later/earlier the farther north you go. But it can get pretty chilly at both ends of that time frame, and you don't want to run the risk of freezing your niblick off. The absolute pluperfect best time is August and September. Even in the "hot" months, morning frosts will keep you from teeing off much before eight-thirty. On the other hand, you can fry your face in the deceptively penetrating sun at that altitude, so be sure to slather on plenty of protective goo. The good news is that, as fine as the courses are, Colorado is still not popularly perceived as a Golf Mecca, and you should have no great difficulty arranging tee times.

OFF COURSE

Except for the odd music festival, just about everything worth doing or seeing in the high country in the summer is found outdoors. Most of the old mining towns have been tarted up to a fare-thee-well, but it can still be a hoot to walk down the streets of **Leadville** (between Keystone Ranch-Beaver Creek and Crested Butte, on your Rocky Mountain High Five Tour) and pretend you've just made a big gold strike. You can **Pan**

for Gold all over Colorado, and you can admire how long-lost wealth was spent in building up such long-since bypassed towns as **Silverton** and **Climax.** Down near Durango there's the **Durango-Silverton Narrow Gauge Railroad** to ride. And there's the scene in **Vail** to compare with the scene in **Aspen.** But mostly what you'll be doing when you're not playing golf is looking at the scenery, of which there is more per square inch in Colorado than just about anywhere. Hiking, biking, fishing, horseback riding, and all the other outdoor things Colorado has to offer in profusion are wonderful, but they all have to be done during golf hours, so somebody else will have to do them.

CHAPTER 4

BLUE RIDGE MOUNTAIN FAIRWAYS

The Mountain Courses of North Carolina

NOBODY READS THOMAS WOLFE ANYMORE. *Tom* Wolfe, yes. They make movies, big movies, out of Tom's books, so people read them. Or maybe it's vice versa. Anyway, Thomas is (way) out; Tom is (relatively) in. (Thomas and Tom aren't related, by the way, except that both grew up in the South and made their marks in New York City.) Outside college American lit classes, nobody knows from Thomas today.

Except for one thing. Just about everybody knows the title of Thomas Wolfe's *You Can't Go Home Again*. That simple but emotionally penetrating sentence has gone into the language and is used all the time by people who haven't read the book, who aren't even sure which of the Wolves wrote it, the guy with the white suits or the one from Asheville, North Carolina.

Oh yes—we know one other thing about Thomas, the Wolfe from Asheville who couldn't go home again. We know he wasn't a golfer.

We know that because Asheville, located in the skillet handle of western North Carolina, has a lot going for it: a wonderful climate, the Blue Ridge and Great Smoky Mountains, a proud literary and cultural tradition, the fabulous Biltmore House and Gardens, and a great ambiance. But if Thomas Wolfe had been a golfer, you can doggone well bet he'd have found a way to go home again, because Asheville is also the point of departure for some mighty fine mountain golf.

No need to make his mistake and go elsewhere looking for fame and fortune when there are so many birdies to be made within a ninety-mile radius of Asheville. There's "Golfer's Row"—Highway 64—running from Hendersonville southwest toward the Georgia border. There's the cluster of courses around Grandfather Mountain to the north. There are the valley courses due west of Asheville on the way to the Great Smokies. Trust me on this one: there's plenty of golf in Thomas Wolfe's old stomping grounds.

From April through October, you couldn't ask for more hospitable golf weather, and year round you can be sure of encountering hospitable people. As paradises go, the Asheville area is relatively undiscovered, at least by golfers, which means you can count on getting in thirty-six holes a day in high summer without feeling like you're firing bolts on an automobile assembly line.

Can't go home again? Maybe not. But unless you're Thomas Wolfe, you can certainly go to Asheville. And you should, if you like golf.

HOME IS WHERE YOU HANG YOUR GOLF HAT

They don't build them like this anymore. Not with four-foot-thick granite and concrete walls. Not from giant slabs of stone hacked out of the nearest mountain. Not with a lobby so big you could stash a 747 next to the piano. Not with furnishings that constitute living homage to an entire artistic and cultural movement. Not with fireplaces that hold twelve-foot logs supported by andirons weighing 500 pounds each. Not with the character, integrity, and sheer power of design of the Grove Park Inn.

Edwin Wiley Grove was a St. Louis patent medicine manufacturer who got rich before World War I peddling such curealls as Grove's Bromo Quinine and Grove's Tasteless Chill Tonic. A native of Paris (Tennessee, not France), he found the climate in Asheville soothed his chronic bronchitis, and consequently decided to put down some instant roots. A man of his ego and fortune needed a monument, and Grove decided it would be the biggest, best resort hotel in the world. A project of that scope couldn't be trusted to mere architects and contractors, who might have ideas of their own, so he recalled his son-in-law, Fred Seely, from one of the Grove business holdings in South America and gave him the job.

Against all odds, it was a terrific choice.

The Grove Park Inn bears its founding owner's name, but it bears Fred Seely's mark. Seely was a man of competence and taste, a former Atlanta newspaperman with an inventive, probing mind. He knew his father-in-law wouldn't settle for any scale less than grand, so he borrowed the basic design from the Old Faithful Inn at Yellowstone Park, which Seely felt combined the rugged and monumental qualities that would suit the old man. Hence the size, the stone facing, the imposing scale of the Grove Park Inn.

But Seely was also plugged into the current architectural and design scene. At the turn of the century, the Arts and Crafts style had emerged to challenge the ornate pretentiousness of the Victorian Era. Seely sensed that furniture designed by the likes of Gustave Stickley and Elbert Hubbard would work well in the type of structure he envisioned. He drew inspiration from the architectural ideas of Charles Greene and Frank Lloyd Wright in his choice of materials for the edifice's interiors. And so, in personally working out the design and overseeing the construction of Grove Park, Seely—a self-taught architect—created a monument both to his father-in-law and to the Arts and Crafts movement in American design. To honor his efforts, the Grove Park Inn was enrolled in the National Register of Historical Places in 1973.

GROVE PARK INN 290 Macon Avenue, Asheville, North Carolina 28804. Telephone: (800) 438-5800; (704) 252-2711. Accommodations: 142 rooms in the historic Main Inn; 368 in two modern wings. Don't go unless you can get a room in the Main Inn. Amenities: 9 tennis courts, 2 pools; sports center with racquetball, squash, exercise gear; golf. Terms: Double rooms from $160 to $220. Special golf package available.

★

Forgive me for going on a bit, but I'm nuts about Mission furniture and Stickley and Wright-thinking architecture and design; and the Grove Park Inn contains the single largest collection of Arts and Crafts furniture in the entire world. Plus it's an immensely dramatic place, a genuine throwback to another era. As you can tell from a single glance at the two new wings added in the last decade, they really *don't* make them like that anymore.

Great, you're probably thinking right about now, but what about golf?

Relax. There is a golf course at the Grove Park Inn, and it's a pip. Laid out originally by Willie Park, Jr., for the Country Club of Asheville in 1909, the course was reworked later by Donald Ross. It's not particularly long, nor particularly tough, but it's particularly enjoyable to anyone who prefers his golf courses simple and direct, with clean lines and no unnecessary ornamentation—like the interior of Grove Park Inn.

GROVE PARK INN AND COUNTRY CLUB

Design: Willie Park, Jr., and Donald Ross

Year Open: 1909
6,301 Yards   69.4 Rating   121 Slope

Information: (704) 252-2711

★

The Grove Park Inn is a great place to begin your Blue Ridge golf odyssey. Start there and fan out in just about any direction on the compass. Just be sure to stop back at Grove Park at the end of your trip, and spend a couple of days reflecting on how much Thomas Wolfe missed by being so stubborn.

SOUTH: ETOWAH VALLEY

Between the Blue Ridge and Great Smoky Mountains near Hendersonville, about fifty miles south of Asheville, there is a fertile valley the Cherokee Indians called "Etowah." The precise meaning of that word has been lost in time, but a pretty good contemporary translation is "too good to be true."

At least that's what some people would call unlimited play

on twenty-seven beautiful holes . . . a large, comfortable room with a screened-in balcony overlooking the golf course . . . breakfast and dinner . . . all for only sixty-five dollars per person a day (double occupancy).

ETOWAH VALLEY COUNTRY CLUB AND GOLF LODGE
P.O. Box 2150, Hendersonville, North Carolina 28793. About 50 miles south of Asheville on Route 64. Telephone: (800) 451-8174; (704) 891-7011. <u>Accommodations</u>: 55 rooms, all overlooking golf course. <u>Amenities</u>: Pool, hiking, climbing, canoeing nearby. <u>Terms</u>: From $65 (weekdays) to $75 (weekends) per person, double occupancy. Unlimited greens fees, breakfast, dinner, and club storage included. Special golf packages for longer stays. No pets.

Yeah, sure, the skeptic in you replies, only the golf course is a cow pasture, the room makes Motel 6 look luxurious, and the meals would cause a riot in your average high school cafeteria. Plus the portions are too small.

I understand. *Etowah*? No way. It's too good to be true.

But seeing is believing, right? So do this: call (800) 451-8174 and ask for the thirty-minute videotape about the Etowah Valley Country Club and Golf Lodge. For a twenty-dollar refundable deposit, you'll get a preview of the too-good-to-be-true golf deal described above. You'll see the tranquil valley streams, the verdant forest, and the surrounding mountains . . . the

---

ETOWAH VALLEY COUNTRY CLUB

Design: Edmund Ault

Year Open: 1967

Three Nines:

3,507 Yards	36.1 Rating	119 Slope
3,601 Yards	36.5 Rating	118 Slope
3,395 Yards	35.9 Rating	118 Slope

Information: (704) 891-7011

---

lighted putting green, the ultramodern but tastefully designed lodge units, and the well-appointed rooms . . . the lush fairways, tree-framed greens, and the rich landscaping of Etowah's three long, demanding nines. What you'll see is both good . . . and true.

The video is rated SG: No one admitted unless accompanied by a Serious Golfer. So is Etowah Valley.

SOUTHWEST: HIGH HAMPTON

If your idea of dressing for dinner after thirty-six holes of golf is to slip on a clean golf shirt, you'll go hungry at the High Hampton Inn, where gentlemen are expected to wear jackets *and* ties to dinner. And no, it won't get you off the hook if you insist that you're no gentleman; they've heard that one before. Fortunately, the traditional Southern food served here makes getting gussied up worthwhile. And if you order the spectacular fried chicken, the tie will come in handy for wiping your fingers.

The High Hampton Inn is steeped in Southern history. It was part of a mountain retreat put together by Carolina planter Wade Hampton II (1791–1858) and his heirs, the most notable of whom was Wade Hampton III (1818–1902), who managed to become a Confederate hero without getting himself killed, a rare feat indeed. (And just a little suspect, if you want the truth of it.) Hampton III went on to become governor and U.S. senator from South Carolina, all the while adding to the family's Blue Ridge holdings, as politicians are wont to do. The 2,200-acre estate was finally sold in the 1920s to the father of the present owner.

HIGH HAMPTON INN Cashiers, North Carolina 28717. Telephone: (704) 733-2411. About 65 miles southwest of Asheville on Route 107. Accommodations: 33 rooms in inn, 99 rooms in 18 cottages on the property. Amenities: Swimming, fishing, boating, tennis, hiking, white-water rafting, horseback riding. Terms: From $62 to $85 per person per day, Full American Plan (room plus all three meals included). Special golf package available.

★

The High Hampton opened in 1933 as a rustic country inn serving the well-to-do golfing set, and not much has changed since then. Each of the inn's comfortable rooms has a private bath, but none has a telephone, a television set, nor are there any plans to install either, thank you very much. Nor is there air conditioning, but don't panic: the Carolina highland nights are so cool you're more likely to need some of the firewood piled outside your door.

The golf course at High Hampton is every bit as genteel and proper as the inn itself, with not so much as a single blade of grass out of place on its immaculately manicured fairways and greens. It almost seems a shame to take a divot from the lush turf, but there seems to be no local rule against it. Designed around two picturesque lakes by George Cobb, the course has a serenity that may get you to daydreaming about those old pictures of Bobby Jones playing golf in long-sleeve shirt, V-necked wool sweater, and tie. High Hampton is a Bobby Jones kind of place.

HIGH HAMPTON COUNTRY CLUB

Design: George Cobb (redesign of course originally laid out in 1924)

Year Open: 1924/1960

6,012 Yards   No Rating   No Slope

Information: (704) 733-2411

Postscript. If you belong to a club, have your home pro try to get you on the new Wade Hampton Golf Course nearby. I haven't played there myself, but people who have say that it's super. Some are touting it as the best course Tom Fazio has ever designed, and that's saying a lot. It's probably not true that only gray golf shirts are permitted in the clubhouse.

WEST: MAGGIE VALLEY

Don't let the name fool you. The Maggie Valley Resort and Country Club may be located in a valley, but the back nine takes you from 2,600 feet up to 3,500 feet, and you don't need to ogle the Great Smokies and the Blue Ridge that provide so scenic a backdrop for your labors to know that you're playing a mountain course. And if you think somebody named "Maggie" is automatically gentle and cuddling, think again. Water comes into play on eleven holes, and the large greens are a lot faster than you normally expect to find at a resort course. Maggie can be a demanding mistress.

MAGGIE VALLEY RESORT AND COUNTRY CLUB P.O. Box 99, Maggie Valley, North Carolina 28751. On Route 19 35 miles west of Asheville. Telephone: (800) 438-3861; (704) 926-1616. Accommodations: 64 rooms in the lodge, 11 cottages. Amenities: Pool, 2 tennis courts. Terms: From $82 to $112 per person, double occupancy, on weekdays, April 1—October 31. For weekends, add about 10 percent. Price includes dinner, breakfast, room, and greens fees. Assorted special packages available for stays of three nights or more.

Take the third hole. If you don't, it'll take you, especially if you're prone to snap hooks when overswinging on 458-yard par 4s. A creek runs the length of the left side of a fairway that doglegs left to a slightly elevated green. Hit it too far right and you make a long hole longer. Hit it too far left and you better hope you catch the fairway bunker, unless your ball knows how to swim.

Don't get me wrong. Maggie Valley is not something to strike terror in the heart of the weekend golfer. The course rating is only 69.8, with a slope factor of 115, from back tees that stretch to only 6,284 yards, so you don't have to be Greg Norman to score at Maggie Valley. It's fun, fair, and playable.

MAGGIE VALLEY COUNTRY CLUB

Design: William Prevost and William Brenner

Year Open: 1960

6,284 Yards   69.8 Rating   115 Slope

Information: (704) 926-1616

The nicest thing about Maggie Valley, at least from this duffer's point of view, is that it's all about golf. There's a pool, should you feel like drowning yourself after a string of three-putt greens. And there's a tennis court or two, should you be driven to take up another, even dumber game. But everything revolves around golf at Maggie Valley.

Heck, I suppose a person *could* stay at Maggie Valley and not play golf at all. (So far as I know, there's no local ordinance prohibiting it, and small Southern towns are usually pretty good about thinking up things to prohibit.) But why? It would be a lot like going to a Burger King and ordering broccoli.

NORTHEAST: ESEEOLA, GREEN PARK, AND HOUND EARS

Nestled next to Grandfather Mountain about seventy-five miles northeast of Asheville, the Eseeola Lodge has the look and feel of an English country inn in the Lake District. Anglophiles will warm to the well-tended grounds, the garden, and the nearby trout stream. Built in 1924, Eseeola is now listed on the National Register of Historic Places, a designation that aptly recognizes its special quality. There are only twenty-four rooms, and they are always in great demand, so book early.

ESEEOLA LODGE Linville, North Carolina 28646. Telephone: (704) 733-4311. Near the Blue Ridge Parkway 70 miles northeast of Asheville. <u>Accommodations</u>: 28 rooms in rustic lodge. <u>Amenities</u>: Heated pool, tennis courts, croquet court, hiking trails, putting green, trout fishing, golf. <u>Terms</u>: From $85 to $110 per person, double occupancy, Modified American Plan (breakfast and dinner included).

There are reasons aplenty for visiting Eseeola—the excellence of its dining room, the impeccably selected antique furnishings that contribute to the inn's special feel, the quiet luxury and simple good taste reflected throughout. But the best reason for coming here is not to pretend you're an English lord, although you should go right ahead if it makes you feel good. The best reason is golf.

Guests of the Eseeola Lodge are extended playing privileges

at the Linville Golf Club and believe me, that's quite a privilege. Two years before the lodge came into existence Donald Ross was putting the finishing touches on the Linville course, and anyone who loves golf should include it on his itinerary, even if it means sleeping in the car.

LINVILLE GOLF CLUB

Design: Donald Ross

Year Open: 1922

6,780 Yards   72.7 Rating   135 Slope

Information: (704) 733-4311

★

The greens are small but fast, as well as subtly contoured and crested so as to reject poorly struck approaches. The fairways are invitingly wide where the tee shots of average golfers are most likely to land, but much tighter where the big hitters go. The few bunkers are perfectly placed to exact a price for a mistruck ball. And the long par 3s and par 4s require frequent and skillful employment of that most quintessential Ross weapon, the long iron. At 6,780 yards from the tips, there's plenty of long in Linville, which always makes both major golf magazines' periodic listings of the top resort courses in the country.

Linville is, in other words, a classic Ross course. Don't miss it.

Show me your average century-old historic country resort hotel, and I'll show you an old-new hybrid that's had 90 percent of its charm modernized out of existence. The Green Park Inn in Blowing Rock, North Carolina, is an exception.

GREEN PARK INN P.O. Box 7, Blowing Rock, North Carolina 28605. Telephone: (800) 852-2462; (704) 295-3141. About 95 miles northeast of Asheville on Route 321. <u>Accommodations</u>: 85 rooms and suites. <u>Amenities</u>: Golf, tennis at adjacent Blowing Rock Country Club. Wilderness hiking, cycling, horseback riding, climbing, and white-water rafting nearby. <u>Terms</u>: From $89 to $155, European Plan. Special golf package available.

Even if it weren't, a good case could be made for staying there, just so your postcards would be postmarked "Blowing Rock," a strong candidate for the Place Name Hall of Fame. But the owners of the Green Park Inn over the years have had the good sense not to tamper with those essential qualities of the establishment that warrant its being listed in the National Register of Historic Places.

This doesn't mean that you're going to have to read by candlelight and use the privy out back in the woods; all modern creature comforts have been well attended to. It's just that the classicly detailed, white-with-green-trim wooden structure, which first opened its doors to the carriage trade in 1882, has been quietly updated over the years in a manner that has left its character and integrity intact.

Located 4,300 feet up in the Blue Ridge Mountains, the eighty-five-room inn has bedded down a who's who of lumi-

BLOWING ROCK COUNTRY CLUB

Design: Donald Ross

Year Open: 1940

6,038 Yards   68.4 Rating   110 Slope

Information: (704) 925-3141

naries, among them Eleanor Roosevelt and Calvin Coolidge (they had separate rooms), not to mention Herbert Hoover and John D. Rockefeller, who lived up to his cheapskate image by giving each member of the serving staff a shiny new dime. Margaret Mitchell was also a guest at Green Park, thereby bestowing the Tara Seal of Approval on the hostelry.

The golf course that guests survey from their balconies is every bit as charming and comfortable as the inn. At 6,038 yards from the back tees, the par-70 walk in the country that Donald Ross designed for the Blowing Rock Country Club will probably never host a U.S. Open. That's okay; I'll probably never play in one. But if it did, and I did, I'd have to be considered at least a longshot favorite, because this is *my* kind of golf course. Generously wide fairways, forgiving rough, not much sand, and medium-slow greens that add up to a heckuva nice round of vacation golf.

Normally, I'm not a big fan of golf resorts that double as ski lodges in the winter. I can't quite put my finger on the reason. It's not that I have anything against other people risking life and limb hurtling down mountains in the dead of winter, so long as they don't ask me to join them. It's not that I'm afraid of stumbling on the decomposed carcass of an inept downhiller while scouring the woods for my ball on the back nine; I assume the resort's cleanup crews and/or the region's indigenous varmints take care of such unpleasantness before the course opens for the golf season. Maybe it has a little to do with architecture: ersatz Swiss chalet is just not a good look.

HOUND EARS CLUB P.O. Box 188, Blowing Rock, North Carolina 28605. Telephone: (704) 963-4321. About 90 miles northeast of Asheville on Highway 105. Accommodations: 28 lodge rooms and suites, all overlooking golf course. Amenities: Pool, horseback riding, hiking. Terms: From $122 to $134 per person, double occupancy, Modified American Plan (breakfast and dinner included). Note: No liquor, beer, or wine is sold; guests may bring their own.

★

Whatever the case, none of my usual qualifications apply to the Hound Ears Club in Blowing Rock, North Carolina, where you can ski your heart out in the winter (or so I'm told) and play golf from dawn to dusk in the summer. For one thing, the lodge itself is unobtrusively modern and utterly lacking in fake Alpine decor. For another, there are stupendous views from all the bedroom windows.

HOUND EARS CLUB

Design: George Cobb

Year Open: 1963

6,165 Yards   68 Rating   113 Slope

Information: (704) 963-4321

★

But the main reason that Hound Ears causes me to set aside my prejudice against golf-ski hybrids is its George Cobb course, a short (6,165 yards), sweet hike over hilly terrain studded with giant boulders and guarded by thick forest. With a course rating of sixty-eight from the back tees, Hound Ears should give your golf ego a boost. But be careful. It's still a golf course, after all, and that means it's capable of giving you a kick somewhere else.

When to Go

Unless you have something against wildflowers, dogwoods, and azaleas in full bloom, **spring** is a great time to go. Just remember that April showers bring May flowers, and you could get wet. **Summer** in the mountains of western Carolina is as cool, green, and refreshing as . . . as summer in the mountains of western Carolina. In the **fall** Mother Nature paints the mountainsides in swatches of gold and red, the way Uncle Walt used to do in the "Wide, Wide World of Disney." Don't tell the folks in the Northeast or it will hurt their feelings, but autumn in western Carolina is every bit as beautiful as autumn in New England.

Golf courses in the mountains around Asheville are closed from (roughly) Thanksgiving to April 1, so don't go in the **winter.**

OFF COURSE

Visitors to **Asheville** are practically required by local law to visit the **Biltmore Estate** (704-274-1776), and for good reason. Built back in the 1890s by George W. Vanderbilt when a million bucks could buy something, the Biltmore was modeled after Versailles, and it shows in every extravagant detail. There are 250 rooms, give or take a snuggery; elaborate grounds and gardens; a winery; enough fine antiques to furnish a small country; and a whole lot more. Put it this way: if you have vowed never again to be dragged through another stately home so long as there is breath in your body, you should make an exception for this one. It's that special.

Drive up and down the **Blue Ridge Parkway** and let yourself be overwhelmed by some of the most gorgeous scenery this side of a Sierra Club calendar. Visit the **Cherokee Indian Reservation** and become depressed by a dramatic recounting of white man's inhumanity to red man in this country. Take a detour every time you see a road sign for a **waterfall,** of which the neighborhood has plenty. None is Niagara, but all are swell.

This is a great part of the world for pottery and for arts and crafts. The **Folk Art Center** on the Blue Ridge Parkway east of Asheville is a good place to start.

Back in Asheville, visit the **Thomas Wolfe Memorial** (704-253-8304). It's the frame home immortalized as Dixieland in *Look Homeward, Angel,* which you should read in preparation for this vacation. Not much golf in it, but a doggone good book nonetheless.

CHAPTER 5

THE PAUL BUNYAN CIRCUIT
Teeing It Up in the Pacific Northwest

IT'S NOT A WIDELY KNOWN FACT, NOT EVEN among students of American mythology, but Paul Bunyan was an avid golfer.

Not in his youth, when most of his time and energy were devoted to clear-cutting New England, but later, in his early thirties, when he took up the game with a passion. Like many of us, Bunyan had a lot of trouble with his short game when he was first starting out: at least 900 of Minnesota's 10,000 lakes resulted from his hitting his L-wedge fat. But he improved rapidly, as a quick glance at the Dakotas and Montana will confirm: there's hardly a lake to be seen.

But it was as a senior golfer in the Pacific Northwest that big Paul fine-tuned his game. Old logging chanteys tell of the lazy summer days when Bunyan and Babe, his loyal Blue Ox and caddy, would play thirty-six in the morning in Oregon and thirty-six after lunch in Washington. As with everything else, Paul Bunyan had a mighty appetite for golf.

Bunyan, as you might expect, was a big hitter. But he was also a little wild, so he usually hit a three-iron off the tee, even on the longest par 5s. It was something to see, old-timers recall. A booming 285-yard tee shot, followed by another 285-

yard three-iron to the middle of a green that ordinary mortals, not even Greg Norman, could ever hope to reach in two. On occasion, though, Bunyan would lose his concentration while standing over his eagle putt, and stroke the ball another 285 yards past the hole!

(What's that? You say you've heard that one, only it was a gorilla? Yeah, well, that's the thing about myths, they get all confused in the retelling. Sort of like that story you've been telling about how you played the sixteenth at Winged Baltusrol Oaks last month. Remember? That great drive, and that great fairway wood, and that great wedge, and that great twenty-seven-foot downhill putt with three breaks that you drained for a bird?)

Now, if you think I might be making all this up, and want absolute proof positive that Paul Bunyan was a golfer, and a dadgum good one, all you have to do is make your way to the Pacific Northwest and play the back nine at Port Ludlow. . . .

But wait a minute. That's getting ahead of the story. Port Ludlow is the final destination on a golfing loop through the Pacific Northwest that will cause you to give serious consideration to pulling up stakes and moving there to start a new life.

SALISHAN

The first stop on the Paul Bunyan circuit is at a place on the Oregon coast called Salishan, which is a Pacific Northwest Indian word meaning "come together from diverse points to communicate in harmony." Really.

Just ask anybody who's ever come from anywhere to the Salishan Lodge at Gleneden Beach, Oregon. About two hours southwest of Portland, Salishan offers quietly luxurious accommodations unobtrusively laid out in a lush forest, a splendid restaurant that may be the best in the entire region, a wine cellar with over 21,000 bottles that's won *The Wine Spectator*'s Grand Award as one of the world's finest, a Five-Star Rating from Mobil and a Five-Diamond Rating from AAA, and a nifty little golf course that's half woodlands, half links, and all fun.

If you can't communicate in harmony at Salishan, amigo, you're going to have a hard time getting along in heaven.

Highway 101 bisects the Salishan Golf Links, and the dividing line is by no means arbitrary. The front nine, to the east of the highway, runs up and around a thickly wooded hillside,

SALISHAN LODGE U.S. Highway 101, Gleneden Beach, Oregon 97388. On the coast just south of Lincoln City. Telephone: (800) 452-2300. Open all year. <u>Accommodations</u>: 201 rooms in 2-story wooden buildings around the main lodge. All have fireplaces, balconies, and covered carports. Views of forest, golf course, or bay. <u>Amenities</u>: A world-class restaurant, The Dining Room, that features seafood, game, and local produce from the Pacific Northwest. Two other, less formal restaurants, The Sun Room and The Cedar Tree. An intimate lounge, The Attic, with piano entertainment and dancing in the evenings. An 18-hole golf course, 4 tennis courts, fitness center, swimming pool; jogging, hiking, beachcombing; clamming, crabbing; ocean, stream, and lake fishing. <u>Terms</u>: Double rooms from $118 to $175 in high season (May—October); approximately 25 percent less the rest of the year. Two-night minimum required on weekends during the summer. For summer months, book well ahead. Reservations also essential for The Dining Room.

whose groves of Sitka spruce, hemlock, Douglas fir, and red cedar trees are lovely to behold but a nasty place to visit if you're trying to make par. The back nine, on the ocean side of 101, hugs the gently curving contours etched by the ocean as it slowly retreated a couple of million years ago. Trees still come into play—this is tall timber country, after all—but the fairways on the back side feel more like Scotland.

SALISHAN GOLF LINKS

Design: John Gray and Fred Federspeil
Year Open: 1965
6,439 Yards   72.3 Rating   129 Slope
Information: (503) 764-3632

To many American golfers, accustomed as we are to the highly manicured look at better courses, Salishan will appear a little shaggy. That's intentional. The Scottish links philosophy is operative at Salishan, where the tees, landing areas, and greens are well maintained, while the coastal and forest vegetation are permitted a relatively free hand whenever possible. This means that the rough is rough, not precisely cut to a uniform height. It also means tight lies, in fairways that aren't billiard-table smooth, on grass that doesn't always behave. Don't cheat yourself by calling "Winter Rules" and rolling the ball in the fairway: play it as it lays, the way Old Tom Morris would do. Otherwise, you'll miss the point.

The longer front nine has two particularly demanding par 4s that give you the same look from a radically different perspective. The seventh is a dogleg-left that seems to go uphill a lot farther than the 426 yards on the card; the ninth is a dogleg-left that plays downhill considerably shorter than the 440 yards it claims to be. On the former you have to make sure you hit enough club on your second shot; on the latter you have to make sure you don't fly the green perched in a little valley down below.

The shorter back nine looks a whole lot easier than it plays. The closer you get to the ocean, the more you have to contend with the wind. It's not just that it knocks your ball down; it also bends it. In the hands of even a mild zephyr coming over the top of the dunes between you and the ocean, a gentle fade turns into a banana slice. And when it really blows, you'll feel like you're hitting boomerangs. The twelfth hole, for example, measures only 414 yards, but on windy days it might as well be in Hawaii.

You should know, straight off, that the golf course at Salishan takes a back seat to the extraordinary food in The Dining Room, and to the magnificent natural surroundings where forest meets sea along this slice of the Oregon coast. Don't take that as a putdown. In fact, the golf course at Salishan is as invigorating as a salty sea breeze, a touch of Scotland on America's West Coast, a delight in all seasons, and a genuine challenge when the westerly winds are up.

But it would have to be Muirfield and Augusta National rolled into one to match the handiwork of Salishan's kitchen, which is so outstanding that, no matter how bad your round, you are guaranteed a great meal at the end of the day. And, since Mother Nature is a better landscape architect than any golf course designer who ever lived, you'll eat it in a restaurant with a great view.

BLACK BUTTE RANCH

The second stop on the Paul Bunyan Circuit looks like the setting for the climactic chapters of *Lonesome Dove*. Just think: if Augustus and Call had only kept on going instead of stopping in Montana, Augustus might not have caught that arrow in his thigh, and they could have lived out their years playing the two gorgeous courses at Black Butte Ranch. So what if it would have spoiled the TV mini-series?

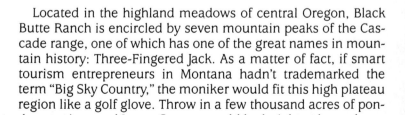

BLACK BUTTE RANCH P.O. Box 800, Black Butte, Oregon 97759. On U.S. Highway 20 about 135 miles southeast of Portland. Telephone: (800) 452-7455. <u>Accommodations</u>: 110 rooms, ranging from hotel-type rooms to 1-, 2-, and 3-bedroom condominium units to larger resort homes. <u>Amenities</u>: The Lodge Restaurant and Lounge, located— as you may have guessed—in the main lodge. Two 18-hole golf courses, 19 tennis courts, 4 outdoor pools, and 16 miles of bike and jogging trails; hiking, fishing, boating, white-water rafting, and horseback riding in nearby Deschutes National Forest. <u>Terms</u>: From $50 for a standard, hotel-type room to $145 for 3-bedroom condominium with 2 baths that will accommodate 6 people. That's in high season (June 15–September 15). Reduced weekly rates make you want to think about staying a long time. No pets. Book well ahead for July and August.

Located in the highland meadows of central Oregon, Black Butte Ranch is encircled by seven mountain peaks of the Cascade range, one of which has one of the great names in mountain history: Three-Fingered Jack. As a matter of fact, if smart tourism entrepreneurs in Montana hadn't trademarked the term "Big Sky Country," the moniker would fit this high plateau region like a golf glove. Throw in a few thousand acres of ponderosa pines and Lorne Greene would look right at home here.

(The smart money says that a foursome of Hoss, Little Joe, Adam, and Daddy Ben Cartwright would be mighty tough to beat in the All-Oregon Scramble.)

Black Butte Ranch is a condo community, and that sometimes spells trouble, conjuring up nightmares of townhouse-lined fairways where even the slightest trace of a teensy little hook might ricochet off the Weber grill on the patio, crash through the sliding glass door to the family room, and conk the much-beloved family mutt right between the eyes. And that could lead to an exchange like this:

> OUTRAGED CONDO-OWNER: Omigod! You've killed Spot! What are you going to do?

> YOU: Well, I think if I open my stance and bring my right hand over just a bit . . .

But you won't need to bring your lawyer with you to Black Butte Ranch—what kind of vacation would *that* be? With a couple of thousand acres to work with, and all those trees that Paul Bunyan overlooked, you don't have to be Frank Lloyd Wright (a six handicap in his prime) to figure out a way to blend nearly a thousand private dwellings unobtrusively into the countryside—and well out of harm's way, even if you're Ben Crenshaw having a bad day.

GLAZE MEADOW AT BLACK BUTTE RANCH

Design: Gene "Bunny" Mason

Year Open: 1980

6,560 Yards   70.6 Rating   125 Slope

Information (both courses): (503) 595-6400

BIG MEADOW AT BLACK BUTTE RANCH

Design: Robert Muir Graves

Year Open: 1970

6,870 Yards   71.6 Rating   125 Slope

★

While You're in the Neighborhood . . .

When I'm en route between principal destinations of a golf vacation, I always think it's a good idea to break up the monotony of travel by stopping every now and then to play a little golf. Here are some names to keep in mind when you hit the open road.

On the western side of the Cascade range in Oregon are two courses open to the public that rank among the top tracks in the Pacific Northwest: **Tokatee Golf Club** in Blue River (telephone: 503-822-3220, about an hour from Eugene on Route 126; and **Elkhorn Valley Golf Course** in Lyons (telephone: 503-897-3368, about forty-five minutes from Salem on Route 226. **Tokatee** is ranked second only to Port Ludlow among golf courses in the entire region, public or private.

Heading north from Portland toward Seattle, plan a rest stop at **Tumwater Valley Golf Course** in Olympia a few miles off Interstate 5 (telephone: 206-943-9500). Its nineteenth hole, a worthy establishment called the Broadmoor, was recently selected by a distinguished panel of experts brought together by the *Seattle Post-Intelligencer* as the best in the state. I'll drink to that.

Way, *way* north of Seattle, north of just about everything—in fact, on the most northwesterly headland of the mainland United States, near the town of Blaine (just off Interstate 5)—is a breathtakingly beautiful layout designed by Arnold Palmer (with Ed Seay, of course, doing all the heavy lifting). Named **Semiahmoo** (after the Pacific Northwest Indian word meaning "half a hmoo"), it's long and lush, with bent-grass fairways that are smoother than half the greens in the country. It's also part of an ultramodern, top-drawer resort with all the trimmings, **The Inn at Semiahmoo** (telephone: 206-371-2000). The only problem with Semiahmoo is that you can't hardly get there from here. But if you do, it's worth the trip.

★

Glaze Meadow, the older and shorter of the two courses at Black Butte (the other is Big Meadow), always makes everybody's list of "Top Five" golf courses in the Pacific Northwest. And with good reason. It's not an especially tough course, nor especially long. But it is especially beautiful. And if it doesn't cause your handicap to go up a couple of strokes, who's to complain? Hey, that's why they call it a *vacation*!

Making suggestions for someone else's vacation itinerary is tough. I don't know where you're starting from, or whether there are any nongolfers in your party whose needs you have to pay lip service to, much less whether you're as obsessive as I am about getting from one golf course to the next, while spending as little time and energy as possible in such frivolous pursuits as sight-seeing and sleeping.

So: you may prefer to make a few detours for some sight-seeing, spend a day or so in Portland and Seattle, take in a Mariners game at the Kingdome, or go fishing in Puget Sound. Fine. But not me. I'm ready for Port Ludlow.

Don't get me wrong—on a nongolf vacation, I'm a major-league, let's-see-everything tourist with a peculiar affinity for obscure places with strange-sounding names. (Someday I want to go to Humptulips in western Washington just to hang out and see what people do for fun.) But when the vacation is built around golf, the only thing I care about is when my next tee time is.

PORT LUDLOW

If you still harbor any lingering doubt that Paul Bunyan played golf, and that his home course was the Robert Muir Graves masterpiece at the Resort at Port Ludlow, proceed at once to the fifteenth hole, and walk down the left-hand side of the fairway about 150 yards. There, well out of play (unless your snap hook is even deadlier than mine), is one of the most extraordinary sights you'll ever encounter on a golf course—or in your nightmares. It's the stump of an ancient cedar tree of gargantuan size, lying on its side and exposing its root structure, an eighteen-foot-wide natural sculpture of gnarls and twists that looks like a huge platter of petrified snakes. It's as if someone had plucked the giant trunk from the ground, then tossed it aside.

Well, someone *did*. It was Paul.

Port Ludlow hasn't been a port since the mid-1930s, when the Pope and Talbot Company (which owned it) shut down its timber-shipping operations. The company kept its land, however, and in the early 1970s set out to build a luxury resort whose main attraction would be a world-class golf course.

PORT LUDLOW

Design: Robert Muir Graves

Year Open: 1975

6,787 Yards   74.4 Rating   143 Slope

Information: (206) 437-2222

★

It wasn't easy. Half the 160 acres designated for the golf course was a peat bog, the other half was solid basaltic rock. In other words, half bottomless pit and half hardpan that wouldn't hold fairway turf. The answer: blast the rock to bits, distribute it over the bog, and haul in hundreds of thousands of yards of sand until everything stabilized enough to plant grass seed. And you do it all on hilly terrain choked with second-growth spruce, cedar, and Douglas fir only after clearing away enough thick underbrush with handsaws and machetes to figure out where to put eighteen fairways.

Unless you like to putter in your backyard, of course, these little details don't matter. You don't want to hear that dynamite was one of the biggest line items of the construction (destruction?) budget. You don't care that it took almost three years to

complete the eighteen-month project. On the other hand, you might care whether they left anything standing. And you certainly care what the end result looks and plays like.

Well, you're in for a treat. Port Ludlow is simply one of the most beautiful golf courses you will ever see. And I'll wager you've never enjoyed on any other golf course the splendid isolation you'll encounter here, smack dab in the middle of this whopping great Pacific Northwest forest. There are a few tastefully designed homes to be seen just off the course on the front nine, but the back nine is nothing but you, the forest, and whatever local fauna decide to cross the fairways. (If you see a mama bear with her cubs, let her play through.)

How many other courses have you ever seen with tree stumps eight feet in diameter smack in the middle of sand traps? With a discreet notice on the scorecard that you get a free lift from wildflower beds? With 250-foot-tall Douglas firs guarding the toughest par 4s? With no two fairways running parallel to each other, so that you practically never see another golfer, except for the bozos in your own foursome? With all this, and an exquisite short hole (the seventeenth) that rivals anything Augusta National can throw up for sheer beauty?

You have to hit the ball straight to score at Port Ludlow. The fairways are wide, much wider than they seem because of the bordering trees. But the rough is . . . well, there is no rough per se: just forest. And if you hit in there, forget about going in to look for your ball. Little Red Riding Hood's grandmother had a better chance of coming out of the forest alive than a golfer does at Port Ludlow. Just drop another, take your stroke and distance, and pray to your lucky stars that you haven't suddenly, finally, stumbled upon a repeatable swing after all these years.

Keep it in the fairway, and you'll discover that pars are tough to come by, but bogeys easy—the way it ought to be, in my view. The pars are tough because the greens are big, undulating, and faster than at most resort courses. Get hot with the flat stick and you can make a good number—*if* you stay out of the woods.

Port Ludlow appears on all the right lists of top courses, ranging from the American Society of Golf Course Architects, to *Golf Digest*, and *Golf*. Even so, it remains less well known than you might expect for a course that's been around fifteen years, and that may have something to do with popular misconceptions regarding the weather.

It's located on the Olympic Peninsula in the Pacific Northwest, and everybody knows that's the wettest spot in continental United States (with the possible exception of Houston when I happen to be there). So that means you never get out of your rain suit at Port Ludlow, right?

Yes and no. Yes, the Olympic Peninsula is pretty moist. Seventy-five miles due west of Port Ludlow, on the other side of Mount Olympus, there's an honest-to-God rain forest, as in over 100 of inches rain per year. That's wet. And in Seattle, just on the other side of Puget Sound, it rains so much that they have to play baseball indoors. Also wet. But Port Ludlow is situated in the "rain shadow" of Mount Olympus, which means that the prevailing westerlies bring moisture in from the Pacific, dump it all at first landfall to the west of Port Ludlow, and don't refuel until they cross Puget Sound. Port Ludlow gets only about twenty to twenty-five inches of rain a year, enough to keep everything green but not enough to spoil a vacation.

Enough meteorology. What about room and board?

THE RESORT AT PORT LUDLOW 9483 Oak Bay Road, Port Ludlow, Washington 98365. About one and a half hours north of Tacoma via Routes 16, 3, and 104. Also accessible from Seattle via car-ferry; check with resort office for precise directions and schedule. Telephone: (206) 437-2222. Accommodations: Approximately 170 rooms in condominium units. Amenities: Full-service marina, with sailports and motorboats available for rent; pool, tennis, handball, croquet, miniature golf; fishing. And, of course, golf. Terms: From $90 on weekdays for a room without a view of the water to $140 on weekends for a 1-bedroom suite with kitchen, living room, fireplace, balcony, and water view. (Spring for the suite.) About 20 percent less between October 1 and May 1. Book early for July and August.

The resort itself is located a couple of miles away from the golf course, on the other side of a little bay that once launched timber-laden schooners out to a world under construction. Guests stay in attractive, well-appointed condo units built on spacious grounds adjacent to a central lodge. All the usual amenities are available, including health club, pool, and tennis courts, and just about any sort of aquatic gear you can think of. Plus there's a huge marina for guests who arrive by water. (To me, Puget Sound is just another water hazard, albeit on a colossal scale. Apparently, the natives see it otherwise. In this part of the country, a lot of people seem to spend all their recreational hours on or in the water.)

Because it's so convenient, give the restaurant in the main lodge, called the Harbormaster, a try. Maybe you'll be lucky, but I found it long on reach and short on grasp. So be prepared to drive down the road a bit to Port Townsend, a delightful port town that has kept the look and feel of its nineteenth-century origins. There you'll find any number of good, solid, unpretentious restaurants specializing in local fish and seafood. My personal favorite: Lido, on the bay at 925 Water Street. (Ask for a table upstairs by the window when you call for reservations; the number is 385-7111.)

But even though this is the land of Dungeness crab and potlatch salmon, of excellent local white wine and Olympia beer, of hiking and biking and birding, of water sports and mountaineering, of the Mariners and the Seahawks and the SuperSonics, of Boeing and big timber, the best reason I can think of for coming to this neck of the woods has to be Paul Bunyan's home course, the crown jewel on the Paul Bunyan Circuit. You have to hand it to old Paul: he didn't know from conservation, but he sure knew his golf courses.

OFF COURSE

Portland and Seattle. Anyone who despairs that American cities are becoming unlivable should pay a visit to these two. I guarantee you'll come away with renewed faith in urban life. In Portland, be sure and visit **Washington Park** to learn why it's called the "City of Roses." Sample the locally brewed beers (**Portland Ale** is a personal favorite). Eat salmon, smoked and otherwise. Walk around and marvel at how good it feels just walking around in a city like this. In Seattle, go up in the **Space Needle**. (Yeah, I know it's corny, but do it anyway. Just make sure it's a clear day.) Eat lunch on the walk at the **Pike Place**

Market, a central market that sells the freshest, best-looking produce, seafood, and other stuff you've ever tasted.

Geography. The biggest attractions along the Paul Bunyan Circuit—other than the golf, of course—are all outdoors. This has got to be one of the most dramatic regions on earth, with everything from rugged seacoast to rain forest to snow-covered mountains to raging rivers to high plateau desert. Maybe the best thing to do is plan another vacation here, one where you leave your clubs at home. (Hey, if you get the shakes, you can always rent.)

Local Color. Near Salishan, you can visit a cheese factory and museum in **Tillamook** (about fifty miles north on U.S. Highway 101). Near Black Butte Ranch, the kids might like **Sisters,** a Western theme town (about ten miles north on Route 20). Near Port Ludlow, you can hike along the entire seven-mile length of **Dungeness Spit,** the world's longest natural sand spit (about forty miles west off U.S. 101).

Warning: There is so much to see and do along the Paul Bunyan Circuit (**Oregon seacoast, Columbia River Gorge, Mount Hood, Mount St. Helens, Puget Sound, Olympic National Park**) that your main problem will be to resist the temptation to let yourself be talked into canceling an afternoon round to do a little sight-seeing. Be firm. Don't let the tail wag the dog.

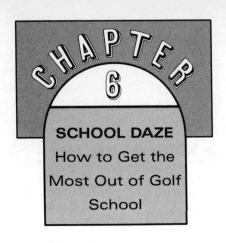

CHAPTER 6

SCHOOL DAZE
How to Get the
Most Out of Golf
School

"HOWZIT GOING? YOU LOOK GOOD. RELAXED.
Healthy."

"Yeah, fine. Just got back from vacation."

"Where'd you go? Must have been somewhere sunny. You've
got a good tan."

"Well, uh, I went to school . . ."

"School? That's great! You finally decided to start work on
your master's, the way you've always said you would? Good for
you."

"No, not exactly."

"You did say you went to school, didn't you?"

"Yeah, but it wasn't that kind of school. It was . . ."

"You went to school but you didn't go to graduate school?
What kind of . . ."

". . . *golf* school."

"*Golf* school? You actually showed that swing of yours to
strangers? I dunno about you. Did it, ah, do any good?"

"You be the judge. Saturday morning, regular time?"

"Sure, sure. You, ah, want me to give you the usual? Two
strokes a side, like always?"

70

"No, I don't think so. Let's play even up. Scratch. Okay?"
"Sure, yeah. Whatever you say."
"Oh, and one other thing. . . ."
"Yes?"
"Bring your wallet."

Guy plays golf pretty regularly, maybe every week when the weather's good. Reads all the golf magazines, even clips out the instructional tips. Buys books like this one that tell about great golf vacations to take. Times his weekend nap for the third round of the Greater Topeka-Andy Rooney-Hyundai Classic. And still his game doesn't improve.

Sound familiar? Somebody you know? Like maybe the guy whose mug you see in the bathroom mirror every morning? Me, too. If you looked up my name in Who's Not Who, the description above would be the entry. At least it was until I finally decided to go to school.

Some people won't even consider going to a golf school because they're afraid it will look like they take the game too seriously. Balderdash. Just because you do something for fun, where is it written that you shouldn't try to do it better and have even more fun? The very nature of golf is to remind you of your humanity, and that to be human is to err. But if you could do something about that horrendous banana slice, if you could fix the damned thing once and for all, why not try? You'd still be human. You'd still find plenty to err about.

But before flipping to the end of this chapter for a list of some top-notch golf schools, think for a moment of how best to get the most out of your golf school, now that you've finally decided to go.

What follows is an extremely loose adaptation of some advice golf writer Pat Seelig gave a couple of years back in an article called "10 Rules to Golf School Success" that appeared in *Golfweek* magazine. I can personally testify that Pat's advice was sound, even though I didn't follow it as well as I might have. Maybe if I had, my golf swing today would look more like a silk purse than a sow's ear.

1. **SHAPE UP.** The fact that you don't have to be in top physical condition to play golf has always been one of its more endearing features. Somehow, I don't think the game would have quite the same appeal to me if I had to run a bunch of

wind sprints and do a lot of calisthenics before teeing off. But if you go straight from winter hibernation to a five-day golf school, where you'll hit more range balls in a day than you normally hit in a year, you're asking for trouble in the form of blisters, day-after joint stiffness, and soreness of muscles you didn't even know you had.

Do yourself a favor: devote a couple of weeks *before* matriculation to getting your body ready for golf school. That means swinging a club in the backyard a hundred times a day or so to remind your muscles what it feels like to play a round. It means toughening your hands to guard against blisters. (Nolan Ryan used to soak his pitching hand in pickle brine. Hitting a couple of buckets of range balls serves the same purpose and is a lot less smelly.) It means doing those flexibility exercises that Gary Player is always swearing about in the golf magazines. (There may be nothing in the world more boring than flexibility exercises. Warm up a little bit, assume a position, feel the stretch, then hold it for sixty seconds. Now do it again. Fun, huh? But if there's a purpose—such as giving you a better hip turn and adding thirty yards to your drive—then even flexibility exercises can be a gas.)

You aren't training for the Ironman Triathlon, but going to golf school is a lot more demanding physically than watching the last round of the Buick Open on TV. Get yourself ready.

2. DON'T EXPECT MIRACLES. If golf schools could turn everybody into scratch players, they'd be harder to get into than Harvard. You are not—repeat, *not*—going to go directly from golf school to the PGA Tour. The more unrealistic your expectations, the sharper your disappointment, so go to golf school *expecting* to learn more about the game and your swing, and *hoping* to shave a few strokes off your handicap.

The good news is that the higher your handicap, the more you can expect to gain from golf school. Pat Seelig figures that a golfer with a handicap between twenty and thirty can realistically expect to drop eight to ten strokes. Note the word "realistically," in conjunction with the numbers "eight" and "ten." I don't know about you, but that sounds pretty doggone good to me.

The lower your handicap, of course, the fewer strokes you can expect to drop by going to golf school. If you sport something between a ten and a nineteen, Seelig says, you're looking

at an improvement range of three to seven shots. And if you're a single-digit player, I hate your eyes.

3. X-RATED: VIEWER DISCRETION ADVISED. Unless you're prone to out-of-body experiences, chances are you've never seen your golf swing. Steady yourself, because at golf school you'll almost certainly see your swing on videotape, and it's likely to be a tad shocking. In my mind, I'm as smooth and effortless as Freddie Couples. On tape, I'm as herky-jerky as a guy with fire ants in his shorts. A picture is worth a thousand words, remember, only nowhere is it written that they have to be nice ones. But don't avert your eyes. Videotape is the golf school's single best teaching tool because it shows you what the instructor is talking about.

4. HEY, THIS DOESN'T FEEL RIGHT! Of course it doesn't. Whatever the flaws in your old swing, it's yours, and a new one is going to feel uncomfortable. Persevere. Practice the new swing, even though it feels funny at first. In due course, your old swing will be the one that feels funny.

5. SEEK AND YE SHALL FIND. Back in high school, the last thing in the world you wanted to do was call attention to yourself by asking a question. Not so in golf school. Your job is to ask questions until you're sure what the teacher is driving at. Speak up.

6. NO WINNERS. NO LOSERS. ONE TEACHER. Golf school is not a golf tournament. You're not competing with anybody, not even yourself, and you're not trying to "beat" anyone. So

try not to pay attention to your fellow classmates while you're in class. Don't sneak looks at their swings to see how good they are. Don't ask them for tips. This isn't a group therapy session. This doesn't mean you can't be sociable at after-class get-togethers down at the root beer stand. But it does mean that the only person you should seek advice from is your teacher.

7. HOW DO YOU GET TO CARNEGIE HALL? Practice, practice, practice. If you're not willing to commit yourself to practicing more than has been your custom to date, then you probably shouldn't spend the time or money going to golf school. You'll learn a lot at any good golf school about the golf swing. But if you come home, stick your clubs in the garage, and don't practice what's been preached to you, what's the point? I'm not saying you should quit your day job and spend all your time at the practice range. I'm saying you should hit a big bucket of range balls two or three times a week to groove the lessons you learned in school. If this means playing a round or two less per month to make time for the practice range, do it. Any pro will tell you that you do more for your game in one hour at the range than four on the course.

8. LENIN WAS RIGHT. Not about world revolution, maybe, but "One Step Backward, Two Steps Forward" pretty much sums up how what you learn at golf school will get incorporated into your game. Back home, expect some very weird golf for a while. (Okay, so you always play weird golf. So do I. Then expect it to be even weirder.) There's a good reason for this. You spent a lot of years developing your bad mechanics, right? Well, it's going to take a while to replace them with good mechanics. Some days you'll be Dr. Jekyll on the front nine, Mr. Hyde on the back nine. Or even both on the same hole. (So what else is new?)

But if you stay the course, if you stick with the program, if you adhere to the lessons you learned in golf school, and if you practice, practice, practice, it will all come together. Just remember that you heard it here first.

9. FOLLOW-UP. They'll throw a lot of stuff at you in golf school, and not all of it will stick. Try to make time for a follow-up session a few months down the pike to make sure you're in synch with the program.

10. ALL WORK. NO PLAY. At a good golf school, you're go-

ing to be in "class" from 8 A.M. until 4 P.M. You're going to concentrate on golf in a way you've never concentrated before. You're going to hit range balls until your arms feel like they're going to fall off. And you think that you're going to try to squeeze in nine holes after school? Think again. For one thing, you're going to be too tired to play well. For another, you need time to assimilate what you've learned. Do yourself a favor and stay away from the golf course.

Go for a leisurely swim. Get a massage. Spend some quality time in the Jacuzzi. Have another massage. Follow a sensible dinner with a nice long stroll. (There's something especially satisfying to the soul about strolling around a golf course on a warm summer night under a full moon. Take off your shoes to get the full effect.) Go to bed early. Dream about birdies.

Going to golf school but not playing a single round of golf sounds like a prescription for acute frustration. After all, the reason for going to golf school in the first place is because you love to play golf, right? If you don't play, what's the point?

Six Questions to Ask Before You Enroll

1. What is the instructor/student ratio?

2. Can I focus on one part of my game or do I have to follow the standard curriculum? (Important for matriculants with low handicaps.)

3. Are high- and low-handicap golfers put together in the same class, or are the students grouped according to skill level?

4. What is the composition, in terms of age and sex, of a typical class? (You may not want to be the only old geezer in a gang of young bucks, or vice versa.)

5. Does the school provide for a short follow-up session a few months after completing the course? (Even if you're a quick study, an hour or two going over key points a few months down the pike could be helpful in keeping you with the program.)

6. Does the school use videotaping as a teaching tool?

★

The point, of course, is that you're not there to *play* golf, but to learn to play golf better. To do that, you need to devote all your physical and mental energy to what goes on in class. There simply won't be enough of either left over for an enjoyable round of twilight golf.

Fortunately, there's a way to have your cake and eat it, too. The longest golf school programs run five full days; many last three days. So why not just tack on a few extra days at the end and put what you've learned to work? First work, then play.

That brings us to the all-important question: which golf school?

Now, some are better than others, of course. Some are better for some golfers than for other golfers. And some are probably lousy, given the facts of life. But pros I've talked to agree that, for the double-digit handicapper, *it really doesn't matter all that much* which golf school you go to. Their feeling is that the focused concentration the student brings to school—whatever school—will lead to a dramatic improvement in his game. It's what *you* bring to the party that matters most.

For that reason, I think the three primary criteria in choosing a golf school should be the same as in real estate: location, location, location. You should definitely check with your local pro, and you should listen to what friends who have been to one golf school or another have to say, and you should do some comparative shopping. But then, after this preliminary screening has produced a short list of possibilities, pick a golf school located at a course you've always wanted to play and/or in a place you've always wanted to visit.

Golf school is work. But it's also vacation.

The following list of golf schools is not definitive, but neither is it arbitrary. Certainly there are other high-quality schools that merit your consideration. But the schools here are ones that I know personally or that come strongly recommended by golfers whose judgment I trust. I believe all can be counted on to give you solid value for your tuition dollar.

Which one is best for you? Hey, I caught enough grief trying to steer my three kids into the college of my choice without begging for more from perfect strangers. Different courses for different horses, right? What's sauce for the goose might be Golf School Hell for the gander, agreed? Call me a wimp, but I'm not telling you which golf school to go to. What if you went to a place I recommended and cut only five strokes off your handicap instead of eight? You'd come looking for me with your two-iron, that's what; and after a week in golf school, you'd probably be able to hit me with it! No, siree, I was born at night, but it wasn't last night. I'm listing these suckers alphabetically, and that's that.

Study hard.

THE BIG EIGHT

Academy of Golf at PGA National

Location: PGA National in Palm Beach Gardens, Florida.

Cost: $609.50 for three days of instruction; lunch included. Lodging and other meals not included.

Information: (800) 633-9950

Ben Sutton Golf Schools

Location: Just south of Tampa in Sun City Center, Florida.

Cost: $1,450 per person, double occupancy. Price includes seven nights lodging, MAP (breakfast and dinner), plus cart and greens fees, instruction, and assorted extras (e.g. cocktail parties and the odd luau).

Information: (800) 225-6923

Golf Digest Instruction Schools

Location: A lot of good places, including Innisbrook in Tarpon Springs, Florida; Quail lodge in Carmel Valley, California; The Cloister at Sea Island, Georgia; Tucson National in Tucson, Arizona; and Mission Hills Resort in Rancho Mirage, California.

Cost: $2,750–$3,100 (depending on season) for five full days of instruction with lodging and meals; $1,850–2,000 for three days with lodging and meals; $1,900–$2,150 for five days without lodging or meals; $1,200–$1,350 for three days without lodging and meals; $525–$575 for three half-days of instruction without lodging or meals.

Information: (800) 243-6121

Grand Cypress Academy of Golf

Location: Grand Cypress Resort in Orlando, Florida; facility designed by Jack Nicklaus.

Cost: $1,040 for three half-days of instruction; $1,635 for three full days; $2,300 for four days. Lodging and meals not included, but Academy students receive reduced rates at Grand Cypress villas and Hyatt Regency Grand Cypress Hotel.

Information: (800) 835-7377

John Jacobs' Practical Golf Schools

Location: A lot of good places, including Dromoland Castle in County Clare, Ireland; the Wigwam Resort in Phoenix, Arizona; Rancho Las Palmas and Desert Springs in Palm Springs, California; the Royal Waikoloan in Waikoloa, Hawaii; the Grand Hotel in Point Clear, Alabama; the Broadmoor Hotel in Colorado Springs, Colorado; the Grand Traverse Resort in Traverse City, Michigan; plus one-week sessions in Austria, Germany, and Portugal.

Cost: At campuses in the United States, from $1,075 to $1,550 per person, double occupancy, depending on location, for a one-week package (six nights). For Germany, $1,814; for Austria, $1,780; for Portugal, $1,595–$2,295. Most meals included.

Information: (800) 472-5007

Jimmy Ballard Golf Workshop

Location: Doral Hotel and Country Club in Miami, Florida.

Cost: $625 for 10-hour instructional program ($500 if you are a guest at Doral). Two-day (Tuesday–Wednesday) or three-day (Thursday–Friday–Saturday) options available. Lodging and food not included.

Information: (800) 327-6334

Pinehurst Advantage Golf School

Location: Pinehurst Hotel and Country Club in Pinehurst, North Carolina.

Cost: $1,190–$1,420 per person, double occupancy, for four-day program (five nights lodging); $875–1,040 for weekend program (three nights lodging). All meals included.

Information: (800) 634-9297

Stratton Golf School

Location: Stratton Mountain, Vermont.

Cost: $387 per person, double occupancy, for two-day mid-week program (two nights lodging); $743 for five-day program (five nights lodging). Meals not included.

Information: (800) 843-6867

CHAPTER 7

THE HAPPY BUDDHA, THE GOLDEN BEAR, AND THE PRINCE

Bali Hai Is Calling

NO WAY WAS I GOING TO MAKE MY TEE TIME.
Since leaving San Francisco on a United Airlines flight at 9 A.M. and changing planes at Honolulu for an Aloha Airlines flight now preparing to land on the Hawaiian island of Kauai, I had become vaguely aware that we'd crossed several time zones and maybe an international dateline or two. For all I knew, having slept most of the way, it was yesterday and I was a day younger, or vice versa. With only the fuzziest idea of how long I'd been in the air, all I really knew for sure was that it was 12:12 P.M. local time and my chances of making a 12:30 P.M. tee time were slim to none.

The plane was on time, but I still faced the traveler's standard arrival drill. You know what I mean. Wait for luggage to come down. Haul it out front. Wait some more for hotel van. Drive from airport to hotel. Straighten out fouled-up reservation. Arrange to have stuff stashed until three o'clock check-in time. Get clubs taken around to golf course. Go to course. Sign in. Buy sleeve of balls at shocking price. Only by then it's nearing midnight, Greenwich Mean Time, well past my tee time.

Sound familiar? Sure it does. But that's not the way it worked this time.

From the time "Flight attendants, please prepare for land-ing" piped through the plane's intercom until I took my first practice swing next to the Happy Buddha on the first tee, ex-actly thirteen minutes elapsed. No joke; I timed it. And don't think I subtracted an hour in a little time zone sleight of hand. We're talking about standard operating procedure for getting guests from the airport to their tee times at the Westin Kauai Resort at Kauai Lagoons, one of the great destination resorts of the Westin world—and an absolute must-stop for the seri-ous golfer planning a golf vacation in Hawaii.

LITTLE GRASS SHACK

What can you say about the Westin Kauai that best describes its essence?

Maybe you talk about the seven white marble horses form-ing the sculptural centerpiece of a fountain that shoots a sixty-foot geyser into the air in the two-acre reflecting pool on the way to the hotel lobby.

Or the fifty outrigger canoes and five thirty-two-passenger and three ten-passenger mahogany launches that ferry visitors along the mile of man-made lagoons and inland waterways. (You'd think such a navy would cause a helluva traffic jam on so small a body of water, but they're not all at sea at the same time.)

Or the $2.5 million (and growing) collection of oriental and Pacific art that's strewn about the public areas, mostly in the form of monumental sculpture and oversized artifacts.

Or the thirty-five horse-drawn carriages being pulled around the eight miles of carriage paths on the property by sixty Clydesdales, Belgians, and Percherons, a *remuda* that gives new meaning to the term "horseflesh."

Or the 26,000-square-foot swimming pool—the largest in Hawaii—patterned after the pool at William Randolph Hearst's San Simeon, with the welcome addition of five Jacuzzis housed in an arc of stylized pagodas around the perimeter, the better to serve the tired swimmer who wants his muscles regener-ated.

Personally, I think the hallmark of the Westin Kauai is the stretch limousine—one of a fleet, of course—that whisked me from the airport to the first tee with plenty of time to spare, a service afforded to all resort guests as a matter of luxurious routine.

THE WESTIN KAUAI AT KAUAI LAGOONS Kalapaki Beach, Lihue, Hawaii 96766. The resort is 1 mile on a private road from the Lihue Airport, where visitors are met by a hotel representative and a stretch limousine. Telephone: (800) 228-3000. <u>Accommodations</u>: 846 rooms, including 41 suites and 46 Royal Beach Club rooms. Guests in the Royal Beach Club receive complimentary breakfast buffets, evening cocktail parties, and assorted other amenities. <u>Amenities</u>: Largest swimming pool in Hawaii; 8 tennis courts; private beach; sailing, other water sports; horseback riding; 12 restaurants and lounges; world-class European-style spa and wellness center; 2 golf courses. <u>Terms</u>: For the standard double rooms, from $185 to $385; for the Royal Beach Club, from $350 to $385; for the 41 suites, $475 to $1,500.

But what's really special about the Westin Kauai, what most aptly sums up its essence, is that all these things—and more, much more—have been brought together in one glorious tropical setting and tied up in a dizzyingly glamorous package. The stupendous excess of everything about the place is so outrageous, so overblown, that it ends up being enormously entertaining. What the Westin Kauai is saying through its cacophony of styles, its overlays of fantasy, its preposterous touches—viz., the little island mini-zoos that dot the artificial lagoons ("Look, Ma! A kangaroo! Are we in Australia?")—is "What the hell, we know it's all a little crazy. But you're on vacation. So take off your shoes, kick back, and have a rum punch. And don't miss the sunset."

What makes the whole greater than the sum of its parts—what makes it all work rather than repulse—is the exuberant, unself-conscious celebration of undiluted excess fueling the vision of Westin Kauai's creator, Christopher Hemmeter. I'm tempted to refer to Hemmeter as the Donald Trump of Hawaii, except that he's much more entertaining, has more style, and builds more interesting playhouses than The Donald. An island legend whose flair for the flamboyant knows no equal, Hemmeter spent $350 million of borrowed money, give or take a small fortune, to make sure that the Westin Kauai was the latest word in conspicuous consumption—at least until the next big deal came his way.

And best of all, he didn't forget the golf.

KIELE

The Eagle makes *poi* on your head. The Gorilla rips off your arms. The Dragon sets your hair on fire. The Alligator bites you on your handicap. The Lion devours your entrails. And when you finally get to the eighteenth hole, the Golden Bear squeezes what's left of you to death.

Aloha, Kiele.

KIELE COURSE AT KAUAI LAGOONS

Design: Jack Nicklaus

Year Open: 1988

7,070 Yards   73.7 Rating   137 Slope

Information: (808) 246-5056

★

Naming golf holes is common in Scotland, where it all began. So there's nothing wrong in principle with the folks at the Westin Kauai for naming theirs. And I suppose if they want to give them the names of animals, that's okay too. (Actually, only sixteen are named for animals; the other two bear the names of deities. The first is called Happy Buddha; the eighteenth is the Golden Bear, after the architect who designed the course.) But when you encounter a white marble statue of the designated animal sitting on a 6,000-pound granite base serving as a tee marker on each hole, it crosses your mind that maybe, just maybe, somebody went too far.

That can't be, though, because the words "too far" are simply not in the vocabulary of mega-developer Chris Hemmeter, the man who gave Jack Nicklaus an unlimited budget and encouraged him to exceed it in building what Brian McCallen of *Golf* magazine calls "the most varied and beautiful resort course Nicklaus has built to date." The course cost in the neighborhood of $20 to $25 million to build, which is a pretty ritzy neighborhood even in the corner of the universe inhabited by

Hemmeter's ego. Probably the tee markers put him over budget.

Kiele is the Hawaiian word for "essence of gardenia." In golfese, that translates as "essence of tough." Stretching to 7,070 yards from the back tees, Kiele has three other sets of tees to give the rest of us a break. But when you're bucking the tradewinds, say, on the Rabbit (ninth hole), it's an overnighter from wherever you start—at 378, 427, 445, *or* 459 yards. As Jack says in his notes for the yardage book, it "will require a little bit of strength to play the hole." (Thanks, Jack. I hadn't noticed.)

Not that he needed much encouragement, but Nicklaus followed the example Hemmeter set with the rest of the Kauai Lagoons project and conceived everything in heroic scale. There's enough sand on Kiele to build another Waikiki. Nicklausian swales and multiple tiering between tee and green make it look as though some giant stubbed his toe on the turf and wrinkled it like a carpet. The greens range in size from big to huge.

Fortunately, the scale extends to the fairways, which are generously wide, but not to the rough, which is rarely punitive. You can hit the ball off line, as I am prone to do once a hole or so, and are able to find it and hit it again, and again, and again. The strokes pile up, what with the fairway bunkers and sheer length to contend with, but at least you don't find yourself taking penalty strokes for balls faxed into the forest.

A baseball player will sometimes talk about having had a "good at-bat," even though he didn't get a hit, if he fouled off

the pitcher's best pitches, hung in there tough, didn't swing at anything outside the strike zone, and eventually lined out hard to the left fielder. At Kiele you can have a good at-bat, even if you don't score well. Odds are, it plays a whole lot tougher than your home course (unless your home course is, say, Pine Valley), but it plays fair. You'll feel better about making bogey at Kiele than you will about making par at lots of other places.

Only twice did I feel utterly inadequate to the task when I first played Kiele, and that was when I did battle with the Eagle and the Gorilla.

The Eagle (Number five) asks you to carry the ball 219 yards from the tips over a mango forest onto the biggest green on the course, an elevated monster protected by a pair of deep traps. But wide as the green is, it's dadburned narrow as a fairway, and if you underclub you're up to your niblick in mangoes. But let's say that you do just make it to the front edge of the green, and that you three-putt from eighty feet for your bogey. Now you have to wrestle the Gorilla.

No problem, says the Golden Bear, who writes in his course notes that "For most people this hole shouldn't play as a difficult three shot five." I guess I'm not most people, Jack, because if I have to carry the ball a couple of hundred yards back over the mango forest, this time into the teeth of the tradewinds, I'm looking at more load than I want to tote. Okay, okay—so the precise yardage is 181 from the gold tees to the closest edge of the cliff on the other side of the tree-filled ravine. But that's as the crow flies, not as the ball slices. A degree or so off dead-center and we're talking another ten, fifteen yards of carry—or more. And don't forget the damned wind! ("Got . . . to . . . swing . . . a . . . little . . . harder . . . on . . . this . . . one! Uh, where's the drop area?")

As you buggy down into the tree-choked ravine that bisects the Rabbit and the Gorilla, take a deep breath. The effect is like sticking your nose into a bottle of "Eau de Hawaii." Actually, you don't have to make a special effort: the heady aroma of mango and guava plum and schefflera blooms will overpower you anyway. The mangoes and plums become overripe and fall to the bottom of the ravine, where they ferment. That's why the wild guinea hens who live down on the forest floor sometimes stagger when they run in front of your golf cart: they're drunk.

Lucky chickens. You're tempted to join them, but there's no

way to play this golf course unless you have your wits about you. Particularly since the *back* nine is a whole bunch tougher than the front.

Take the tenth, a 562-yarder into ocean winds that like nothing better than to push your approach to the green into the enormous waste bunker down the left side. Driver, three-wood, four-iron, sand wedge, sand wedge, putt, putt. Make that a double! No wonder the tenth is called the Hippo.

But even when they're short, like the Dragon (Number 11) at 366 yards from the gold tees, the holes on Kiele's back nine are no day at the beach. Bunkers cutting diagonally across the middle of the Dragon's landing area give you a choice: boom it over them to the right side, where you'll have a clear view of the front of the green; or hit a safer drive down the left side, where you'll be shooting over mounds to the narrowest part of the green. Short, yes; easy, no.

And so it goes: a long, graceful downhill ride into the Alligator's mouth at Number 12, a powerful par 4 that ends on a cliff; then over the ocean at the par 3 Frog, 207 yards from the back tees but with a helping wind; a bit of a breather at the Peacock, a birdie opportunity even for the likes of me; and then back to the ocean for the Lion and the Turtle, a par 5 that plays easier than it looks followed by a par 4 that plays harder than it looks.

The Tiger (Number 17) looks hard and plays that way. The marker says 171 yards from the gold, 147 from the blue, 130 from the white, and 111 yards from the red tees. But figure at least twenty yards longer than that when picking a club, unless you want to get wet. The tradewinds are right in your face, and the only thing between the lagoon and the green is a U-shaped sand trap that wraps around the entire right half of the putting surface.

If you had any lingering doubts about which animal is the King of the Beasts, the Golden Bear (Number 18) dispels them. The landing area for your drive is wide enough so that you can come out of your shoes on your tee shot. And you'd better do just that, because you need every yard of distance in your big stick to have any second shot at all. The scorecard says 431 yards from the back tee, but the strong wind in your face says, "In your dreams, sucker!" Belt it as far as you can and you still have a long iron over the lagoon to a well-trapped boomerang-shaped island green. (Actually it's an isthmus, if it'll make you any less nervous.) There's a bailout area to the left, but even then you'll have a tricky wedge to play and not much green to play it to.

But what the hell—you didn't come all this way to lay up. You can do that back home at Podunk Muni. Figure your distance, add two clubs or more, and give it a mighty lash. If it goes into the water, you're out $1.75 and a penalty stroke. Big deal. But if not, and if you walk away from the Golden Bear with a 4 on your card, you'll become an instant island legend, and they'll write hula songs about your feat.

Go for it.

THE LAGOONS

Poor Lagoons. It's a doggone good golf course, a links-like layout spread over a former sugarcane plantation with sweeping vistas and a grand, open feel. Yet, inevitably, it's pegged as the "other course" at the Westin Kauai, and nobody gives it the respect it deserves because of its more spectacular sibling.

LAGOONS COURSE AT KAUAI LAGOONS

Design: Jack Nicklaus

Year Open: 1988

6,942 Yards   72.8 Rating   135 Slope

Information: (808) 246-5056

★

The Lagoons is a Jack Nicklaus course; Kiele is a Jack Nicklaus "Signature" course. The difference? For starters, about a million bucks. (Not bad for an autograph. A man wouldn't have to sign many to make a decent living.) Beyond that, the Lagoons is Nicklaus's conception of a golf course that's playable by ordinary mortals. At first I was stumped: how could he possibly know anything about the golf games of people like us? Then the answer hit me: it must be all those pro-ams he played in over the years. Nicklaus is notorious for concentrating so fiercely on his own game that an invasion from outer space wouldn't crack his train of thought when he's over a shot. But somewhere along the way he must have caught something out of the corner of his eye, because he got the Lagoons course dead-solid perfect. It's a Nicklaus course for just plain folks.

But this is no Jose Canseco-Ozzie Canseco deal. It's not that one's a great course and the other is just a course. The Lagoons has a lot going for it in its own right. Plenty of length (6,942 yards from the back tees). Tough greens (smaller than Kiele's, with more dips and curves). A lot of roll to the fairways (Nicklaus had Scottish links in mind when he gave the bulldozers their marching orders). It's a course you can breeze around, shoot your usual score, and somehow feel a lot better about it than you normally do.

I like it. So will you.

BALI HAI WILL CALL YOU

"You mean to say you're not going to Hanalei?" The white-haired lady in the seat next to me on the plane was incredulous. She and her husband were old Hawaii hands from way back—"This is our fourteenth, no, fifteenth trip"—and she was giving me more tips than both major golf magazines combined. "Oh, that's a big, big mistake," she said in a kind but insistent Midwestern twang. It was my first trip to Kauai, and I hadn't scheduled a trip to the northern end of the island. She was having none of it. "It's the most beautiful place on earth," she said, checking her watch to see how much time there'd be to set me straight. She and her husband had boarded in Honolulu, and the flight to Kauai takes about forty minutes. Plenty of time, as it turned out, because I was a pushover. Thank goodness.

Before Chris Hemmeter took over the slightly run down Kauai Surf Hotel and its links course and transformed them into his vision (at the time, at least) of Golf Heaven on Earth, *the* place to play golf in Kauai was on the north end of the island overlooking Hanalei Bay. Remember Bali Hai in *South Pacific*? Well, the movie model for it is the island of Makana in Hanalei Bay, and the best vantage point for viewing it is a former coffee plantation high on cliffs overlooking the sea. And it is there, almost twenty years ago, that Robert Trent Jones, Jr., made his solo debut as a golf course designer by creating twenty-seven holes of surpassing beauty—and of sufficient quality for the Makai Course at the Princeville Resort to be ranked among *Golf Digest*'s Top 100 courses in America every year from 1973 through 1989.

(Makai fell out of the Top 100 in 1990, but it's still the same course, which means it's still plenty wonderful.)

MIRAGE PRINCEVILLE RESORT P.O. Box 3040, Prince-ville, Hawaii 96722. Located on the northern coast of the island of Kauai at Hanalei Bay. Take Route 56 north from Lihue Airport; or fly direct from Honolulu to Princeville Airport. Telephone: (808) 826-3040. Accommodations: 300 rooms in Sheraton Mirage, plus 1,100 condominium units. Go for the condos. Amenities: Tennis, health spa, all water sports, horseback riding, hiking trails, cycling, guided nature tours. Terms: From $250 to $450, depending on view and size.

The Mirage Princeville, as the resort has been named since being taken over by an Australian company in 1987, has recently undergone a multimillion-dollar restoration that, by general agreement, was long overdue. In any event, the result was worth waiting for. In its new incarnation, the Mirage Princeville is a world-class establishment, and once again worthy of its golf course.

The three nines that make up the Makai Course are named Ocean, Woods, and Lakes, and that pretty much sums up their salient features. What the names don't make clear is how well any two of them blend together to form a single, harmonious eighteen. A $3 million renovation program completed last year has brought all into top shape.

MAKAI COURSE AT MIRAGE PRINCEVILLE

Design: Robert Trent Jones, Jr.

Year Open: 1971

Ocean	3,401 Yards	72.4 Rating	131 Slope
Lakes	3,363 Yards	72.6 Rating	131 Slope
Woods	3,377 Yards	71.8 Rating	129 Slope

Information: (808) 826-3580

But good as the Makai most certainly is, the best reason for the traveling golfer to include the Mirage Princeville on his itinerary is Jones's new Prince course, opened in the winter of 1989–90 to virtually unanimous acclaim. Brian McCallen of *Golf* magazine, who knows as much about resort golf courses as anybody who's ever swung a club, says Prince will "blossom into one of the most challenging layouts in the Pacific." Jones himself calls it "one of the top five courses I've ever designed," and that's saying a lot, inasmuch as he's laid out 150 courses (and counting) in twenty countries.

PRINCE COURSE AT MIRAGE PRINCEVILLE

Design: Robert Trent Jones, Jr.

Year Open: 1989

eighteen holes, par 72

7,309 Yards   75.6 Rating   144 Slope

Information: (808) 826-3580

The new course at Princeville was named after a nineteenth-century Hawaiian prince, Albert Edward Kauikeaouli Leiopapa A Kamehameha. History is silent on the subject, but you have to figure his subjects called him Al for short. (Just think: if the folks who used to sponsor what once was the San Diego Open ever decided to shift their sponsorship to a Hawaiian event, it could be called the Shearson Lehman Hutton Prince Albert Edward Kauikeaouli Leiopapa A Kamehameha Open.)

When I saw that Prince played at 7,309 yards from the back tees, it was almost enough to send me back to the mainland, particularly since I knew the tricky tradewinds would make some of the long holes play even longer. But there are five sets of tees at each of the holes, with some of them having as many as nine different teeing areas. Plus the back two tee boxes are limited to single-digit handicaps, which took me off the hook. I felt sort of like you do when you've agreed to fight the school bully after school—following the peculiarly adolescent logic that the best way to save face is to have your nose broken—

only he fails to show up because he's found somebody more interesting to beat up.

If playing golf on a great, challenging course in a verdant tropical paradise with spectacular views of the ocean and volcanic mountains holds even passing appeal, you will love playing Makai and Prince at Princeville. And if it doesn't, what in the world are you doing with this book in your hands?

When to Go

The north side of Kauai is the wet side, and that means really, truly, seriously *wet*. On the summit of Mount Waialeale, at 5,080 feet the highest point on the island, it rains literally all the time, from a fine mist to cats-and-dogs. Sometimes it seems like that at Princeville, where in the winter (i.e., from October to May) it might rain hard all day for five or six days straight. At the Makai and Prince courses, little pagoda-like rain shelters are almost as common as bogies. Unless you like sweating inside a rain suit, plan your trip to the north in the summer.

To the south and southeast, where the Westin Kauai is situated, there's less rain in the winter, and summer rains are usually of short duration, which is probably why Nicklaus and Hemmeter didn't even bother putting in rain shelters. We know it certainly wasn't because they were trying to cut costs.

OFF COURSE

Resorts such as the Westin Kauai and the Mirage Princeville are designed to have everything that the tourist could possibly want, from shuffleboard to shopping. (I think they have shuffleboard; I know they have shopping.) That's why they call them "destination" resorts: you go there, and you stay. That would be a pity in Kauai, one of Hawaii's least developed islands, where there is still so much of "Old Hawaii" to see in the smaller towns. If you must take a day off from golf, rent a car and follow your nose. You can't go wrong, and you can't get too far from home—Kauai is a small place, after all.

CHAPTER

8

ALOHA!
CAPTAIN COOK!
FORE!
Golf on the Big
Island

N O SOIL: JUST MILE AFTER MILE OF HARSH, black rock. No rain to speak of: a little shy of eight inches a year on average. Not exactly hospitable conditions for a pitch-and-putt, much less a world-class golf course. But Laurance Rockefeller had asked Robert Trent Jones to build one, right there on the leeward side of the Big Island, and the dean of American golf course architects agreed to fly out and have a look-see.

Locals call the Island of Hawaii "the Big Island" because, in Hawaiian terms, it really is *big.* At 4,000 square miles the Big Island has twice the land mass of all the other islands in the Hawaiian archipelago combined. And yet—here's the good part—despite accounting for two thirds of the state's land area, the Big Island has a population of less than 100,000 people, or only one tenth of the state's total. (Lots of land—and not many people. I don't know about you, but that sounds to me like the beginning of a great vacation, provided there's a golf course nearby.)

The Big Island is also large when it comes to Hawaiian history. It was home to Kamehameha the Great, a warrior-king who brought the islands under unified rule by force of arms and personality. And it was where Captain James Cook, who visited the Hawaiian Islands a thousand years or so after the first Hawaiians put down roots there, met a violent death. (Legend has it that Cook, whose notorious slowness around the greens was of Nicklausian dimensions, wouldn't let the group behind him play through on the third hole at Mauna Kea. The brave captain died as he would have wished, with his putter in his hand.)

But what was Robert Trent Jones going to do with the wasteland of black rock that surrounded him? Compared with getting fairways and greens to grow on this other-side-of-the-moonscape, turning a sow's ear into a silk purse would be a snap. Over time, the forces of nature would turn the hardened lava into wonderfully rich soil that could grow just about anything. But this stuff was already 5,000 years old, and Mr. Rockefeller, like all developers, was an impatient man. At the top of his powers, world-renowned for his vision and ingenuity, Jones was stumped.

Then, local legend has it, Jones squeezed hard in frustration on a couple of small, black rocks he was holding in his hand. And they crumbled.

Eureka!

Mr. Watson, come here; I want you.

Shazam!

Just like that, Jones had the solution: he would make his own soil. And so he did, crushing tons of lava into small pebbles, then covering them with a layer of even more finely crushed lava, and finally covering that over with a sandy loam mixture—after first installing an unprecedentedly elaborate underground watering system capable of pumping more than a million gallons of water a day onto the soon-to-be fairways and greens.

The rest is golf history. In the less than three decades since Jones proved once again that necessity is the mother of invention, a tiny sliver of ostensibly inhospitable coastline on the leeward side of the Big Island of Hawaii has given birth to three world-class golf resorts and some of the most astonishingly dramatic golf you could ever imagine, even if you had the imagination of a Robert Trent Jones, who described the course he crafted on *manufactured* soil as his "crowning achievement."

WAIKOLOA BEACH WONDERLAND

Want to go swimming with dolphins? No problem. Just check the appropriate box in the *Vacations by Design* pamphlet, drop it off at the Aloha Services desk, and the friendly staff at the Hyatt Regency Waikoloa will make all the arrangements. All you do is show up at the lagoon at the appointed hour, follow some simple instructions (e.g., "Put your hand out slowly and let them come to you"), and splash! Oh, one thing: the dolphins love to have their bellies caressed. (Who doesn't?)

Actually, it's not *quite* that easy. Swimming with the dolphins is the most popular activity at the mind-boggling $360 million resort, so popular that selection of each day's forty lucky participants is by lottery. But don't worry if your number doesn't come up; there are a few other things to do at the Hyatt Regency Waikoloa.

HYATT REGENCY WAIKOLOA One Waikoloa Beach Resort, Island of Hawaii, Hawaii 96743. About 30 miles north of Keahole Airport in Kona. Telephone: (808) 885-1234. <u>Accommodations</u>: 1,279 rooms in 3 towers (Ocean, Palace, Lagoon), plus 128 "exclusive rooms, offering the finest VIP service" on Regency Club floors. <u>Amenities</u>: A cornucopia of amenities and activities, including all you've ever heard of and then some. The best: swimming with "tame Atlantic bottlenose dolphins." (As opposed to what, one wonders. Ferocious dolphins? And why did they go all the way to the Atlantic to get dolphins? The Pacific is, after all, rather nearby. Never mind. Which way is the first tee?) <u>Terms</u>: From $215 to $315.

The talk of the islands since it opened in 1988, the Hyatt Regency Waikoloa makes Donald Trump's Taj Mahal in Atlantic City look like a warehouse. It makes even the original Taj Mahal look like it could stand a refurbishing. If there is such a thing as "too much" in the fantasy resort business, then the Hyatt Regency Waikoloa could be just that.

Carved out of black volcanic ash on sixty-two oceanfront acres, the latest vision to leap from Christopher Hemmeter's overheated imagination has a mile-long museum walkway stuffed with Pacific and oriental *objets d'art* ranging in size from huge to colossal, and a mile or so of Hemmeter-made waterways clogged with canal boats hauling guests who might otherwise be exposed to the shocking fact that the shortest distance between two points is a straight line. (So what? You're on vacation, right? You *should* be protected from reality.)

Hungry? Try one of the seven restaurants. Thirsty? Thirteen lounges and counting. Workout? Check in at the 25,000-square-foot health spa and go for the burn. Tennis, anyone? Eight courts at your disposal. Helicoptering? Deep-sea fishing? Snorkeling? Windsurfing? Sailing? I'm not sure, but I think they even have Ping-Pong.

What I am sure of is that they have golf aplenty at two adjacent courses, both of them dandies.

BEACH COURSE AT WAIKOLOA GOLF CLUB

Design: Robert Trent Jones, Jr.

Year Open: 1981
6,507 Yards   71 Rating

Information: (808) 885-1234

★

KING'S COURSE AT WAIKOLOA GOLF CLUB

Design: Tom Weiskopf and Jay Morrish

Year Open: 1990
7,064 Yards   75 Rating

Information: (808) 885-1234

★

The recently renovated Beach Course, a Robert Trent Jones, Jr., design, is simply spectacular, with lava formations incorporated into the layout of every hole. Although it opened in 1981, there are certain features of the Beach Course that have been around a lot longer: ancient Hawaiian burial grounds bordering the driving range, a large petroglyph field between the sixth and seventh holes, and ruins of a centuries-old fishing village preserved on the twelfth fairway. Tight, rolling fairways, seventy-six sand bunkers, and three lakes make the Beach Course unusually exacting for a resort course. (Hang around the eighteenth green for half an hour, and you hear practically every golfer say the same thing as he comes off the course: "Whew, what a Beach!"

On the other side of the resort complex, and also available to its guests, is the brand-new King's Course, which opened in 1990. King's is longer than the Beach (by some 500 yards) has more traps (eighty-three), more lakes (six), and more designers (Tom Weiskopf and Jay Moorish teamed up to blast it out of the lava). Time will tell whether it's also tougher.

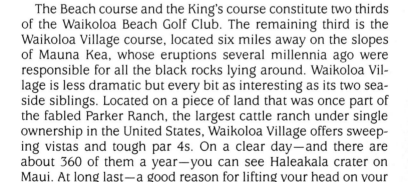

WAIKOLOA VILLAGE COURSE AT WAIKOLOA GOLF CLUB

Design: Robert Trent Jones, Jr.

Year Open: 1972

6,687 Yards   72.1 Rating   129 Slope

Information: (808) 883-9621

The Beach course and the King's course constitute two thirds of the Waikoloa Beach Golf Club. The remaining third is the Waikoloa Village course, located six miles away on the slopes of Mauna Kea, whose eruptions several millennia ago were responsible for all the black rocks lying around. Waikoloa Village is less dramatic but every bit as interesting as its two seaside siblings. Located on a piece of land that was once part of the fabled Parker Ranch, the largest cattle ranch under single ownership in the United States, Waikoloa Village offers sweeping vistas and tough par 4s. On a clear day—and there are about 360 of them a year—you can see Haleakala crater on Maui. At long last—a good reason for lifting your head on your swing!

By the way, Waikoloa Village bills itself (informally, at least) as "The Best-Kept Secret on the Big Island." If I could take a stroke off my handicap for every "Best-Kept Secret" I've run across, I'd almost be in single digits. But in this case, there's as much truth as sloganeering involved. In the high tourist season, from January through May, when the courses down by the ocean are chock-a-block with golfers, it's often easier to get a tee time up at the Village. Keep it in mind.

"MOUNTAIN REACHING HEAVEN"

Frances H. I'i Brown was, by any measure, a colossal figure. Half Hawaiian and half English-Scottish, he was a scion of a family that owned a big chunk of Oahu, including what is now Schofield Barracks and Pearl Harbor. By all accounts, he knew how to spend money as well as any other immensely wealthy heir to a fabulous fortune. He owned fourteen expensive cars (all at the same time) and maintained luxurious estates in Pebble Beach, on Diamond Head in Honolulu, and on the Big Island. He was on a first-name basis with assorted European royalty, and numbered among his friends Babe Ruth, Bing Crosby, Howard Hughes, John Wayne, and Bob Hope. A world-class athlete, he excelled at polo, swimming, and surfing. When he wasn't playing something or just hanging out with the rich and famous, he took time to be a big shot in Hawaiian politics. To top everything off, he was tall, good-looking, and, by all reports, a helluva nice guy.

Now, while I'm pretty sure that third name of his would have gotten him into a few scraps back where I grew up, I have to say that Frances H. I'i Brown comes as close as anybody I've ever heard of to having it all.

Oh yes, he was a good golfer to boot. Good enough to win the Hawaiian Amateur Championship a record nine times in the 1920s and 1930s. Good enough to win the Japan Amateur title in 1929 and the California Amateur at Pebble Beach in 1930. Good enough to have set course records at Pebble Beach *and* at St. Andrews. Plenty good.

So what I want to know is, why did the people who own Mauna Lani Bay, one of the world's great golf resorts, take a wonderful golf course named after France H. I'i Brown and cut it in half?

Mauna Lani Bay sits on part of a 3,200-acre chunk of lava that Brown bought from the Parker Ranch in 1930 for $3,700. The name comes from the extinct volcano looming in the east.

MAUNA LANI BAY RESORT P.O. Box 400, Kohala Coast, Island of Hawaii, Hawaii 96743. About 35 miles north of Keahole Airport in Kona. Telephone: (800) 367-2323. <u>Accommodations</u>: 351 guest rooms, plus 4 luxury villas complete with their own pools, saunas, and hot-and-cold running house servants. <u>Amenities</u>: Everything, which is not a whit less than you'd expect from a Mobil 5-star resort. <u>Terms</u>: From $195 to $395.

In Hawaiian Mauna Lani means "mountain reaching heaven," which sounds about right. In one of his last business deals before his death in 1976, Brown brought in a Japanese developer to build the spectacular resort on the best stretch of coastline on the entire leeward side of the Big Island. Since its opening in 1981, it's been ranked by *Golf* and *Golf Digest* as one of the world's finest golf resorts. With 351 large, beautifully appointed guest rooms and 4 bungalow suites (complete with private pool, sauna, and cadre of servants), Mauna Lani is nonetheless modest in size compared with the Hyatt Regency Waikoloa next door, and that's all to the good. Even if you have your own candidate, it's easy to see why the fatuous twit who dishes up "Lifestyles of the Rich and Famous" named it the Most Popular Luxury Resort in the World in 1990.

The golf course to go with it was named, appropriately enough, the Francis H. I'i Brown Course, whose most distinctive feature is the lava it was built on. The fairways are plenty wide, as befitting a resort course, but if you do hit one astray, be prepared to dodge the ricochet as your ball pings around in the lava. Forget visors and caps; wear a hard hat.

The two nines of the "old" Brown Course are (were) quite different in personality. The front nine, fairly flat, runs nearer the ocean, through lava black as the devil's heart. The back nine, whose fairways have a lot more roll, runs through older, brownish lava dotted with trees and brush. Each side has a signature hole: the famous Number 6, a 199-yard par 3 over an ocean inlet to a sprawling, heavily bunkered green; and the almost equally famous Number 17, a 136-yard par 3 guarded by a big brown boulder the size of Rhode Island sitting in a bunker at front left.

FRANCIS H. I'i BROWN COURSE
AT MAUNA LANI

Design: Original 18 by Raymond F. Cain; second 18 by Cain with Bell Collins & Associates.

Year Open: 1981, 1990

North Course: 6,968 Yards

South Course: 7,015 Yards

Information: (808) 885-6655.

At least, that's the way it used to be. In 1990 Mauna Lani opened a second eighteen holes, only instead of building an entirely separate course, they grafted one of the two new nines onto the front side of the Brown Course and the other onto the back side. The thing makes good real estate sense, and it's not as if we were talking about the splitting of Cypress Point or some other piece of hallowed ground. But it is a bit disconcerting. The famous Number 6 is now the famous Number 15 on the new South Course, while the almost equally famous Number 17 remains the almost equally famous Number 17 on the new North Course.

Don't mind me. The whole thing is still called the Francis H. I'i Brown Course. If you've never been there, it won't make any difference anyway. And even if you have, there's now twice as much spectacular golf to be played, so who could possibly be upset? Not me.

MAUNA KEA

As golf resorts in Hawaii go, Mauna Kea is positively ancient— and therein lies one of the main sources of its powerful appeal. The place is luxurious in every respect, right down to the perfect orchid placed on your pillow every night. But if it were to be built today, that wouldn't be enough. It would have to be bigger, louder, glitzier, more opulent to meet a contemporary developer's misguided sense of what luxury should be. All you have to do to understand what I'm driving at is to walk through the public spaces of the Hyatt Regency Waikoloa just down the beach and then walk through the airy, refined lobby and halls of the Mauna Kea. It's the difference between a state-of-the-art discotheque and New York's Rainbow Room—and I'm a Rainbow Room kind of guy.

MAUNA KEA BEACH HOTEL P.O. Box 218, Kohala Coast, Island of Hawaii, Hawaii 96743. About 40 miles north of Keahole Airport in Kona. Telephone: (800) 228-3000. Accommodations: 310 guest rooms. Amenities: 3 major-league restaurants that serve dinner only, plus 3 less formal places for lunch and breakfast; 13 tennis courts; pool; health spa; horseback riding, deep-sea fishing, helicopter flight-seeing, snorkeling, cycling, jogging, napping. Terms: From $230 for a mountain-view single room to $365 for an ocean-view double. (Spring for the ocean view; look at mountains on your Colorado trip.)

Take the ventilation system. (I know, I know: you didn't buy this book to read about ventilation systems. But bear with me. You'll understand what I'm driving at in a minute.) In each large, comfortable room there are three sets of sliding doors leading out to your small terrace overlooking the beach. Option One: close the glass doors and let the AC keep you cool. (Usually a mistake, but there may be times when it's necessary.) Option Two: open the glass doors and let the ocean breezes in through the screen doors. (Ahhhh . . .) Option Three: same as Option Two, except you close the slatted wooden doors, blocking out ambient light from full moons and low-cruising stars. (Ahhhh . . . Zzzzz). Did I mention that the entrance to your room has a second, slatted wooden door that lets you leave the outside door open, thereby ensuring a steady flow of gentle ocean breeze to freshen and cross-ventilate your room?

There, I told you ventilation system could be revealing—and what it reveals is an exceptional attention to detail that is evident throughout Mauna Kea, a monument to the best in modern design.

But most of what is so appealing about the Mauna Kea is a lot more obvious: the teak used for all interior woodwork (including the famous slatted wooden doors); the museum-quality oceanic art pieces in the hallways and public spaces (unlike the artifacts in the Hemmeter palaces, the artworks in the Mauna Kea weren't chosen primarily for their size, but for their artistic significance); the small, perfect, utterly private cove on which the hotel is situated, with its crescent of white sand; the clean, simple architectural lines of the multilevel hotel as it steps down through lush gardens to the beach; the impeccable efficiency and warmth of the staff; the excellence of the cuisine in the elegant restaurants; the overall sense of intimacy, comfort, and understated luxury that makes Mauna Kea richly deserving of all the top ratings it routinely receives from AAA, Mobil, and other self-appointed monitors of resort excellence in the travel world.

The truth is, Mauna Kea is such a great place that it wouldn't matter if it didn't have a world-class golf course just the other side of the garden terrace. Fortunately for you and me, though, it does.

MAUNA KEA GOLF COURSE

Design: Robert Trent Jones

Year Open: 1964

7,114 Yards   73.6 Rating   133 Slope

Information: (808) 822-7222

The golf course that Robert Trent Jones built once he proved he could grow grass on crushed lava rock is one of his best— maybe *the* best he ever designed. It was from the outset big, demanding, and heroic, one of the toughest tests of golf to be found at any resort course in the world when it opened. Given an overhaul in 1975 by the original designer's son, RTJ Jr., to make it a little less demanding, it's still plenty tough, a championship course in every sense of the term. It's the only Hawaiian course ranked by *Golf Digest* among its Top 100 courses in the world.

Just as every new name-brand course built in Florida these days must have an island green to attract well-heeled condo buyers, so every island course has to have at least one over-the-ocean par 3. At some of the newer Hawaiian courses, it

almost seems as if the ocean were diverted to build such holes. Not at Mauna Kea. Its spectacular third hole looks like it's been there forever, perhaps serving as some ancient Hawaiian test of manhood until Robert Trent Jones came along and decided to build seventeen more golf holes to keep it company. One of the half dozen most photographed holes in the world (you've seen it in a lot of ads, whether you know it or not), it has everything: crashing waves, rocky cliffs, a huge undulating green, trees on a hill behind to give it definition, gaping bunkers—and a bailout area to the right in case you peel off a banana trying to get too much oomph behind your swing. It has four tee boxes set at 210, 200, 180, and 140 yards, but do yourself a favor and at least have a look from the tips, even if you decide to fire from closer in. It's quite a sight.

Not all wine improves with age. Many wines, in fact, lack the character, substance, and structure to grow beyond a certain point. They can be perfectly enjoyable, but from the outset what you see is what you get. It's the same with golf courses, sort of. For some, perhaps most, older doesn't mean better: what you see on Day One is all you're ever going to get. (Fortunately for us golfers, the analogy breaks down here, because a modest, unpretentious little golf course isn't going to turn to vinegar even if left in the bottle too long.)

Like a great, voluptuous burgundy, Mauna Kea is an exception, a golf course whose maturity has given it immense depth and soul. It is, remember, positively venerable indeed by Hawaiian resort standards. Compare it with the Kiele Course at the Westin Kauai or Kapalua on Maui, and I think you'll see what I mean. They are good courses, maybe great ones, and certainly beautiful, but they have, in comparison with Mauna Kea, a young, undeveloped feel to them. And unlike its nearby neighbors at Waikoloa Beach and Mauna Lani, which appear to be pasted onto the black lava like photos in an old-fashioned album, Mauna Kea is a living part of the bluff, seeming to have evolved as a natural element of a gorgeous environment.

There are many memorable holes—a long par 3 (the eleventh), with *four* tees ranging from 247 to 166 yards, that drops over a hundred feet toward the water to a crowded, elevated green that rejects more far balls than it accepts; a short, relatively easy par 4 (the thirteenth), where the difference between the blue tees (323 yards) and the black tees set back in the woods (409 yards) is the difference between night and nightmare; and a deceptively tough par 4 (the sixteenth), whose 422 yards seem half again as long when you turn right on the gentle dogleg into the wind off the ocean.

But my personal favorite is the seventeenth, a long, gallumping fiver that bends, dips, and roller-coasters its way over hill and dale, not to mention valley and swale, to an elevated green framed by trees and protected by three deep traps. Although at 555 yards it's long enough to require some big booms, placement is more important than power on the seventeenth. If you don't get your second shot far enough to the left, you don't see the green for your third shot. But if you get it too far, you end up in a valley that makes the green look like Mauna Kea (the volcano) herself. Take it from someone who took advantage of a virtually empty course one September afternoon and played this single hole four times, one after the other, two balls per try, in something like forty-five strokes: the seventeenth at Mauna Kea is a whole bunch of golf hole.

And Mauna Kea is a whole bunch of golf course. Both the major golf magazines rate it as the best course in Hawaii. There are others out there in the middle of the Pacific that are flashier, more dramatic, even more scenic. But there's none better. It's my favorite course in Hawaii, and among my top ten favorites in the world. I'm just happy that Robert Trent Jones's hands were strong enough to crush that lava almost three decades ago.

When to Go

It rains less than eight inches a year on the western, leeward side of the Big Island, so you don't have to worry about your golf vacation being washed away no matter when you go. But all golf courses get heavy play in winter, spring, and summer by tourists from Japan and the U.S. mainland, so you want to schedule your trip for September to November.

OFF COURSE

Scenery. Rent a car and take a spin around the Big Island. It's not all that big, when you get right down to it, and you can get all the way to the wet side in a few hours. Marvel at the flora. Admire the waterfalls and rainbows. Have a cup of coffee. (Kona coffee is the best in the world, if you ask me.) Then hightail it back around to the dry side for a quick nine before cocktails.

Take a Helicopter Ride Over an Active Volcano. If you want a firsthand account of what it feels like to hover over an active volcano's crater in a helicopter, then you're asking the wrong tour guide. The nearest I've ever come to a helicopter ride in Hawaii (or anywhere else, for that matter) was watching Magnum and T.J. chase crooks on TV. The nearest I'm likely to come in the future is watching reruns. If it's not big enough to have at least four flight attendants, it'll just have to go without me. As a responsible journalist, though, I have to report that helicopter riding is a very big deal in Hawaii, and braver souls than I rave about it. Your hotel concierge will be happy to arrange a flight for you. Just don't ask me to come along.

Parker Ranch. Check it out—we're talking far, *far* west here, and the Parker spread offers land, lots of land, 'neath the starry sky above. The cowboys are called *paniolos*, and the cows are called cows. The ranch covers just about all the slopes and valleys upland from the beach resorts, so you can't miss it. Get directions from your hotel concierge about specific spots to visit.

Pie. A few years ago, Sonja and Steve Bakalyar traveled all the way from California to the Big Island, and then to the tiny village of Kapaau, located a couple of hours north of Mauna Kea on Highway 270, to eat coconut pie from **Holy's Bakery.** Pretty great, huh? It wasn't the only reason they came to

Mauna Kea, I suppose, but Steve in particular is serious about his pie, and he'd heard stories about Holy's from a friend back in California who'd grown up on the Big Island. So he and Sonja asked around the hotel, discovered that Holy's is indeed a local institution loved by everyone, and made the pilgrimage. Their informed judgment (and my gut tells me they know what they're talking about when it comes to pie) is that Holy's coconut pie (they even brought a toaster oven with them to heat it) is "good, interesting, different . . . but not great." Was I disappointed to hear this? Not a bit. Nor, I believe, were Sonja and Steve. It just proves what medieval knights who sought the Holy Grail established long, long ago: it's the quest that's important, not reaching the goal itself.

Postscript: Maui? Zowie!

Three island golf paradises divided by two weeks equal too much hopping on and off airplanes. That's my view at least, which is why I've focused in this chapter and the last on the Big Island and Kauai, respectively, and why I've neglected Maui. That was a tough call, because Maui boasts some mighty fine golf—namely, the Bay and Village courses at Kapalua Bay (plus the new Ben Crenshaw course that opened last year); and the fine Robert Trent Jones layout at Royal Kaanapali (the North Course), too often overlooked by island-hopping golfers.

But Maui itself certainly hasn't been overlooked by many developers, and it's hands-down the glitz capital of the fiftieth state. This is where Carol Burnett, Tom Selleck, Dinah Shore, and a few thousand other Beautiful People have *pied à isles*, so part of Maui has a Palm Springs feel to it. But it's also where the charter planes drop off most of their sardine-packed human cargo in high season, when parts of it feel more like Myrtle Beach.

The place is knock-'em-dead gorgeous, which is why it's so popular. But *because* it's so popular, I'd rather build my Hawaiian golf vacation on some other lava flow. The Big Island and Kauai aren't exactly underrun with tourists like me, but I believe you have a better chance of stumbling onto a slack time on either of them than on Maui.

   "Different courses for different horses" is a truism among golfers, however, so here are some useful Maui names and numbers, should you decide to find out for yourself whether I've been spending a little too much time in the sun:

Kapalua Bay Hotel and Villas

1 Bay Drive

Kapalua, Maui

Hawaii 96761

Telephone: (800) 367-8000

Royal Kaanapali Golf Courses

Kaanapali Beach Resort

Lahaina, Maui

Hawaii 96761

Telephone: (808) 669-5656

Maui Prince Hotel

5400 Makena Alanui

Kihei, Maui

Hawaii 96753

Telephone: (800) 321-MAUI

★

CHAPTER 9

ARIZONA FAIRWAYS
Color the Desert Green

LONG, LONG AGO, WHEN I WAS A KID GROWING up in Texas, one of my favorite magazines was a monthly called *Arizona Highways*. It was published by the Arizona department of transportation to lure tourists. This was before air conditioning and before the interstate highway system, so it must have been a pretty tough sell back then. It's still around, but I associate it with the *Saturday Evening Post* and *Collier's*, which disappeared when I was a teenager and had my back turned. Anyway, *Arizona Highways* was a great magazine, filled (I recall) with vivid color pictures that brought the desert alive in ways that not even John Ford movies could do. Rugged mountains, immense vistas, giant rock formations, and all sorts of wildlife, from prairie dogs to deer to bobcats (night photography) and snakes (uggh!). A mining town here, a ghost town there, but no cities. Not even many people; mostly landscape. I remember seeing one photo of some movie star or other standing next to this giant, twelve-foot-tall saguaro cactus and wondering how anything could be so tall and not be a tree.

Imagine my shock when I first visited Phoenix about forty years later.

It takes some getting used to, Phoenix does. For starters, you have to wonder about the decision to put a town there in the first place, smack dab in the middle of nowhere, on a flat-as-a-pancake former ocean bed where temperatures reach 110-plus degrees in the summer and where, when it does rain, it floods. If you'd visited the Valley of the Sun, as the area calls itself, on a mid-July day about 100 years ago, you'd probably have concluded that this arid, featureless, beastly hot desert-scape was unfit for human habitation. You could still make that argument today, except that nearly 2 million inhabitants of the Greater Phoenix metropolitan area would probably disagree.

A boomtown for the last three decades or so, Phoenix is a city with its own peculiar set of contradictions. For example, a lot of people moved there in the first place for its clean air, but the Environmental Protection Agency says now that Phoenix has the highest level of carbon monoxide pollution in the country. Nothing much used to grow there but sagebrush and cactus, but irrigation and the importation of plants not native to the desert have now made it the pollen capitol of America. A great sprawl of a town that would be unthinkable without the automobile—here's yet another example—Phoenix has too few freeways (an American first!) and too few main thorough-fares to handle its staggering number of private cars. (If you need to cross Phoenix from one side to the other, better pack a lunch. On second thought, there are more than enough fast-food outlets to sustain the entire population of Minnesota, which seems to descend on Phoenix every winter.)

And, for a fourth and positively final example of Phoenix's internal contradictions, consider this: while the average annual rainfall is less than eight inches a year, and the scarcity of water has long been perceived as the region's most serious long-term problem, there are to be found in the Phoenix metropolitan area over eighty large, irregularly shaped expanses of lush, rich, green grass that would seem to have no obvious agricultural purpose.

These desert oases are called golf courses, and they are evidence of Phoenix's emergence in the last decade as one of the half dozen most important popular destinations for traveling golfers in America.

Arizona highways, meet Arizona fairways.

MARK CALCAVECCHIA PLAYED HERE

The more you play golf, the more you want to play the best courses. In the older metropolitan areas of the country, about the only way to get on the best golf courses is to live there a few generations, be worth a few zillion dollars, and make a lot of well-connected friends so they'll sponsor you for country club membership. In *nouveau riche* cities like Phoenix, the variation on that theme is to plunk down a few hundred thousand for a housing lot twenty miles from nowhere filled with cactus and scorpions so that you'll qualify for . . . country club membership. You don't have to build anything, mind you—you just need the lot. The sign outside the gatehouse reads "Private— Members Only" at places north of Phoenix like Desert Highlands and Troon, and the traveling golfer who isn't best pals with a member in good standing is usually invited to go whistle up his two-iron.

Fortunately, that doesn't matter so much in Phoenix, because one of the best courses in the Phoenix area—*the* best course, according to some experts—is the Tournament Players Club in Scottsdale. And you don't hae to buy a piece of property just to play there. Designed by Tom Weiskopf and Jay Morrish, TPC-Scottsdale is the home of the Phoenix Open and probably the finest of all the stadium courses commissioned by Deane Beman and the PGA Tour. What's more, this terrific track is open to the public. That's you and me, bub, so take advantage.

(There's a second Weiskopf-Morrish course just next door. It's shorter, easier, and a whole lot of fun to play. It's also a lot less crowded, because everybody wants to tackle the Stadium

---

STADIUM COURSE AT TPC-SCOTTSDALE

Design: Tom Weiskopf and Jay Morrish

Year Open: 1987

6,992 Yards   73.9 Rating   130.7 Slope

Information: (602) 585-3600

★

Course. Keep it in mind if your spirits need a little late afternoon boost. The slope factor is 112 from the back tees versus 130.7 across the street. The difference could do wonders for your cocktail hour, not to mention your handicap. But it's not a course you want to structure your whole vacation around.)

DESERT COURSE AT TPC-SCOTTSDALE

Design: Tom Weiskopf and Jay Morrish

Year Open: 1988

6,552 Yards   71.4 Rating   112 Slope

Information: (602) 585-3600

The first hole of a good golf course ought to get you out of the chute in a good frame of mind. It needn't be a pushover, but neither should it be a rally killer. A golfer has enough burdens to bear without having to start the morning with a big number. What he needs at the top of the day is a little salve for his endemically fragile ego. There'll be plenty of time for humiliation on down the line.

By that measure, the first hole of the Stadium Course at TPC-Scottsdale may be the quintessential opening hole. From the tips it's just 410 yards, and from where nonmembers of the PGA Tour will be hitting it's only 366 (Championship), 341 (Regular), and 311 (Forward). But that's only the beginning of the good news. The fairway is a generous swath of green bordered by desert, but it takes a near boomerang to find the sand and rocks. The green is another oasis, smaller than the fairway but bigger than most greens. Keep it away from the monster trap on the right and you can walk to the second tee with a solid par under your belt, perhaps even a birdie if your approach is true.

But the Lord giveth and the Lord taketh away, and the second hole is all about taking away. At just about the point where a decently struck tee shot finally yields to gravity, the fairway pinches in like the waist of a voluptuous woman, just enough so that you notice. To the left of the pinch is a single deep pot bunker, to the right three fairway traps. Depending on the wind and the amount of curve in your drive, you could buy yourself some quick trouble. Like the first hole, the second is also short (416 from all the way back), and it also has but one trap protecting the green. But the green is smaller, the trap is deeper, and the odds a lot greater that you discover in a hurry why *this* is a stop on the PGA Tour and your average resort course isn't.

Weiskopf and Morrish are also responsible for Troon, one of the region's finer private courses located about twenty minutes north at the foot of the mountains. One big difference between the two courses is that Troon is an inherently dramatic site where mountain meets desert, with sweeping vistas and interesting terrain, while the TPC-Scottsdale began with a couple of hundred acres of barren, flat flood plain.

How flat? Well, if you dropped a marble on the ground it wouldn't roll anywhere. At least it wouldn't have before Weiskopf and Morrish brought in the 'dozers and started digging lakes and building hills and otherwise giving the land some features. You still know you're in a flood plain, though, because of the bordering levee on the south side of the course. It's there to keep all those fancy stores and expensive ranch-styles in Scottsdale high and dry (well, at least dry) when the floodwaters cut loose. The levee makes you feel, from certain vantage points, that the course is laid out in a moon crater, but with this one big difference: a crater on the moon is a whole lot more scenic than a flood plain in Phoenix. (Okay, okay—so it's *Scottsdale*, not Phoenix. For my money, it's a distinction without a difference, except in the price of a three-bedroom ranch.)

What are lakes doing in the middle of the desert? Good question, one you might well ask yourself in mid-waggle on the eleventh tee. Well, when you move around a few hundred thousand tons of dirt to build mounds for spectators to sit on— it's called a Stadium Course, remember—then you're going to leave some pretty big holes in the ground. If you don't fill them with water, you're going to have some mighty strange lies for second shots. Hence the lake on the eleventh hole. Better a little bit of water, the thinking goes, than a baby Grand Canyon.

Thoughts like that will be of small comfort as you stand on the tee at eleven, the number-one handicap hole on the course. What you see 469 yards away (if you're a pro), or 439 yards (if you're a single-digit handicapper), or 408 yards (if you're playing with me), is a skinny fairway with a right-to-left tilt bordered all the way down the left-hand side by Lake Weiskopf-Morrish. It's not very deep or very big as lakes go, but it sure is wet, and any kind of hook will end up there. But even if you play safely to the right (not that there is much safety to the right, unless you like sidehill lies in the rough or hitting out of waste bunkers), you still have a tricky second shot because of the way the green is perched out on a little 'dozer-made bend in the shoreline. A slightly pulled second shot might not make it to the water, however, because of the immense left-side bunker protecting a green that just coincidentally has a little right-to-left pitch to it.

No doubt about it: the eleventh at TPC-Scottsdale is stronger than the noonday sun. When you see it for the first time, just imagine trying to play it with a Sunday pin placement (extreme left) on a gusty day (the Phoenix area figures on a couple of hundred of them a year) from the back tees. Makes you wonder whether rattlesnake wrestling wouldn't be a safer desert pastime.

A good start deserves a great finish, and TPC-Scottsdale delivers both. Remember that par on the first hole? Savor it as you walk up to the tee on eighteen, because finishing the way you started is going to be a lot tougher. Better still, get it out of your mind altogether, and concentrate instead on cutting off as much of the lake on the left as you dare on this dramatic dogleg where bravery pays big dividends. If you have to comfort your tee shot too far to the right to be sure of staying dry, getting home in 2 becomes well-nigh impossible. But if you airmail it over enough water, you stand a good chance of putting for a birdie to close out your round. The big green has a deep bunker on its right-hand side, but from the left-hand side of the fairway you can run the ball on with a well-struck middle iron. But everything—your chances of finishing with a 3 or a 4, any hope of salvaging the round, maybe your entire vacation—depends on a solidly smitten, precisely directed tee shot.

Don't be nervous.

A PRINCESS IN THE DESERT

Looking for a convenient place to bunk while you bring the TPC-Scottsdale to its knees? How about right across the street at the Scottsdale Princess Resort, the first American venture for Princess Hotels International, which has left its luxurious mark on Acapulco, the Bahamas, and Bermuda. With 525 rooms to fit all budgets, provided that they're at least big, the Princess is royally appointed, with the usual cacophony of resort design styles (Mexican, Southwestern, "international") blended this time into a sonorous desert harmony.

SCOTTSDALE PRINCESS RESORT 7575 East Princess Drive, Scottsdale, Arizona 85255. On the north side of town just east of Scottsdale Road; you can't miss it. Telephone: (800) 255-0080. <u>Accommodations</u>: 525 rooms, casitas, and suites. <u>Facilities</u>: 10 tennis courts, including a 10,000-seat stadium court if you have a big match scheduled; 3 restaurants and 8 bars; a health spa with every piece of exercise equipment known to man (or woman) should either of you spend too much time in the restaurants and bars; pool (the big news, of course, would be if there weren't any pool); 480 stables and a polo field at Horseworld, just a short canter away. <u>Terms</u>: From $200 for a standard double to $260 for a deluxe to $475 for a villa suite to $1,500 for the presidential suite. That's in high season, from January 1 through mid-May. In the summer, when only mad golfers and Englishmen go out in the noonday sun, the tariff is reduced by more than half. There are various splendidly named packages, including "Royal Escapade," "Honeymoon Majesty," and the one you want to hear about, "Royal Tee."

For the golfer, of course, the primary advantage of the Princess is its convenience to the two TPC courses. For my money, you can't beat stepping out of a comfortable room directly onto the first tee. But there are other, smaller touches that are also impressive about the Princess.

If you bring a letter of introduction from your club or your home pro, for instance, the Princess promises to try to get you a tee time on one of the local private courses in the area. The Princess is the only resort in the area to state publicly its willingness to make such an effort. This could be important to you, as all three golf courses in the Phoenix-Scottsdale area that *Golf Digest* ranks among "America's 100 Greatest Courses"—Desert Highlands, Troon, and Desert Forest—are private.

The Princess also has enough facilities and activities to make the nongolfers in your party beg to stay an extra few days. Naturally, you accede to such entreaties: "If you insist, dear . . ."

CAMELBACK

Everybody's heard of Camelback, a national landmark that first opened its doors in 1936. Located way to hell and gone up on a bluff north of Phoenix, Camelback gave instant definition to the "Western resort" with its stucco casitas, Southwestern and Indian decor, desert surroundings, towering saguaro cactus, and splendid isolation.

MARRIOTT'S CAMELBACK INN RESORT 5402 East Lincoln Drive, Scottsdale, Arizona 85262. About 20 minutes north of Phoenix's Sky Harbor Airport. Telephone: (800) 24-CAMEL. (I hate it when they do that. Since telephone exchanges—BUtterfield, TRafalgar, and ACademy, to name just three in New York—have gone the way of the dodo bird, nobody knows the letters on a phone dial any more, never mind that it's not even a dial but three rows of buttons. It takes me twice as long to find 24-CAMEL as it does to dial—sorry, punch—242-2635. Someone in the Camelback promotions department is guilty of serious overcreativity.) <u>Accommodations</u>: 423 rooms and suites in casitas fanning out from a main lodge. <u>Amenities</u>: Pool; tennis; health spa; pitch-and-putt course on premises; 2 golf courses 10 minutes away at Camelback Golf Club; cycling and jogging trails. <u>Terms</u>: From $95 to $250.

Today, Camelback is surrounded by sprawling exurbia, as well-heeled Phoenicians (do you suppose they call themselves that?) over the past decade have striven to give new meaning to the term "Living Desert." It's still a swell place, though, mellowed by age and buoyed by a recent refurbishing by Marriott, its current owner. (One wonders—that is, *I* wonder—why the Marriott people, who surely don't have an identity problem, felt compelled to put their name above the title. Do they think Marriott enhances the Camelback name, or are they hoping for a little vice versa?) The Chaparral is still one of Phoenix-Scottsdale's best restaurants, the motto on the white stucco tower over the main entrance still says "Where Time Stands Still," and Camelback still garners every conceivable star and diamond doled out by the resort rating specialists—and deserves every single one.

PADRE COURSE AT CAMELBACK GOLF CLUB

Design: Red Lawrence

Year Open: 1970

6,559 Yards   71.2 Rating   123 Slope

Information: (602) 948-0931

INDIAN BEND COURSE AT CAMELBACK GOLF CLUB

Design: Arthur Jack Snyder

Year Open: 1978

7,014 Yards   73.4 Rating   125 Slope

Information: (602) 948-0931

The only problem is that I don't think the two Camelback courses are anything to write home about. It's not that they're down the road apiece, instead of just outside my front door. I'm spoiled, but not that spoiled. It's just that they are, well, sort of boring. The Indian Bend Course runs a long way out and a long way back along something that Camelback publicists call a "verdant natural wash," but that looks to me like a long drainage ditch. The Padre Course is older, prettier, more interesting, and shorter, but it's just another resort course compared with the TPC-Scottsdale, about ten minutes away.

My suggestion? If you want a little taste of history, stay at Camelback, but play at TPC-Scottsdale.

CAREFREE

Andrew Harper's Hideaway Report is a monthly newsletter that bills itself as "A connoisseur's guide to peaceful and unspoiled places." In that capacity, it reviews and ranks high-ticket resorts around the world and passes the word along to people willing to pay a hundred bucks a year for guidance in planning their next luxury vacation. They can afford it. According to the *Hideaway Report*, the average annual income of its 15,000 subscribers is $302,000. (I am not one of them, much to my regret.)

Now, the point of this little detour is that each year the *Hideaway Report* polls its readers and asks them to rank the top luxury resorts in America, about which they can reasonably be expected to know a thing or two. For the last *four* years, the same resort came out on top: The Boulders in Carefree, Arizona.

THE BOULDERS 34631 North Tom Darlington Drive, Carefree, Arizona 85377. North of Phoenix-Scottsdale just off Scottsdale Road; about 50 minutes from Sky Harbor Airport. Telephone: (800) 553-1717. <u>Accommodations</u>: 136 casitas supplemented by several patio homes (1, 2, and 3 bedrooms) scattered around the property. <u>Amenities</u>: All the basics—pool, tennis, and (of course) golf, plus just about everything imaginable to ride (hot-air balloons, jeeps, helicopters, horses, bicycles, gliders) except ostriches. <u>Terms</u>: From $250 to $445 for a double room, with breakfast and dinner for two persons, depending on the time of year. Several packages available.

(Carefree is not, as you may have guessed, a loose translation from the Apache or a name conjured up for a trading post by nineteenth-century prospectors looking for the Lost Dutchman Mine. Carefree is the happy-face moniker invented by the environment-rapers who set out to turn a few square miles of rough, untamed desert into a playground for the rich back in the late fifties. But their silliness didn't end with the town name. In Carefree, you could live on Languid Lane, visit friends on Never Mind Trail, shop at the intersection of Ho and Hum, and check your balance at the bank on the corner of Easy Street and Wampum Way. It's enough to gag a maggot.)

Nestled in the foothills of the high Sonoran Desert about forty miles northeast of downtown Phoenix, the Boulders seems to have been sculpted rather than constructed. All its 136 rooms are in stucco casitas whose curved shapes and desert tan color echo the giant boulders from which the resort draws its name. The word "unique" is bandied about a lot by travel writers and resort publicists, more often than not with blatant disregard for correct usage (as in "very unique"), and usually out of sheer laziness (travel writers) or purposeful puffery (resort publicists). But sometimes the shoe fits: in conception and design, The Boulders resort is unique.

Not surprisingly, considering that the average net worth of the *Hideaway Report* readers who rank it as top resort is $2.7 million, The Boulders does not stint on luxury. Chances are you can't think of a creature comfort that isn't provided, and you aren't likely to get bored. Helicopter over Grand Canyon? Soar over the desert in a glider? Get away from it all in a hot-air balloon flight? Bounce into the desert on a jeep? Horseback riding? Fishing? Tennis? Hiking? Shopping tours with lunch? You name it, The Boulders has it—or will get it.

All this swellness comes at a price, of course: $200 for the Grand Canyon helicopter ride; $140 per person for the hot-air balloon ride (two and a half hours), $50 to $95 per person for the desert jeep ride (depending on duration), $35 to $50 per person for the shopping tour with lunch (depending on whether you have dessert). And double rooms (including breakfast and dinner for two persons) range from $345 to $445 during high season.

(Keep in mind that you're picking up part of the tab, even if you never set foot in Arizona. The Boulders is much valued by corporate CEOs and high-level business muckety-mucks as a center for blue-ribbon conferences, which are pursued by the Rockresorts management team at The Boulders the way sidewinders pursue desert mice. Figure that a whole bunch of those top dollars spent at The Boulders for "business" meetings are tax deductible—which is more than you can say for the greens fees a Podunk Muni.)

All right, already—The Boulders is a great resort . . . a *unique* resort, even. What about the golf?

Not so great. At least that's my take on the three Jay Morrish nines (called Saguaro, Lake, and Boulders). Don't get me

THE BOULDERS

Design: Jay Moorish

Year Open: 1983, 1984

Boulders-Lake:	7,266 Yds.	75.1 Rating	134 Slope
Lake-Saguaro:	6,982 Yds.	74.7 Rating	132 Slope
Saguaro-Boulders:	7,012 Yds.	74.9 Rating	138 Slope

Information: (800) 553-1717

Note: Course open to members and resort guests only.

wrong: Each layout is astonishingly beautiful; each has its share of vividly dramatic holes; each is doggone tough, with slope ratings (from the tips) of 132, 134, or 138, depending on which two nines you play; and Jay Morrish is a heckuva fine golf course architect (he and Weiskopf did TPC-Scottsdale, remember). But desert golf is, almost by definition, target golf; and target golf is just not my cup of tea.

At desert courses in general, and at The Boulders more than most, the rough consists of, well, *desert*. You look out from a tee box and what you see on a lot of holes is patches of green in a sea of brown. It looks like some giant had cut out irregular swatches of lush, green fabric and scattered them at his feet on the desert floor. On most nondesert golf courses, if you should (God forbid!) hit a ball into the rough or into the woods, you go find it and hit it out. But on desert courses, and even

more so at The Boulders, this can be unnerving, if not down-right dangerous. I don't know about you, but when I'm addressing the ball before trying to knock it back from rough to fairway, I've got enough on my mind without having to worry about whether a rattlesnake is getting set to curl up on my Foot-Joy.

Snakes aside (which is exactly where I want them), the exigencies of golf course design in the desert make for a whole different kind of game. After decades of rampant development the residents of the Valley of the Sun have come to their senses—at least a little—about the need to conserve water. Mind you, if the folks who own golf courses in Phoenix had enough of it, they'd create oceans of green and let the fragile desert ecology go to hell. But they don't, and new restrictions on how much of a golf course's total area can be irrigated, and how much water can be used, have forced desert course designers into target golf—of which The Boulders is merely an extreme example.

Play TPC-Scottsdale. Then play The Boulders. And then tell me whether you don't agree that there's a big, big difference between a course built in the desert and a *desert course*. I prefer one; you may prefer the other. Who's right? Hey, that's why they have nineteenth holes.

When to Go

A friend of mine who used to live in Tucson always insisted that summer golf in Arizona was great. "Sure, it's hot," he would say, "but it's dry heat. All you have to do is play early in the morning or late in the day." By "early" and "late," it turns out, he meant 6 A.M. and 5 P.M. Sorry, Charlie, but when I'm on vacation I want to play golf *all* day. And I don't care whether the heat is dry or wet—when it's 110 degrees outside, I'm inside.

The best time to go to Arizona for golf (or anything else) is January through mid-April, when it's cold and/or wet and miserable in two thirds of the rest of the country. But that's also the most expensive and the most crowded time. Try mid-September through November, when rates are softer and the snowbird migration hasn't commenced from colder climes. It can still get plenty hot during the day, but it's . . . ah, dry heat.

OFF COURSE

Living Desert. The Sonora Desert is one of the great natural wonders of America. Because it receives at least some rainfall both winter and summer, the Sonora is rich in plant and animal life. In the foothills north of Phoenix-Scottsdale, giant saguaro cactus tower over the rugged landscape. See them at dusk, when the fading rays of the sun cast their immense shadows across the sagebrush, boulders, and bare-limbed paloverde trees. All the major resorts can arrange a jeep tour of the desert. Do it.

Grand Canyon. If I were going to take a helicopter ride of my own volition, and I'm not, I would take one that swoops down into the Grand Canyon. The people I spoke with who did it raved about it. If I had yielded to their entreaties and gone along, I'm pretty sure I would still be raving.

Shopping in Scottsdale. I have it on good authority, though not from personal experience, that shopping in Scottsdale in general is great and that in something called the Borgata (a high-class mall, I suppose) it is exceptional. Expensive, too, I should imagine.

Spring Training. If you go in March, be sure to catch a ball game. Even if you're not a particularly avid baseball fan, there's something incredibly appealing about spring training. The pace is lazy, the players actually seem to be having fun, the ballparks are small, and you get a good feel for why the game is the national pastime. After golf, of course.

CHAPTER 10

HEARTLAND
Playing Through Middle America

SAY THE WORDS "FOUR-STAR GOLF VACATION" and what places come to mind: Florida? Arizona? Hawaii? California? Sure. That's automatic. Those places are known for their incredible golf, and rightly so. But sometimes the automatic answer is incomplete, and no review of great golf vacations would do justice to the subject without a close look at golf in the American Heartland.

That's right, the Heartland—the American Midwest. Far from the Sunbelt, thousands of miles from the ocean, nobody's automatic answer to the question, "Where's a great place to go on a golf vacation of a lifetime?"

Now, this is going to sound weird, but to me an especially appealing thing about the four places discussed below is that you could cram them all into one two-week vacation—and drive from one to the other. Let me put it another way: You *could*; I *would*. That's right. Throw the clubs in the trunk of the Hertz buggy and *vrooom!* From O'Hare to southwest Indiana to northwestern Illinois to eastern Wisconsin. Piece of cake. Have I lost my mind? No. But I have been living in Manhattan for the last couple of decades. I never drive anywhere. I don't even own a car. For me, getting behind the wheel of a car provides the same jolt of freedom and excitement that it did when I was a teenager, even though drive-in movies have gone the way of the buffalo. Now that I'm older, it spells vacation.

If you drive to work every day (I walk), you may not want to log as many miles on the family wagon as would be necessary to get from Cog Hill to French Lick to Eagle Ridge to Blackwolf Run, the components of the Heartland Tour. That's okay. Except for Cog Hill, all are destination resorts where you can spend your entire vacation without fear of boredom. Plus there's a distinct advantage of staying put: the hours I spend on the highway you can spend on the practice range.

Even so, I think you ought to hit the road. You may not be able to get your kicks on Route 66 anymore, but you sure can get in a lot of golf in the Heartland.

COG HILL

"Attention, campers: the first stop on our deluxe, 5-star golf tour of the American Heartland is at a public course in . . ."

Whoa! Stop right there! Did you say public course? Hey, Mac, I can wait four hours for a tee time to play a five-hour round on a scruffy, crowded, poorly maintained, unchallenging, indifferently designed course *without even leaving town*. Where do you get off tossing around words like "deluxe" and "5-star" and "public course" together in the same sentence?

Quiet on the tee, please. Look, I know the golf boom has overtaxed the country's public courses, and that playing on many of them—perhaps most—is not what it was a decade or more ago. I also know that anyone contemplating a 5-star golf vacation, which is what this book is all about, is prepared to spend a few extra bucks *not* to have to put up with all the aggravation customarily associated with public courses, at

COG HILL 119th Street and Archer Avenue, Lemont, Illinois 60439. About 30 miles southwest of Chicago off I-55. Telephone: (708) 257-5872. Cog Hill is a privately owned golf complex that is open to the public: 4 golf courses, driving range, golf shop, restaurant.

★

least those in most major metropolitan areas. I understand all that, and I'm here to tell you that Cog Hill belongs on your Heartland tour. Why? Because of the *golf*.

Located thirty miles southwest of Chicago, Cog Hill consists of a large, comfortable, Old World-style clubhouse with three dining rooms; a large practice range; a golf shop; and four well-maintained courses—three of which are short, sporty tracks that are fun to play if you're in the neighborhood but which are not, taken alone, worthy of a special detour, much less inclusion on the itinerary of a deluxe, 5-star golf vacation.

The fourth course is another matter.

Ranked among America's best golf courses since it opened in 1964, Cog Hill Number 4 is called "Dubsdread," which is even harder to play than it is to say. (Go ahead, say "Dubsdread, Dubsdread, Dubsdread" three times, fast, while patting your head and rubbing your stomach. Now go play it. See what I mean?) True, *Golf Digest* recently dropped Cog Hill Number 4 from its "America's 100 Greatest," but that has to do with the emergence of some great, newer courses in the last quarter century, not with any weakness in the fine Dick Wilson design.

COG HILL NUMBER 4 (DUBSDREAD)

Design: Dick Wilson

Year Open: 1964
6,992 Yards   75.4 Rating   142 Slope

Information: (708) 257-5872. Tee times may be made up to 6 days in advance (up to 90 days with prepayment).

Indeed, "weakness" and "Cog Hill Number 4" do *not* belong in the same sentence. With a 75.4 course rating and a 142 slope, Dubsdread (as in "I *dread* the *dubs* this course causes me to hit") is 6,992 yards of trouble. Beautiful, too, and impeccably maintained, but as tough as a true championship course ought to be.

Appropriately enough, a storied championship event will be contested on Cog Hill Number 4 in 1991. When the members of Butler National in Oak Brook, Illinois, decided that they didn't want to be hurried into the twentieth century with regard to their restrictive membership policies, the PGA Tour went looking for a course of championship caliber that didn't find anything wrong with women and blacks walking on the same fairways as rich WASP males. And so it came to pass that Cog Hill Number 4 will host the 1991 Western Open, the oldest (except for the U.S. Open) and one of the most prestigious golf tournaments on the PGA Tour.

There's no hotel at Cog Hill, but that shouldn't present a problem for the traveling golfer. Just play until dark, then head back to the freeway and look for one of those places where they keep the light on for you.

FRENCH LICK

The toughest challenge about the next stop on your Heartland Tour is not smirking when you tell the guys down at the office you just got back from playing French Lick.

("You were playing *what*? I thought you were going on a *golf* vacation!")

Okay, okay. Got it out of your system? Can we be little mature for a minute?

The correct name is the French Lick Springs Resort in French Lick, Indiana. Nobody ever adds the "Springs Resort" part, of course, any more than people refer to Sixth Avenue in New York as Avenue of the Americas. The name was changed from "French Lick Hotel" to "French Lick Springs Resort" some years back for reasons that undoubtedly make perfect sense to people who specialize in hotel marketing. But to everyone in Indiana except the telephone operators at the place, it's just good old French Lick.

FRENCH LICK SPRINGS RESORT French Lick, Indiana 47432. About 110 miles southwest of Indianapolis and 60 miles northwest of Louisville. Telephone: (800) 457-4042. Accommodations: 485 guest rooms. Amenities: 2 pools; spa, with mineral water baths; horseback riding; 18 tennis courts; fishing, boating, and swimming in nearby Patoka Lake. Terms: Golf package available. From $105 to $295.

★

To avoid any possible misunderstanding and/or sophomoric joking about the name, we might as well deal with the business of its origins right now.

Long, long ago, when the Midwest was just the West, herds of buffalo roamed (and deer and antelope played, no doubt) in what is now southwestern Indiana; and they would come from miles around to lick the rocks caked with salt from underground mineral springs. French explorers discovered the waters in the late 1600s, and nearly a century later pioneers moving west came upon them as well. A noted adventurer of the day, General George Rogers Clark, named the area "French Lick."

Passing over a colorful but golfless stretch of French Lick history in the nineteenth century, during which a greedy entrepreneurial physician built a hotel and hyped the therapeutic qualities of the water (Pluto's Water, he named it) before dying in scandal and disgrace, we fast forward to 1901, when the mayor and political boss of Indianapolis, one Tom Taggart, bought the site where the original hotel had stood before it was destroyed by fire, built a new, much larger one, and turned the place into a refuge for the Hoosier state's rich, regionally famous, and politically connected, as well as a summer retreat for the *crème de* Indianapolis and *haute* Terre Haute society.

French Lick became more than merely a local getaway in the 1920s, its golden age. Rolls-Royces, Stutzes, and Packards from all over the Midwest turned up at French Lick's front doors to disgorge their wealthy passengers, who came by the droves to take the waters, gamble at nearby casinos, drink Prohibition-era cocktails in public without fear of arrest, cut political deals, pay off corrupt public servants—and play golf at the new championship course designed by Donald Ross that was opened for play in 1920.

HILL COURSE AT FRENCH LICK SPRINGS COUNTRY CLUB

Design: Donald Ross
Year Open: 1920
6,625 Yards   71.5 Rating   119 Slope
Information: (812) 935-9831

★

Golf wasn't exactly new to French Lick. A shorter, easier course—the oldest in the Midwest, it's alleged—had been around since before the turn of the century. But the new Ross course, with its rolling fairways and small, humpbacked greens, was a strong enough layout to host the 1924 PGA Championship, won by the great Walter Hagen. Golf became one of French Lick's major activities, right up their with swigging Pluto's Water and rigging elections.

The stately old hotel went into a steep decline after World War II, a victim of changing fashion and obsession with the sleek and modern. The turnaround came in the early 1980s. Nostalgia for the traditional, new capital, major renovations, clever marketing, and the beginning of the golf boom all played a part in bringing back some of the old glory, albeit in modern packaging, of the French Lick Hotel (sorry, the French Lick Springs Resort).

Located in a beautiful, quiet, bucolic corner of the Heartland, French Lick has a good, unpretentious feeling to it. It's a grand old place, one that has borne its face-lift well. Plus, of course, it has that grand old name.

EAGLE RIDGE

All right, class, time for our American geography quiz: In what midwestern state is the town of Galena?

My guess is that more than half of the readers of this book who are under thirty years of age don't have a clue where Galena is. At least that's what I'm led to believe by report after report about how little geography Americans know, and how the situation is getting worse. Shocking, if you ask me, and I think it's about time somebody did something about it. So, in the spirit of public service, right here and now I'm going to give a mini-geography lesson. (Readers who know where Galena is may skip the following paragraph.)

Galena is 153 miles northwest of Chicago, 175 miles southwest of Milwaukee, 280 miles southeast of Minneapolis/St. Paul, and 210 miles northeast of Des Moines. It's also about 20 miles from Dubuque, the town that most New Yorkers, the most parochial of our countrymen, usually have in mind when they talk about someplace "out there" in America. A lead-mining town of some importance in the nineteenth century, Galena was the home of U. S. Grant when the Civil War began. Today,

Galena is virtually a living museum whose grand Victorian homes and nineteenth-century church spires make it seem frozen in time. Oh yes: Galena is in *Illinois*.

Enough geography; let's talk golf.

EAGLE RIDGE INN AND RESORT Box 777, Galena, Illinois 61036. About 20 miles southeast of Dubuque on Route 20. Telephone: (800) 323-8421. <u>Accommodations</u>: 66 guest rooms in the inn and over 200 resort homes (1 to 4 bedrooms). <u>Amenities</u>: Tennis, fishing, horseback riding, sailing, swimming, hiking, fitness center. <u>Terms</u>: From $150 for a ''deluxe'' double room (actually, their lowest-priced standard room; you need to know Hotelspeak to understand why) to $190 for a ''superior.'' (A superior with fireplace costs another $35, but you're going to be there in the summer or fall, so you don't need the fireplace.) Golf package available.

The Eagle Ridge Inn and Resort is the flagship of the Galena Territory, a 6,800-acre recreational resort community six miles east of Galena. Located on a bluff in some of the Heartland's most beautiful hills, Eagle Ridge is as modern as Galena is Victorian. The inn itself is small (sixty-six rooms), but the complex is large, with just about every recreational and sports activity known to man, with the possible exception of the luge. (And just because I didn't see a luge run there doesn't mean there isn't one.) Best of all is the golf.

NORTH COURSE AT EAGLE RIDGE INN AND RESORT

Design: Roger B. Packard

Year Open: 1978

6,836 Yards   73.3 Rating   130 Slope

Information: (815) 777-2500

The two Roger Packard courses at Eagle Ridge would constitute a heckuva entry if two-course golf resorts were judged on the individual strengths of their layouts rather than on the better of the two. Most such resorts, as noted elsewhere, have an "A" course and a "B" course. The Eagle Ridge courses are "A" and "A minus"—and there is no unanimity of opinion about which is which, although the North Course generally receives the higher grade.

SOUTH COURSE AT EAGLE RIDGE INN AND RESORT

Design: Roger B. Packard

Year Open: 1984

6,762 Yards   72.6 Rating   125 Slope

Information: (815) 777-2500

★

Opened for play in 1978, the North Course is the older of the two. It's also generally considered to be the tougher. The South Course, six years younger, has its devotees, though, who believe that when it matures it may well be the equal of the North. Neither is exceptionally long (6,836 and 6,762 yards from the back tees, respectively), but there's a lot of up and down as both stretch over rolling hillside. The North Course is ranked fifteenth among all Illinois courses, and that includes some of the country's best (e.g., Medinah, Olympia Fields, Butler National, Kemper Lakes, all in *Golf Digest*'s top 100 American courses); the South is ranked thirty-seventh.

Together, the two Eagle Ridge courses have earned the resort *Golf* magazine's silver medal. Only forty-two other resorts in America received silver in the magazine's most recent ranking (twelve got gold medals), so the award really means something.

It means you should learn where Galena is and how to get there.

BLACKWOLF RUN AND THE AMERICAN CLUB

"State of the art bathrooms, usually encountered only in magazines, come alive for your enjoyment . . . Also unique to each of the rooms are the exceptional plumbing fixtures . . . Special suites include Infinity and Super Bath whirlpools, for one or two, or our remarkable Habitat enclosures, an exotic escape into a relaxing environment of sun, steam, and rain."

In my line of work you read a lot of promotional brochures extolling the virtues of this or that golf resort, but I don't recall ever seeing a single brochure that even mentioned bathrooms, much less extolled their plumbing fixtures with the zeal and specificity employed in describing the johns at the American Club in Kohler, Wisconsin. In addition to the direct message that the bathrooms at the American Club are alone worth the trip, I suspect that the sales literature is laced with subliminal suggestions as well. How else to explain this overpowering, double-barreled urge I have to play golf and buy a new bathtub?

The tipoff to this loo obsession, of course, is the location of the American Club. Kohler, Wisconsin, is the company town and national headquarters of the Kohler Company. Check out your toilet: the odds are pretty good that it's a Kohler or a Sterling (the other brand name used by Kohler). Founded in 1873 by John Michael Kohler, the company moved to its present location from Sheboygan in 1920, and the rest is plumbing history. For a long time the Kohler Company, one of the largest companies in America still in private hands, has been the

THE AMERICAN CLUB Highland Drive, Kohler, Wisconsin 53044. About 55 miles north of Milwaukee just west of Interstate 43. Telephone: (800) 458-2562. <u>Accommodations</u>: 160 rooms, each with a private bath. <u>Amenities</u>: 6 restaurants; Sports Core, a large, comprehensive fitness center with a wide range of programs and classes in addition to the latest and best in exercise gear; River Wildlife, a 600-acre wildlife preserve with 30 miles of hiking trails; hunting, fishing, canoeing, cycling. <u>Terms</u>: From $122 to $292 for a double room in the summer. Numerous special packages available.

country's leading and best-known manufacturer of plumbing products.

Constructed in 1918 by the son of the company's founder, the red-brick, neo-Tudor building that now houses the only AAA 5-diamond resort in the Midwest began life as a dormitory for immigrant workers in the Kohler factory. Actually it was more than just a shelter. Billiards and bowling highlighted leisure time activities, while classes in English and citizenship helped bridge the gap between Old World and New. By day, you fabricated commodes; by night, you read Emerson in your bowling shirt. A worker's paradise, smack dab in the Middle Border.

Or so it was in the romanticized, well-scrubbed version of the past preferred by the people who own the Kohler Company. In fact, Kohler was the object of the longest, bitterest strikes in American history. It started back in the fifties and was still going on back in the sixties. (It may still be going on, for all I know.) If Kohler had ever been a workers' paradise, it had surely become something else in the decades after World War II.

But all that's blood under the bridge. Anyway, except for the exterior, it's not likely that the former residents of what is now the American Club would recognize the place. Completely renovated between 1979 and 1981, the interior of the handsome structure reflects a degree of luxury that immigrant workers in the 1920s could not even have imagined. Especially the bathrooms.

The primary reason for going to Kohler, Wisconsin, and staying at the American Club is not, of course, to become a little part of plumbing history, but to play golf at one of the best resort courses in the country, Blackwolf Run.

Named the "Best New Public Course of 1988" by *Golf Digest*, Blackwolf Run is actually two eighteen-hole courses, the River and the Meadow Valleys, both designed by the redoubtable Pete Dye. Sculpted from land formed by glacial runoffs some thousands of years ago, Blackwolf Run is Dye at his best—and toughest. Indeed, both of the courses amply live up to the legendary toughness of their namesake.

Black Wolf, chief of the Winnebago tribe, was a great warrior of the early 1800s who successfully fought off attempts by the Chippewa and Menominee Indians to conquer the Winnebago homeland, one of the richest hunting and fishing grounds in the whole region. In a famous battle against their numerically superior foe, Black Wolf and his Winnebagos crept down the Sheboygan River to Lake Michigan, circled around behind the Chippewas and the Menominees, and forced them off the road. (Keep that in mind as you scramble to save par.)

The two tracks at Blackwolf Run are of comparable quality. Meadow Valleys is really two terrains—meadow and valley, get it?—but both have the feel of a subtly rolling Scottish course because of the work done by the glaciers long ago in shaping the land. The greens range from small (20 yards in length) to immense (the eighteenth is a whopping 55 yards from stem to stern); most are well guarded by sand or pot bunkers. Men can play the course at 7,142, 6,735, or 6,169 yards, with the score-

---

MEADOW VALLEYS AT BLACKWOLF RUN

Design: Pete Dye

Year Open: 1988–90*
7,142 Yards   74.7 Rating   143 Slope

Information: (414) 457-4446

*Two nine-hole layouts, the original Valleys and River nines, opened in 1988; another nine holes were added in 1989 (Meadow); a fourth nine came on line in 1990, at which time the entire course layout was restructured.

card recommending a handicap of zero to five for the black tees, six to fourteen for the blues, and fifteen to twenty-three for the whites. As the course has a 132 rating from the *white* tees, no one need feel in the least diminished by walking up to the front to tee off. My suggestion: get a grip on your ego and follow the scorecard's advice.

If that's sound advice for Meadow Valleys, it's darn near a categorical imperative for the River Course. The River is a little bit shorter, but a whole lot tougher. Water comes into play on twelve holes, but usually as a lateral hazard, so it is possible to reach most of the greens by surface mail. There are pot bunkers, sand traps, plenty of dogwood and willow trees, and the Sheboygan River to contend with, not to mention multiple landing areas you must choose from for your tee shot.

RIVER COURSE AT BLACKWOLF RUN

Design: Pete Dye

Year Open: 1988–90

6,991 Yards   74.9 Rating   151 Slope

Information: (414) 457-4446. Guests of the American Club may reserve tee times when booking hotel reservations. Nonguests may make reservations up to 1 month in advance.

The best hole? Dye himself says it's Number 9, called "Cathedral Spires" on the scorecard. (I could have done without names for the holes. It seems right in Scotland; it seems forced and artificial at a water closet manufacturer's company course.) A short (337 yards from the *back* tees) par 4, Cathedral Spires gets its name from the 90-foot dogwoods standing guard down the middle. You have three distinct fairways to shoot at, each providing a different level of difficulty for your second shot. What makes Number 9 so special is that it forces you to think *and* pull off career shots. That's asking an awful lot of a golfer, if you ask me.

It's too early to tell (the final nine holes weren't opened for play until the summer of 1990), but the River Course at Blackwolf Run just may be the most challenging resort course in the country. Look at the slope ratings: 137 from the *front* tees, 146 from the blues, and 151 from the tips—the highest slope rating for any course in America.

If your game is on, playing these two beautiful, tough, splendidly groomed new courses at Blackwolf Run will be among the most exhilarating experiences of your golf career. But if your game is off, you'd better be the kind of person who enjoys beautiful scenery no matter how you score, or it's going to seem like a long, hard day at the office.

Either way, of course, you'll have at least one thing to look forward to back in your room at the American Club.

A nice, hot, state-of-the-art bath.

When to Go

Cog Hill, French Lick, and Eagle Ridge have longer golf seasons than Blackwolf Run, where cold blasts of air from Canada in mid-autumn make you think the glaciers are coming back. For my money, September is the perfect time for all of them because the crowds have thinned out a bit, but a strong case can also be made for smack in the middle of summer. What could be more appropriate than spending the Fourth of July at the American Club?

OFF COURSE

French Lick. I'm told there is a House of Clocks Museum somewhere nearby, but I don't know what its hours are.

Eagle Ridge. For a glimpse of late-nineteenth-century America, Heartland division, Galena can't be beat (You do know where that is, don't you?). There is even a Mississippi Paddle Wheeler to tempt the riverboat gambler in your soul. But for my money, the best thing to do here besides play golf is to take a long, slow drive in the country. It doesn't get any prettier.

The American Club. Thinking about adding a new bathroom? Pop over to the Kohler Design Center (414-458-6144), a 36,000-square-foot tribute to state-of-the-art plumbing. The place has a museum, a theater, and twenty-three designer kitchens and baths to admire . . . Want to commune with some mighty fine-looking nature? Take a walk in River Wildlife, a stunning, 600-acre nature preserve with 7 miles of scenic rivers and more than 30 miles of woodland trails, immediately adjacent to Blackwolf Run . . . Want to know more about the Kohler family's roots? Visit Waelderhaus, an architecturally faithful replica of the Kohler ancestral Austrian home. (Visiting Austria without leaving home! What could be more American?) . . . Like cheese? Eat some when you tour the Gibbsville Cheese Company (414-564-3242) just south of Sheboygan Falls . . . Looking for something a little spicy and exciting? Spend the afternoon with your travel companion indulging your senses with cycles of sun, steam, soft rain, and gentle breezes in your Kohler Habitat Masterbath.

CHAPTER 11

VALHALLA IN THE SANDHILLS
Pinehurst and Environs

PINEHURST *IS* GOLF.

For beans, go to Boston. In peaks, think Pike. Need 500, try Indy. When it comes to corn, there's no place like Kansas in August. For skyscrapers, take Manhattan. Want a lobster, make for Maine. Smog? L.A. Brotherly Love? Philly. Mud Hens? Toledo, of course. And for chili, beautiful women, plumb ignorant state legislators, barbecue, chiggers, and the Alamo, head for the Lone Star State of Texas. (Okay, I'm prejudiced.)

But *Pinehurst* is golf.

It didn't start out to be. Back in 1895, when James Walker Tufts, a wealthy Boston entrepreneur and philanthropist, bought 5,000 acres of barren, sandy wasteland in the Sandhills region of central North Carolina, golf was the last thing on his mind. Tufts paid a dollar an acre for land that all the locals knew was puredee worthless for the simple reason that he liked the climate. Tufts thought this big hunk of real estate stuck out in the middle of nowhere would make a jim-dandy site for a health resort that would attract hordes of Northerners looking to escape the winter cold.

Problem was, there wasn't any *there* there, and so Tufts started from scratch. He began putting in streets and sewers and water lines, all the while daydreaming about what to call this fantasy he was turning into reality. For a while, he called his village-in-the-making Tuftown, but fortunately his ego didn't need that kind of feeding. (If such an enterprise were to be undertaken today, it would be called "Trumphurst.") Then, while at his summer home in Martha's Vineyard, Tufts's eye fell on the winner in a contest to name a local real estate development, and bingo!—Tuftown was no more, and Pinehurst was born.

(A nice bit of luck that was, when you think about it. Somehow, I don't think a place called Tuftown would ever have become the Golf Capital of America. Tuftown sounds more like the nickname for a reformatory. Or, if you pronounce it *Tuf*-ton, like a tony New England boarding school.)

Pinehurst was nothing but a sandy expanse of stumps and scraggly trees where a thick pine forest once stood before the timber industry had its day, so Tufts hired the New York architectural firm Olmsted, Olmsted, and Eliot to design a village and create a landscape plan. The firm's head, Frederick Law Olmsted, was the man who designed New York's Central Park; you have to say that Tufts made a good call.

Within a year, Pinehurst had a general store, a dairy, about twenty cottages, a boardinghouse, and a small hostelry, the Holly Inn. (Jack Nicklaus stays there when he visits Pinehurst.) The whole thing was supposed to look like a New England village, and it does, sort of, minus the maple trees. Almost from the first day, a wide range of sporting activities was provided for guests of the new Pinehurst health resort. Just about everything, as a matter of fact, except golf.

Tufts was something of a sportsman himself. He also believed in the therapeutic value of vigorous activity. Riding, archery, hunting, lawn bowling, polo, bicycling, and tennis were heavily emphasized in those early days. But the Boston-bred Tufts didn't know beans about golf, and if it hadn't been for a handful of temperamental cows, Pinehurst might today be known as the Lawn Bowling Capital of America.

Some of his guests, hip to a new game recently introduced in the Northeast from Scotland, began playing an improvised version of golf out in the field alongside some otherwise affable Guernseys. (Some of my drives have ended in places like that, but it never occurred to me to play a whole round there.) The historical records are vague, but the experiment didn't work out. The cows became huffy about nonmembers taking over their course, while the hotel guests complained about the hoof marks the cows left on the greens. The cows stopped giving milk, and the hotel guests demanded replacement of shoes ruined by cow, uh, hazards.

To resolve the crisis, the ever-ingenious Tufts hired a New York friend, a Dr. D. LeRoy Culver, to design a proper golf course for Pinehurst. Right instinct, but wrong man, for Dr. Culver knew a lot more about unnecessary gall bladder operations than he did about constructing greens and placing fairway bunkers. The nine-hole track that opened in early 1898 took the cows out of play, but Tufts knew he had to do more to satisfy the heightened expectations of his golf-crazy customers. And so, in 1901, he took the momentous step of hiring a bona fide professional to head up golf operations at Pinehurst, a young Scot named Donald Ross.

For almost five decades, until his death in 1948, Donald Ross remained at Pinehurst. Under his guidance, Pinehurst became the nation's first resort to specialize in golf. In time, Pinehurst became synonymous with the game. But Ross's influence on American golf spread far beyond the Sandhills of North Carolina. In the first half of this century he designed or redesigned more than 400 golf courses throughout the North American continent. He was to golf in America what Leonardo da Vinci was to the Renaissance.

Today, Pinehurst is the biggest, most efficiently run golf factory in the world. When I use the word "factory" to describe Pinehurst, by the way, I don't intend to imply anything derog-

PINEHURST HOTEL AND COUNTRY CLUB P.O. Box 4000, Pinehurst, North Carolina 28374. About 65 miles south of the Raleigh-Durham Airport. Telephone: (800) 334-9560. Accommodations: 310 rooms in the hotel, plus more than 160 condominiums (ranging from 1 to 3 bedrooms) on the property. Amenities: Seven 18-hole golf courses; 28 tennis courts; riding club; gun club with 9 trap and 6 skeet fields; 5 swimming pools; health spa. Terms: $315 per person for the basic golf package (2 nights/3 days, with dinner, breakfast, and unlimited golf).

★

atory. I specifically don't mean to imply impersonality, or dull routine, or mobs of golfers, lunch pails in one hand and drivers in the other, lining up to punch the clock. What I *am* talking about is an entire organization, well trained and highly professional, focusing single-mindedly on one thing and one thing alone: creating the best possible golf experience for Pinehurst clientele.

The worst fear that traveling golfers rightly feel when they hear the term "golf factory" is of endless lines of foursomes backed up, waiting to tee off. Too many golfers, insufficient intervals between tee times, no rangers on the course to keep play moving, and maybe a dense morning fog to make your day even more miserable. Have you been there before?

So have I, but not at Pinehurst. Remember, there are *seven* courses at Pinehurst. The main hotel is relatively small, as resort hotels go, with only 310 rooms. So even when you throw in another 160 condominium units ranging from 1 to 3 bedrooms and factor in local members of the Pinehurst Golf and Country Club, you're still dealing with a manageable number of golfers for seven courses—without even taking into consideration the other nearby courses that resort guests can play. Sure, Pinehurst Number 2 figures to be booked solid every day during high season. But resort guests can reserve tee times up to sixty days before arrival, whereas local club members can book only five days in advance, so for once in a setting where the traveling golfer and the club golfer are competing for tee times, the traveling golfer gets a break.

While You're in the Area . . .

There are 35 golf courses (and counting) in the Pinehurst area, all but 2 of them open to the public. First let's talk about how to get on one of the privates, then take a look at the two best publics.

The **Pinehurst National Golf Club** is a Jack Nicklaus "Signature" course, his first venture into the Carolina Sandhills. As the prime draw for an exclusive residential community (houses start at a small fortune and go up), it is very private, public keep out, no trespassing, that-means-you, Buster. Unless, of course, the public might be interested in buying a residential lot, in which case there's a way. If you can convince the Pinehurst National real estate sales people that you're a serious potential buyer, and if you'll sit through a 3-hour sales spiel, they'll take $85 from you and let you play the course. If you're interested, call (800) 633-2685 and ask for information about the "Pinehurst National Guest Program." Who knows, it might be worth it.

Definitely worth a stop is **The Pit Golf Links,** ranked by *Golf Digest* as one of the country's top 50 resort courses and a truly extraordinary golf experience. Built on the site of a 70-year-old sand quarry, this Dan Maples layout has to be seen to be believed. If they could grow grass on the moon, this is the kind of course they would build there. Target golf with a thyroid condition. Not a course you'd want to play every day for the rest of your life, unless you're an irredeemable masochist. But certainly worth a look. Call (919) 944-1600 to arrange for your descent into The Pit.

Built in 1921 to compete with Pinehurst, the **Mid-Pines Resort** has a Ross course. Apparently his boss didn't mind Ross moonlighting for the opposition—or couldn't stop him. The number is (800) 323-2114.

Dick Taylor, former editor of *Golf World* magazine and one of the game's preeminent salty dogs, claims to have played the Ross jewel at the **Pine Needles Resort** over 4,000 times and says, "I have never gotten bored with it."

Okay, he's a bit prejudiced, but Taylor has seen a few other golf courses in his day, and his opinion counts. He loves the course (blade by blade of grass, by now), *and* he loves the casual, intimate, homelike resort it's part of. The founder of Pinehurst, James W. Tufts, built **Pine Needles** in 1927 to compete with upstart **Mid-Pines,** which was situated a few miles nearer the Southern Pines railway depot than Pinehurst, and thereby posed a threat. Warren "Bullet" Bell (a former NBA player) and Peggy Kirk Bell (an LPGA star) bought the hotel in 1953, and it's been owned by the Bell family ever since. It's not exactly a secret — *Golf Digest* ranks it among the top 75 resort courses in the country, and a British golf magazine a few years ago called it "The Greatest Little Resort in the World" — but it's a fact that **Pine Needles** doesn't get the recognition it deserves in most accounts of golf in the Pinehurst area. **Pine Needles'** 67 rooms are spread through 10 comfortable, homelike lodges; it has a quiet, easygoing pace; it serves good, solid, traditional food; and it has a world-class bar. The number is (919) 692-7111. Book a room for me, too.

Everybody who was ever anybody has played at Pinehurst over the years, which for a couple of decades was a stop on the PGA Tour. But Pinehurst didn't seem suited for the new era, big bucks Tour — too isolated, too small to handle big crowds, no big corporate sponsor — so it hasn't been the site of a regular tour event for years. That will change in 1992, when Pinehurst hosts the PGA Tour's "Champions" tournament, the season-ending event that replaces the Nabisco Championships. Two years later, Pinehurst Number 2 will be the field of battle for the U.S. Senior Open. And there's even talk of bringing the U.S. Open there some time in the mid-1990s.

From its first days, whether a tour stop or not, Pinehurst has remained a favorite among top amateurs and touring professionals. Golf pros do not, as a rule, play golf for fun, but most make a point of dropping by Pinehurst for a round if they are in the neighborhood. (Even then they play for plenty of long green, of course, although it doesn't count as official money and may not make it onto their income tax returns. You play enough two-dollar Nassaus, they mount up.) Sam Snead still rates Pinehurst Number 2 as "my number-one course," and that means something, because the Slammer has seen a few. From your 6:30 A.M. made-on-the-spot-to-your-specifications omelet (with hot biscuits) served to early-bird golfers in the Carolina Room to your last sip of brandy in the hotel lobby after the evening's golf seminar conducted by a member of the Pinehurst golf school's teaching staff, everything about the place centers around golf. The Carolina Room serves good, traditional Southern fare in a pleasant, turn-of-the-century setting, but nobody other than local residents weary of Pizza Hut comes to the Pinehurst Hotel for the food. The rooms are large, well appointed, and comfortable, but there's no view of oceans or mountains to bedazzle. There are all the usual facilities and activities associated with a swell luxury resort, but frankly I have no first hand experience of any of them.

The simple truth is you go to Pinehurst for one reason, and one reason alone—to play golf from dawn to dusk. And here, without further ado, are the courses where you will do just that.

PINEHURST NUMBER 1

Originally laid out as a nine-hole course in 1898–99, Number 1 was redesigned over a period of years by Ross. Don't let its shortness fool you: Number 1 is tree-lined, tight, and murder on hookers and slicers. If you've got your crooked ball working, you'll spend more time in the woods than Daniel Boone.

PINEHURST NUMBER 2

Curtis Strange calls it one of his five favorite courses in the world. *Golf Digest* ranks it twelfth among "America's 100 Greatest Golf Courses." *Golf* puts it fifteenth among the "100 Greatest Courses in the World." But chances are, after playing it the first time, you'll ask, "Where's the beef?"

That's because the character of Pinehurst Number 2 is so subtle as not to be readily discernible to the eager first-timer. The fairways are deceptively wide, and you think to yourself (I know *I* certainly thought to *my*self), "If this is such an all-fired great course, how come I can get away with spraying the ball all over creation?" And the greens are small, not the aircraft carrier flight decks that certain modern golf course architects think are obligatory.

So, where *is* the beef?

Yes, the fairways are wide, at least where the average golfer's tee shots land, but that's because Ross believed in giving golfers a chance to play the game. He didn't believe in making par a pushover, however, so within fifty yards of the hole Pinehurst Number 2 is one of the toughest courses in the world. For starters, those small greens are almost all elevated and crowned, so an approach shot that's a little off line will hit the green and run off. Not only that, but the rough around the greens is clipped short, so a poorly hit approach will run off a long way.

On most PGA Tour stops, by way of contrast, the rough around greens is long enough to hold the ball close. When he misses a green, all the pro has to do is open up an L-wedge and flop the ball up near the hole. We "ooh" and "aah" because we can't do that shot, but it's almost a no-brainer nowadays for the pros. Things would be different if the same slightly errant approach to an elevated green were to skitter ten to fifteen yards away instead of getting caught in the grass a few feet off the fringe. The pro would have a tough choice to make: try to stop a softly hit lofted club, or bump and run the ball up to the hole in the Scottish manner. The pro would have to think and he would have to have a variety of shots in his bag of skills—two good reasons why a pro like Curtis Strange likes Pinehurst Number 2 so much.

Once on the small greens, the really nerve-wracking work begins. It never occurred to Ross to bury a Model-T in the middle of one of his greens, or to create a miniature golf putting surface minus the windmill. But he did believe that skill with the short stick should separate the wheat from the chaff, so he built in enough slope and undulation to make an inchworm seasick. Not that the double breaks and right-left dips are all that easy to see, much less read correctly—"I could have sworn that was going to break right" you will say to yourself as your putt curls left.

Play Pinehurst Number 2 a couple of times and you'll come to see that the wide fairways, the deep bunkers, the loose, sandy soil that always gives a fair lie, the hilariously misnamed "love grass" in the rough (if that's love, give me hate), and the small, undulating, crowned greens all add up to one of the world's greatest courses.

(*Postscript:* Do yourself a favor and use a caddy when you play Pinehurst Number 2. Carts are restricted to the cart paths, so you'll be doing a lot of criss-crossing the fairway on foot anyway. There is no better way to get the feel for any course than walking it, but that's especially true at Pinehurst Number 2.)

PINEHURST NUMBER 3

This is the shortest of the Pinehurst layouts, and the one with the greatest variety of design. It was finished by Ross in 1910, but some of the original holes were grafted onto courses number 4 and 5. Current layout dates from the 1960s. Number 3 begins in hilly, forested terrain, then opens out into a more Scottish setting, with rolling fairways and whins in the rough. Back into the forest and up a hill for a dramatic finish. The par 3s are a bit of a shocker: two are more than 200 yards long, while the 175-yard ninth plays to a postage stamp lying on its edge.

PINEHURST NUMBER 4

A lot of tinkering has gone on here over the years. The original Ross design was short and tight, much like Number 1. In 1973 Robert Trent Jones stretched it out to 7,000 yards for use by the PGA Tour for its World Open tournaments. Ten years later his son, Rees Jones, chopped it back down to a size that ordinary folks could enjoy, plus he enlarged the greens and converted half the bunkers to grassy mounds. You'd expect a hodgepodge after all that, but Number 4 is actually a naturally flowing, seamless web of a course that plays like it's been there forever. Indeed, it's the favorite of local members of the Pinehurst Golf and Country Club.

(Can you imagine, by the way, a sweeter deal than belonging to the Pinehurst Golf and Country Club? You have a choice of seven courses to play, including one that's among the best in the world, and your dues are ridiculously low because of greens fees paid by traveling golfers!)

PINEHURST NUMBER 5

The original Number 5 was designed in 1928 but abandoned in 1935 when the Depression forced major cutbacks at Pinehurst. Ellis Maples designed the current course, to which Robert Trent Jones added new tees, bunkers, and water hazards in 1974. Of all the courses at Pinehurst, Number 5 has the most water. The most beautiful hole? The fifteenth, a 175-yard par 3 from an elevated tee over water to a green framed by towering pines. The course record is held by the best golf color commentator on TV, Gary McCord, who shot a 67 in 1975.

PINEHURST NUMBER 6

Opened in 1979, Number 6 is a long, narrow George and Tom Fazio design that snakes up and down through a hilly forest. It's located about three miles away from the main clubhouse and has an entirely different look from the other Pinehurst courses. Budget troubles during the construction of the course forced some serious compromises of the original design, including cutting down the size of the greens. Despite its striking vistas and some magnificent golf holes, Number 6 was unpopular among members and traveling golfers alike. So last year the course was closed for a major renovation to bring it more in line with what the Fazios originally intended.

Number 6 only reopened for play in March 1991, so I haven't seen or played it since the renovation. But I shall always remember—usually in my nightmares—one hole there in particular. It was my first time to play Number 6, and we were starting on the back side, so my first hole was the tenth, a 522-yard par 5, straight as an arrow and downhill. Piece of cake, you're probably thinking, a short fiver *and* downhill. Right, except that you come out of a tree-lined chute to a narrow fairway. Then your second shot has to be plumb-bob straight *or* carry two lakes that pinch in at both sides at precisely the distance that second shots like to travel. Assuming all has gone well to this point (it hadn't, trust me), your approach to a severely elevated green has to be right on the money or it bounds into one of two deep traps. Are you still with me? Well, if you'd been with me back then you'd have watched me write a 10 on my scorecard. It's always great to start a round with double figures on the first hole, don't you think? Sort of focuses your attention on the rest of the day.

Fact is, I'm looking forward to seeing what they've done to Number 6. Only this time I plan to start on the first hole.

PINEHURST NUMBER 7

Number 7 is the newest of the Pinehurst courses and—next to Number 2—the best. It's long (7,206 yards from the gold tees) *and* narrow, with marshes, streams, rolling terrain, dogwoods, and tall, tall pine trees providing supporting scenery. It was designed by Rees Jones, who no longer labors in the shadow of his father or his more flamboyant brother, and who someday may be the Jones that everybody tries to keep up with.

Postscript: Still wondering if Pinehurst is really all that special? Try this: before you make your reservations, have a gander at a little brochure called *What You Can Expect from the Weather in Pinehurst.* It's provided to potential guests contemplating a visit, and it's chock full of everything you could possibly need—or want—to know about the subject. For each month of the year you are told the mean, mean maximum, and mean minimum temperatures; the number of days that are clear, partly cloudy, and cloudy; the average relative humidity; and the direction of the prevailing wind. And you don't just learn how much it rains in the month; you learn how many days in the month it rains .01 inches or over and how many days it rains .25 inches or over. (All this for *each* month of the year, mind you.) Finally, you get a comforting explanation of why you shouldn't worry about a little rain on your parade:

The sandy character of the soil makes for a greater spread between the low night temperatures and the highs of the daytime than are generally found. The sand heats up rapidly under the sun's rays and radiates quickly after sunset. The result is warm days and cool nights with lower humidity especially during the daylight hours. Rain disappears into the ground about as fast as it falls so outdoor sports can be enjoyed immediately after the rain ceases.

Get the picture? When it has to do with golf, Pinehurst becomes obsessively thorough, for one simple reason.

Pinehurst *is* golf.

When to Go

Fall is the busiest season, spring is the next busiest. June and July are the hottest, and July and August are the wettest. It can get pretty nippy at night in the dead of winter, but play goes on year round. (Although I do recall one occasion, between Christmas and New Year's, when I'd have been flat out of luck if one of the savvy local members I was playing with hadn't thought to bring along a hammer to drive our tees into the ground. But when you check your weather booklet, you'll discover that such conditions are extremely rare.)

My recommendation: November. The days are crisp, the nights are nippy, there's less precipitation than in any other month, a lot of the crowd will be gone, and the Carolina Room is a great place to eat Thanksgiving turkey.

OFF COURSE

Not long ago one of the zillion golf publications I see regularly published an article entitled "Ten Other Reasons to Visit Pinehurst." The subhead was even more explicit: "There's Much More to Pinehurst Than Incredible Golf Courses." With a pretty good idea of what her reaction might be, I held up the magazine so my wife could see the headline, whereupon she broke into hysterical laughter.

There is nothing—I repeat, *nothing*—to do or see in the Pinehurst area besides play golf. And if you don't believe me, ask my wife. Just be prepared to have your ears pinned back by an extended, colorful, and loud account in no uncertain terms of just how much nothing there is there for the nongolfer.

Yes, the resort offers a solid lineup of sports and activities: horseback riding, shooting, swimming, tennis, and so on. Yes, you can eat yourself into a stupor and drink yourself into a rehab clinic. Yes, you can catch up on your reading. (And mine, too, for that matter.) But once you leave the compound, don't expect a lot of thrills and chills, or a whole bunch of interesting places to visit and things to see and do.

Wait! I almost forgot one major off-campus attraction. Just down the road from Pinehurst Number 2 is the **PGA/World Golf Hall of Fame,** a swell-looking modern building with nicely maintained grounds. Sorry, but that's all I can tell you about it firsthand. It's never rained when I've been in Pinehurst, so I've never had enough spare time to go inside.

But I've got to believe it's a pretty exciting place after reading the following ad: "Walk among the enshrined legends, saluting their contributions to the game, and explore the history of golf from its ancient beginnings, up to the present, and on into the future." Now, I don't care all that much about its ancient beginnings, but I would *love* to explore the history of golf *into the future.* Don't you think it would be nifty to know if Greg Norman will ever win another major? Whether anyone will ever break 60 in competition again? Who will be the Masters champion in 1997? (My guess is José-María Olazábal, who will beat Jack Nicklaus by a stroke when Jack finally figures out how old he is and *has* a stroke.)

On second thought, maybe it isn't such a hot idea to tout the PGA/World Golf Hall of Fame (919-295-6651) to a nongolfing traveling companion as a super thing you can do together when you're not on the course. It might work in your household, but it sure wouldn't work in mine.

My advice, if you want to go to Pinehurst and your traveling companion is a nongolfer, is to book two single rooms: one in Pinehurst, the other in Paris.

CHAPTER 12

ISLAND
HOPPING
Caribbean
Golfaways

SOME YEARS BACK THERE APPEARED FOR THE first time a brilliant ad campaign for a line of fur coats based on a single question: "What Becomes a Legend Most?" The ad typically featured a large, dramatic photograph of a famous woman enveloped in a fur garment. There was very little ad copy. Just this strong picture of a woman in fur looking, well, legendary.

(Some of the stars of those ads, which began to run before our consciousnesses were raised by animal rights activists, would just as soon we didn't recall their blatant huckstering in favor of the wholesale slaughter of defenseless animals, all in the service of personal vanity. They needn't fret. Except for Lillian Hellman, who is dead, I don't recall the name of a single one. Too bad.)

All this comes to mind because, in thinking about golf vacations in the Caribbean, it dawned on me that three powerful individuals—each a legend of sorts—were responsible for the three best golf courses in the islands. Each of the three men built a luxurious retreat, intended primarily for himself and his friends. (One, in fact, was originally a private club.) Each made sure that his creation embodied his interests and dreams. Each was an active, hands-on manager who made sure everything was done his way. And each saw to it, by hiring two of the best golf architects in the world, that the golf course built as the star attraction of his resort was of world-class distinction . . . a course befitting a legend.

COTTON BAY

"The legendary Juan Trippe . . ."

Tell me, have you ever seen the name of the larger-than-life aviator, the founder of Pan Am, the multimillionaire bon vivant, the bosom buddy of kings and presidents, mentioned *anywhere* in print without the adjective "legendary" affixed to it? Neither have I. Maybe it's just wishful thinking, but I have to believe it must have been fun along the way, living the kind of life that invariably gets you referred to forevermore as "the legendary . . ."

One way to become legendary, or one of the things you do when you *are* legendary, is to find a semi-deserted tropical paradise, build yourself a magical playhouse there, and have all your friends come over for a party. That's just what the legendary Juan Trippe did back in the 1950s when he built the Cotton Bay Club in the Bahamas as a private getaway for a few hundred of his best pals. A specially outfitted Pan Am 727 was officially dubbed the *Cotton Bay Special* and used exclusively to cart club members to and from Cotton Bay. (Not that they couldn't afford airfare, mind you; it's just that getting there was—and is—a bit of a schlepp.)

No longer private, as you undoubtedly surmised from the fact of its inclusion in this book, the Cotton Bay Club is located on a 450-acre peninsula of white sand and tropical greenery at the southern tip of Eleuthera, an outlying Bahamian island settled in the seventeenth century by colonists from Bermuda. Eleuthera means "freedom" in Greek, and in modern terms that translates as freedom from the hustle-bustle, high-rise glitz, and crowds that turn too many island paradises into tourist hell. If you want casinos, discos, and a dazzling night life, Cotton Bay is definitely not for you. But if you want seclusion, quiet, and understated luxury surrounded by a fine Robert Trent Jones golf course, read on.

COTTON BAY CLUB Rock Sound, Eleuthera, the Bahamas. About 30 minutes by air from Nassau, with regularly scheduled direct flights from Miami, Fort Lauderdale, and Nassau. Telephone: (800) 334-3523. Accommodations: 77 guest rooms, some in motel units and others in cottages. Ask for a cottage. Amenities: Golf, 4 tennis courts, pool; secluded, private beach; snorkeling, scuba diving, sailing, windsurfing; deep-sea fishing and bone fishing. Terms: From $125 for a golf-view double in the fall to $310 for an oceanfront room in the winter. Assorted packages available. Add $45 per person for MAP (breakfast and dinner).

★

If you like your Caribbean golf getaways intimate, consider this: there are only 77 guest rooms in the entire resort, half of them in large cottages tucked away among the palm trees. The highest rise the eye can see is the peaked white roofs over the bar and the dining room, which tower maybe one and a half stories into the azure Caribbean sky. If you were expecting Miami Beach, you're in for a big letdown.

Don't you just love it when potboiling novels set in tropical climes talk of "water as clear as gin?" The water lapping up the edge of Cotton Bay's one-mile stretch of dazzling white beach is as clear as, well, vodka. The finely crushed pink coral and tiny shells of assorted hues give the vodka—sorry, the water— an alluring backdrop of tropical pastels, but the water itself is as clear as a windowpane. (Clearer than mine, if you want the truth of it.) Spend a few hours walking up and down the Cotton Bay beach line and the clean water washing over the clean sand will definitely clean your spirit.

An idyllic natural setting is all well and good, the impatient golfer (and name one who isn't) might ask, but what about the golf?

As clear as the water is, as white as the sand is, as blue as the Caribbean sky is, that's how good the golf at Cotton Bay is. And why not? Among the legendary Juan Trippe's many friends was the legendary Robert Trent Jones, and naturally enough one legend turned to the other when he needed a golf course designed. And when a friend is asking, naturally enough you do your best, which is exactly what Jones did at Cotton Bay.

Oh, he won't come right out and say it's his best golf course. In the first place, there've been so many great ones that it would be virtually impossible to judge, even for him. And in the second place, it wouldn't be very nice to the Mauna Keas of the world if he were to single out any one course as his "best." But in interviews over the years Jones has always included Cotton Bay among his personal favorites, and I have to believe it will be one of yours as well.

COTTON BAY GOLF CLUB

Design: Robert Trent Jones

Year Open: 1958
7,068 Yards

Information: Play restricted to members and guests of Cotton Bay Club.

The course plays a long 7,068 yards from the back tees, but there are three other sets of tees, so it won't be necessary for you to pack a lunch. With thirteen ponds, a hundred and twenty-nine sand traps, and one Atlantic Ocean coming into play if you're not careful, there's more than enough trouble to keep your mind from wandering. The sixth and seventh holes, built on a bluff overlooking the ocean and the rest of Cotton Bay, form the most dramatic duo on the course, with the other sixteen holes depending more on the designer's creative imagination for their character and inner beauty.

Knowing that shifts in the Caribbean trade winds would have an enormous impact on the way the course plays, Jones varied the directional lines of the eighteen holes to ensure a rich variety of challenges. There's only one course at Cotton Bay, but if you play a morning round and an afternoon round, you'll swear there are at least two.

The Director of Golf at Cotton Bay, Sean O'Connor, has a name familiar to followers of the European professional tour. His uncle, Christy O'Connor, is one of the great figures of Irish golf; he still holds the record for the most appearances in the Ryder Cup. After stints as playing pro at the Royal Dublin and other Irish clubs, Sean came to Cotton Bay with the idea of spending a single season in the tropical sun. That was twenty-five years ago.

But for as long as golf is played (and talked about) in the British Isles, Sean's cousin, Christy O'Connor, Jr., also a touring pro, will always be remembered for a shot he made in the 1989 Ryder Cup at The Belfry in England. With the matches between Europe and the U.S.A. tied on the last day, Christy Jr. drilled a 205-yard 2-iron to 6 feet from the cup on the eighteenth hole of his match with Fred Couples, then drained the putt for a 1-up victory that sent the English Midlands into bedlam. Only a final match victory by Curtis Strange over Ian Woosnam salvaged a tie for America, but the Ryder Cup stayed in England—thanks, in great measure, to Christy O'Connor Jr.'s heroics.

An especially nice feature, one perfectly in keeping with Cotton Bay's origins as a private club, is that walking is permitted. Yep, that's right—walking. They have carts, of course, but do yourself a favor and use a caddy instead. (Be sure to request one in advance.) For one thing, an experienced caddy's help in reading Cotton Bay's tricky greens will prevent a lot of three-putt nightmares. More important, you will get the opportunity to experience Cotton Bay the way a course this fine was meant to be played. On foot.

TEETH OF THE DOG

He may not qualify as a legend, at least not on the scale that the legendary Juan Trippe does, but in his day Charles Bluhdorn took up a lot of room. As chairman and big stick of Gulf & Western during the 1970s, he was a certified big cheese who swaggered through corporate America acquiring companies the way a country hound picks up ticks. He had strong opinions on just about everything, and one of them was that the CEO of a major international mega-corporation ought not to stint himself on corporate perks.

To that effect, Bluhdorn spent several score millions of G&W dollars to build a playpen called Casa de Campo, an exclusive retreat for himself, his friends, and people like them (i.e., rich) on 7,000 acres of scruffy ranchland on the southern shore of the Dominican Republic, about sixty miles from Santo Domingo. The resort opened in April 1972 with seventy-eight rooms designed by Miami architect William Cox and decorated by Dominican-New York haute couturist Oscar de la Renta. Almost immediately Casa de Campo developed a certain cachet among movers and shakers of the business world, not to mention certain Beautiful People who do their darnedest whenever possible to slop at the same trough as the rich and richer. Jacqueline Onassis became a Christmas-week regular. So did Henry Kissinger, never one to miss an opportunity to suck up to the corporate establishment in America.

CASA DE CAMPO P.O. Box 140, La Romana, Dominican Republic. About 90 minutes east of Santo Domingo International Airport. Telephone: (800) 223-6620 (Miami sales office). <u>Accommodations</u>: 700 rooms in casitas and 2- and 3-bedroom villas. <u>Amenities</u>: 19 pools; 13 tennis courts; 3 private beaches, including one on an offshore island; an immense equestrian center; 4 polo fields; deep-sea fishing, scuba diving, snorkeling; fitness center; trapshooting. <u>Terms</u>: From $110 for a double room in a casita to $375 for a 3-bedroom villa. Golf package available. Best bet: rent a villa and bring all your friends.

From the outset, the general idea was to make Casa de Campo "the world's ultimate sports-oriented resort," as the promotional literature puts it. If you're an American CEO, that means starting with golf—and at Casa de Campo, Bluhdorn started with a bang.

Pete Dye, surely the most controversial and arguably the best golf-course builder in the world today, has in some quarters become the symbol, albeit unfairly so, of the worst excesses of whiz-bang gimmickry in modern golf course design. Much of that bad rap stems from doing what various employers, from Deane Beman to the Landmark Corporation, have asked him to do (i.e., push the envelope of golf course design). Part of it comes from the way his ideas (e.g. the use of railroad ties à la Prestwick) have been taken over and misused by designers of less ability and taste. But he is also responsible for some of the finest courses of the last twenty years, including two of particular interest to the traveling golfer that rank among the finest in the world. One is Harbour Town at Hilton Head (see Chapter 16). The other is the Teeth of the Dog at Casa de Campo.

TEETH OF THE DOG AT CASA DE CAMPO

Design: Pete Dye

Year Open: 1972

6,888 Yards   74.1 Rating   140 Slope

Information: Play restricted to resort guests.

The original name for Dye's Casa de Campo masterpiece was Campo de Golf Cajuiles, after the cashew (*cajuil*) grove that had to be thinned out to make room for fairways. But almost from the beginning the course was called Teeth of the Dog, and widely considered the best golf course in the Caribbean. *Golf* magazine in 1989 ranked it Number 31 in its "100 Greatest Courses in the World." No other Caribbean course is on the list.

If you have any doubt that the Dog's Teeth are sharp, take a look at the Slope rating: 140 from the back tees. I don't know where you play most of your golf, but to me 140 is stronger than taxes. Part of the difficulty has to do with length: 6,888 oceanfront yards play at about four feet each when the wind is coming strong off the water. (This is the part of the world where storms grow up to be hurricanes, remember.) I don't mind telling that I was pretty happy to discover that the white tees play almost half a mile shorter (6,057 yards).

But length is not the main reason for the Dog's sometimes vicious nature. Seven holes lie close enough to the ocean that a serious hook or slice becomes just another pebble on the beach. What's more, Dye's fairways twist and turn at most inopportune times, and his greenside traps always seem to be between you and the pin. The greens themselves, though, are where the load gets heavy.

Trying to putt at the Teeth of the Dog without a caddy helping you read the greens is tantamount to walking barefoot across a floor full of tarantulas—blindfolded. (You're blindfolded, that is; not the tarantulas.)

It's not that the greens at the Teeth of the Dog are unfair. Actually, they're quite fair, with nary a Volkswagen Beetle buried anywhere. It's just that Dye has shot the greens so full of subtlety that they're unbelievably hard to read. ("What do you think, Martín? Three balls to the left, right?" "Three balls, right . . . but to the left." If I had some version of that conversation once in the dozen times I have played the Teeth of the Dog, I must have had it fifty times. And I was having it as often on the last round as on the first.) Did I also mention that the Dog's greens are super fast? Well, they are, particularly in the afternoon, once the wind has had its way with them all day.

The Links, Dye's inland course on the Casa de Campo grounds, is shorter and easier, and a soothing balm for Dog bites. It has some good holes, and it's certainly no pushover. If it were the only course there, you'd end up praising it as a mighty fine resort course. But like the Lagoons course at the Westin Kauai (see Chapter 7), the Links is destined to suffer from comparison with its more famous stablemate.

THE LINKS AT CASA DE CAMPO

Design: Pete Dye

Year Open: 1976

6,461 Yards   70 Rating   124 Slope

Information: Play restricted to resort guests.

But for all the toughness of the Teeth of the Dog, it's a joy to play. Making a par there is, for me, the equivalent of making a birdie at most other courses. Neither event happens often enough for me to become blasé, and I savor every delicious moment.

So did Bluhdorn savor his creation. By all accounts, he loved the Casa de Campo with the same hell-for-leather passion he brought to buying companies. While he initially let the lodging development side expand at a measured pace, he drove the sports side hard. Tennis, anyone? There are thirteen tennis courts, ten of them lighted for night play. Want to go for a swim? There are three beaches, including one on an offshore island, and nineteen pools scattered around the property. (You can scatter a lot of things around 7,000 acres.) Horseback riding? Yeah, and how: Bluhdorn saw to it that Casa de Campo became one of the major *polo* centers of the world. There are now four polo fields there, three for matches and one for practice. And so it goes, across the board: just about every conceivable resort sport facility, each of top-notch caliber.

There's one feature of the vast Casa de Campo complex that I just don't get, and that's Altos de Chavón, a fake sixteenth-century village built high on a cliff overlooking the Chavon River, about fifteen minutes from the Casa proper. Altos de Chavón has posh art galleries, cutesy shops, cobblestone streets, great views, numerous restaurants, housing for artists and craftsmen, a school affiliated with the Parsons School of Design in New York, and a Potemkin village feel to it. My best guess is that it's intended by the Dominican Tourist Board to be a way for rich Anglos to "see" the Dominican Republic, the second poorest country in the Caribbean after its island neighbor, Haiti, without having to stray far from the compound. Like EPCOT Center, which lets Americans "visit" other nations without having to leave the country, Altos de Chavón banks on timid tourists preferring a sanitized counterfeit experience to a potentially unsettling real one. People always prefer fantasy to reality, don't they? Especially when they're on vacation.

Casa de Campo was purchased in 1984 by the Fanjul family of Palm Beach (formerly the Fanjul sugar barons of pre-Castro Cuba). From the day they took over, the new owners have cranked up development plans to full speed ahead. Too much, too fast, some old-timers complain; and it's certainly true that the complexion of Casa de Campo has changed. Not only does it have its own airstrip (you drive across it on the eighteenth hole), but now it has direct service to Miami, Fort Lauderdale, and New York. And if you go during the off-season (the weather's great from April to December, too), Casa de Campo changes from exclusive retreat to hustle-and-bustle package-tour centers—at reasonable rates.

The almost-legendary Charles Bluhdorn would not be amused at this turn of events. His intent from the start was to create a hideaway—a big hideaway, but a hideaway nonetheless—for people like himself. I can't see him smiling benignly at the likes of us—well, at least at the likes of me—turning up in his backyard.

That won't happen. Charles Bluhdorn died of a heart attack in 1983 as he was flying to New York in his private jet . . . from Casa de Campo.

DORADO BEACH

The closest Laurance Rockefeller ever got to being legendary in the traditional, swashbuckling sense was his last name. But that turned out to be plenty close enough, because the name let him sign some really big checks, and they in turn permitted him to make some major waves in the golf world. While brother David was running the American economy, and brother Nelson was running New York and the liberal splinter of the Republican Party, and brother Winthrop was dabbling in Arkansas, brother Laurance—the least well known of the chips off John D. Jr.'s block—was building luxury resorts, most of them with world-class golf courses. Who's to say his contribution to society won't prove at the end of the day to be more enduring?

Laurance Rockefeller's own favorite of all the glittering stars in the Rockresort constellation was his beloved Dorado Beach, the resort he created in Puerto Rico, about a million light-years from downtown San Juan but only minutes from Pontantico Hills and Park Avenue.

The Dorado Beach Resort, which opened its doors on December 1, 1958, with a party of Rockefellerian proportions, was built at the edge of the ocean on part of a 1,000-acre swath of prime, undeveloped coastline. Its 300 rooms, each with a patio or balcony and most with ocean views, are artfully fitted into a two-story structure and surrounded by enough exotic trees and lush tropical flowers to suggest an impeccably manicured botanical garden. The smallness of scale created a sense of intimacy and quiet. If you want to get down and boogie, the Dorado made clear, go somewhere else.

HYATT DORADO BEACH Dorado, Puerto Rico 00646. On the north shore of Puerto Rico, 22 miles west of San Juan. Telephone: (800) 233-1234; (809) 796-1234. <u>Accommodations</u>: 300 rooms in main hotel, plus 17 casitas. <u>Amenities</u>: Six restaurants, 2 bars; casino; 21 tennis courts, 4 lit for night play; all the usual water sports; health club; and 4 golf courses. <u>Terms</u>: From $225 to $295.

For as long as Dorado remained Laurance Rockefeller's personal playground, you could only admire his taste in toys. But in the late 1970s and early 1980s, Dorado began to slide downhill. By 1985, when Hyatt bought it, Dorado was in a serious state of disrepair.

"The condition of the hotel was so bad, one more year and the place would have closed," Victor Lopez, Hyatt's regional vice president for Caribbean operations told Roger Schiffman, a writer for *Golf Digest*. "We're trying to restore Dorado to the way it was when Laurance Rockefeller opened it. And, of course, we're adding a few touches to bring it up to date."

HYATT REGENCY CERROMAR BEACH Dorado, Puerto Rico 00646. On the north shore of Puerto Rico, 22 miles west of San Juan. Telephone: (800) 233-1234; (809) 796-1234. <u>Accommodations</u>: 504 rooms, including 1 presidential suite, 3 deluxe suites, 15 VIP suites, 4 junior suites, 4 conference suites, 16 petite suites, 45 nonsmoking rooms, and 58 Regency Club rooms. (Whew!) <u>Amenities</u>: The Hyatt Dorado and the Hyatt Regency Cerromar Beach share sports facilities, so look for the same 21 tennis courts, 4 lit for night play; all the usual water sports; health club; and 4 golf courses. Cerromar Beach has its own restaurants (4), plus the 2 at the golf complex it shares with Dorado; 3 bars; 1 disco; and its own casino. <u>Terms</u>: From $165 to $340.

Today called the Hyatt Dorado Beach, and operated in tandem with the seven-story, 504-room Hyatt Regency Cerromar Beach a mile away, the apple of Laurance Rockefeller's eye has survived its midlife crisis. Times have changed, and so has the Dorado, but all the essentials are still in place: serenity, intimacy, quiet luxury . . . and great golf.

(By way of contrast, the Hyatt Regency Cerromar Beach is bigger, brasher, and glitzier. Both have casinos, but only the Cerromar Beach has a disco. Indeed, there's a lot more nightlife to be had at the Cerromar Beach. But since my nightlife consists of reading and sleeping, I prefer the Dorado by a margin not quite as large as Kansas.)

The Hyatt Dorado Beach-Hyatt Regency Cerromar Beach complex has four Robert Trent Jones courses, the largest single concentration of resort golf in the Caribbean. While this can give the place something of a factory feel in high convention season, it also affords the traveling golfer plenty of options and variety.

THE COURSES AT HYATT DORADO/ HYATT REGENCY CERROMAR BEACH

Design: Robert Trent Jones

Year Open: East, 1958, 1963; West, 1958, 1959; North and South, 1972

East Course:	6,985 Yards	72.3 Rating	127 Slope
West Course:	6,913 Yards	72.6 Rating	127 Slope
North Course:	6,841 Yards	73.5 Rating	127 Slope
South Course:	7,047 Yards	73.7 Rating	127 Slope

Information: (809) 796-1234 (ext. 3713 for East and West; ext. 3213 for North and South)

Note: All of the courses were scheduled to be recharted and given new USGA ratings and slope ratings in the winter of 1990–91. The ratings for the East and West courses are not expected to change because course length has not been altered since they were originally rated.

The North and South courses are well maintained, efficiently run, attractive resort layouts of no great distinction. That sounds like a put-down, but it's really not. Lots of sun, plenty of ocean breeze, lush vegetation, and medium-length par 4s add up to swell times on the golf course, in my book. But North and South, which belong to Cerromar Beach, are simply not the same points on the compass as the Dorado's East and West.

The East and the West are the courses that Jones designed for his pal Laurance Rockefeller, and—as at Cotton Bay—Jones always seems to give a little something extra to his friends. The back nine of the East and the back nine of the West were the original eighteen when the course first opened in 1958. By 1966, the two separate courses were completely operational. Both are long, both have huge greens, both have long "runway" tees that permit holes to be shortened or lengthened as required, and both are exceptionally beautiful.

The East is the more famous of the two, having been the site of various Senior PGA Tour and LPGA Tour events. It has one of the strongest finishing stretches this side of Churchill Downs, as in a 205-yard par 3 (the fourteenth) followed by four par 4s ranging from 415 to 455 yards. That's stronger than yesterday's coffee.

The East also has the single most exciting hole, and one of the best anywhere, the famous double dogleg thirteenth, a 540-yard beauty that invites the bold golfer who would fly with eagles to take two trips across water. The thirteenth makes Jack Nicklaus's list of top ten holes in the world because two daring shots will leave you (yes, you!) putting for an eagle, while two more conventional shots will pay off with a solid par.

(That assumes, of course, that both shots—daring or conventional—are also *good* ones. And that, if you don't mind me saying so, is assuming a helluva lot.)

You know what to do. Unless there's a tropical gale blowing right in your face, fly your tee shot over the water on your left side. (The carry is 185 to 220 yards, depending on which tees you hit from, but you need to hit it a good ways beyond that.) Then pull out a long iron or a fairway wood and hit the shot of your life over the water on your right, over the sand trap on the front right of the green, and onto the putting surface.

Do *that*, my friend, and you'll feel positively legendary.

When to Go

Everybody in the snowbelt wants to visit the Caribbean between December 15 and April 1, so that's when it's the most crowded and the most expensive. Nobody wants to go there between mid-August and early October, because that's hurricane season. (If you really like to play in wind, I suggest Turnberry in Scotland as a safer alternative.) That leaves a lot of the months of the year, all of which I prefer to high season and the possibility of being blown away. Contrary to popular misconception, it's only a few degrees hotter in the summer than in the winter on the southern shore of the Dominican Republic and in Eleuthera. The northern shore of Puerto Rico is another matter, but even there the sea breezes keep things comfortable. Uncrowded, off-season golf is always preferable, in my book, even if the trade-off is a little more sweating.

OFF COURSE

In Eleuthera (Cotton Bay) . . . You could, I suppose, hop a plane to Freeport or Nassau and hit the casinos. But if that's what you're looking for as a corollary to your golf vacation, why not play a high-stakes skins game instead? My suggestion: bring a lot of books for the time you aren't playing golf.

In the Dominican Republic (Casa De Campo) . . . If you're there in the winter, go to a baseball game in La Romana, the town where the Casa de Campo is located. They take their baseball very seriously in the Dominican Republic, and you'll see a lot of stateside stars in action. In Santo Domingo, sixty miles away, you can visit **Christopher Columbus's Tomb** in the **Cathedral of Santa María,** an appropriate pilgrimage for traveling golfers in the region in 1992. The **Market** in La Romana offers the freshest tropical fruits imaginable, including the best pineapple this side of heaven. In terms of sports and activities, though, there's no reason to leave the Casa de Campo complex.

In Puerto Rico (Hyatt Dorado Beach and Hyatt Regency Cerromar Beach) . . . A trip to **Old San Juan** is a must. The town was the heart of Spain's Caribbean empire for 300 years, and its narrow, cobblestone streets carry you back to that time. Unless you're a teetotaler, a visit to the **Bacardi Rum Distillery** is a heady experience. There's always shopping and nightclubbing for the restive members of your party, but I can't be of much help to you on either front. Do have the hotel concierge arrange a guided tour of **El Yunque Rain Forest** so that you will be able to tell your grandchildren what a rain forest was.

CHAPTER 13

GRAND HOTELS
Legendary
Settings
for The Grand
Old Game

SOMETIMES ALL YOU NEED FOR A REALLY GREAT golf vacation is a single good golf course and an endless supply of balls. It doesn't matter where you sleep—the car will do in a pinch—or whether you eat anything fancier than a Double Whopper with Cheese.

But other times require more for a really great golf vacation than reserved tee times and a grooved swing. Maybe it's your honeymoon, or your wedding anniversary, or Christmas, or Mother's Day, or the vernal equinox—whatever the special occasion, you need a special venue for your golf vacation.

You need a Grand Hotel.

To qualify for the designation "grand," a hotel must meet certain essential criteria. Among them:

★ *It must be of grand scale. An intimate little inn can be wonderful, but never grand. A grand hotel is, by definition, a big hotel.*

★ *It must have a great setting. One of the things that makes the Plaza in New York a great hotel is its location, on Fifth Avenue, and across from Central Park. Move the Plaza to Atlantic City and it's just another Trump property.*

★ *It must be of a certain age—nothing younger than fifty years old need apply.*

★ *It must have unsurpassed service, every modern convenience, luxurious appointments, great restaurants, at least one terrific bar, a couple of public places where you can sit and watch the world go by, and every conceivable activity. You pay an arm and a leg, you want to be sure body and soul are well provided for.*

★ *It must have a personality. Maybe it derives from the architecture, maybe from the place's history. Wherever it comes from, a grand hotel's character should be distinctive and strong.*

And since we're talking about golf vacations here, a grand hotel must provide good golf. Not necessarily great golf, because the emphasis here is on the whole enchilada, the "grand hotel experience," and not exclusively on the quality of the golf course. But good golf, and plenty of it, on the premises.

There are probably only a dozen or so hotels in America that meet all these criteria. Two are treated elsewhere in this book (The Balsams in Chapter 1, Pebble Beach in Chapter 18). Others deserve to be mentioned but can't be because of space limitations. Here I'm going to talk about just four: one in the Arizona desert, one in the Colorado Rockies, and two separated only by a few hills and hollers in the Allegheny Mountains in Virginia and West Virginia.

THE ARIZONA BILTMORE

Every time I drive up the long, curving driveway that leads to the main entrance of the Arizona Biltmore in Phoenix, my first thought is the movie *Tall in the Saddle*, which should have starred my boyhood hero Randolph Scott, even though it really featured John Wayne.

ARIZONA BILTMORE Twenty-fourth Street and Missouri, Phoenix, Arizona 85016. On the northern side of the city, about 20 minutes from the airport. Telephone: (800) 228-3000. <u>Accommodations</u>: 551 guest rooms. <u>Amenities</u>: Everything you would expect in a grand hotel. <u>Terms</u>: From $195 to $320.

★

Since 1929 the Arizona Biltmore has stood, well, tall in the saddle, towering up from a gently rising mountain slope north of the featureless, flat desert hardpan on which most of Phoenix squats. If ever a collection of buildings yearning to be a city needed a touch of grandness, it is Phoenix, so the Arizona Biltmore was a godsend. It is now, and always has been, the classiest joint in town.

The great Frank Lloyd Wright inspired the Arizona Biltmore's strong, lean, angular lines. His spirit presided over the marriage of plane geometry and desert textures that give the Arizona Biltmore its quintessentially Western look; Mrs. Frank Lloyd Wright selected the interior color schemes; the architectural firm devoted to Wright's ideals, Taliesin Associated Architects, directed major recent additions and renovations; the great man himself created the molded concrete blocks, based on ancient Aztec designs, used to face the main building; and the architect of record, Albert Chase MacArthur, was a Wright disciple.

For me, the Arizona Biltmore, thrusting into the dazzling desert sky, will always be the quintessential Grand Hotel, wild west division. It was a Mecca for Hollywood stars of the 1930s and 1940s who always stopped at the "Jewel of the Desert" when they were in the area. The most famous was Clark Gable, who once lost his wedding ring while playing golf on the Biltmore's Adobe Course. (How, I wonder? In a bet? Did he use it as a ball marker and forget to pick it up? Did he swing so hard it came flying off?)

Spreading out just to the south of the hotel like a large, lush front lawn, the Adobe is the quintessential resort course: only a few steps from the front door, perfectly maintained, and a tonic for the golfer's ego. It's not that it's easy. As I've already mentioned, you're asking for trouble anytime you use the words "easy" and "golf course" in the same breath.

Adobe's fairways are wide and inviting, the trees that have grown in over the years are more decorative than dangerous, the rough is short, and there's about as little water as you'd expect in a desert but nowhere near as much sand. And yet, at 6,767 yards from the back tees, the Adobe has enough length so you don't feel like you're whipping up on an overgrown pitch-and-putt.

ADOBE AT THE ARIZONA BILTMORE

Design: Bell & Associates
Year Open: 1930
6,767 Yards   71.5 Rating   121 Slope
Information: (602) 955-9655

The Links, the Biltmore's other course, is in my view just that: the *other* course, the one you play in the afternoon if you feel like a second round. Built in 1977, the Links has the feel of an afterthought, though many club members prefer it. The front nine wraps entirely around the Adobe Course, while the back nine follows a condo line around the north side of the hotel. The Links is a bit tougher than Adobe even though almost 400 yards shorter; and it offers scenic vistas—as, for example, from the fifteenth tee, looking down on Phoenix to the south.

LINKS AT THE ARIZONA BILTMORE

Design: Bill Johnson
Year Open: 1977
6,300 Yards   69.3 Rating   122 Slope
Information: (602) 955-9655

But you don't go to the Arizona Biltmore for its golf courses. They're plenty of fun to play, but they'll never be confused with championship tracks, and that's okay. With TPC-Scottsdale only twenty minutes away, not to mention any number of other good courses in the greater Phoenix area, playing lights-out golf while staying at the Arizona Biltmore is not a problem (see Chapter 9). The concierge makes the arrangements; all you provide is the game. Chances are, however, that after one round at the Adobe you won't be in a hurry to line up tee times anywhere else—particularly if every now and then your golf ego appreciates a little jolt of confidence. You go to the Arizona

Biltmore to experience a grand hotel, with golf as the olive in your martini.

As strong and distinctive as the Biltmore's exterior is, it's the quality of what you find inside that makes it a truly grand hotel—and that earns it the highest ranking from AAA and Mobil when it's time each year to ration out stars and diamonds. Brian McCallen put it this way in *Golf* magazine a few years back when awarding the Arizona Biltmore the magazine's silver medal as one of the nation's best golf resorts: "Any resort hotel with the world's largest gold leaf ceiling and an annual budget of $100,000 earmarked just for petunias . . . must be reckoned with."

THE BROADMOOR

The phrase "larger than life" might well have been invented to fit Spencer Penrose.

A wealthy Philadelphia blue blood (one brother became a United States senator), Penrose found life in the effete East too confining, so soon after graduating from Harvard in 1885 he drifted West looking for adventure, fame, and fortune, in roughly that order. A young man of his ambitions, will, and talent couldn't have picked a better time to turn up in Colorado then on the eve of its last great gold rush. Penrose knew he was home the first time he walked into a boomtown saloon. After a few years spent learning the ropes in the gold mining business (i.e., going dead broke), Penrose struck it rich in the 1890s with the C.O.D. gold mine in Cripple Creek. It was as if some primal force of nature had been unleashed by the opening of the C.O.D.'s main vein. From that moment, in an era filled with larger-than-life figures, Penrose took up more space than anybody. Over the next three decades, Penrose built an immense mining and real estate empire, became a kingmaker in Rocky Mountain politics and the most prominent spokesman for the region's mining interests, and generally roared through life at full volume.

(Who could play him in a film biography? Nobody around now. Gable, maybe. Or Welles. Yes! The Welles of *Citizen Kane.* He'd have made a perfect Penrose.)

It surprised no one who knew him that when Spencer Penrose, a man who had barnstormed through the most famous

hotels and spas in the world, was invited on one notably cele-
bratory occasion to remove himself along with his boisterous
dinner companions from Colorado Springs' finest hotel, the
Antlers, and when the owners of the Antlers spurned the out-
raged Penrose's attempt to buy them out, that he decided in
1916 to build his own hotel, and not just any hotel, by God, but
the best damned hotel west of Philadelphia.

THE BROADMOOR 1 Lake Circle, Colorado Springs, Colorado 80901. Telephone: (800) 634-7711. <u>Accommoda-
tions</u>: 500 guest rooms, 60 suites. <u>Amenities</u>: No scuba
diving, no deep-sea fishing, but just about everything else.
<u>Terms</u>: Rooms in Broadmoor Main start at $180, parlor
suites at $225. Rooms in Broadmoor South and Broad-
moor West start at $210.

The construction of the Broadmoor Hotel on a site four miles
southwest of downtown Colorado Springs was a colossal undertaking, given the complexity of the project, the fact that it
was wartime, and the size of Penrose's vision. Consider, as an
indicator of the importance Penrose placed on making his new
hotel the best anywhere, the architectural talent he brought in
at one stage or other to work on the project: Frederick J. Stern
of New York, who had designed The Greenbrier in West Virginia
among other famous hotels; Warren and Wetmore of New York,
who were responsible for Grand Central Terminal, the Biltmore, and the Ritz-Carlton in Manhattan; Olmstead Brothers of
Brookline, Massachusetts, the founder of which firm was Frederick Law Olmstead, designer of New York's Central Park; and
Donald Ross, who was brought west to design the golf course.
Not a bad team.

From the day it opened in 1918 the Broadmoor has stood
among the grandest of America's grand hotels, a paragon of
luxurious splendor, all done up in creamy pink stucco and
topped with red tile in a style best described as Mediterranean
Eclectic. ("Riviera of the Rockies" is the PR slogan that's had
the most staying power over the years.)

Today, the Broadmoor stands less splendidly isolated than it
once did. All I remember of my first sighting in 1952 is that it

towered over the surrounding countryside, the only building of consequence on the horizon. That couldn't last, of course, and now the Broadmoor's veranda takes in Broadmoor South (next door), Broadmoor West (across the lake), and a mountainside speckled with expensive houses and luxury condos. Out front there's a whopping big conference center, and down the way there's a . . . well, you get the picture. Ain't progress grand?

Two of the three courses are delights to play. Ross completed the first eighteen in time for the 1918 opening. Robert Trent Jones added another nine in 1950, and a fourth nine in 1965, at which time the four nines were integrated to form the East and West courses that you play today. While plenty long enough from the back tees, both have wide, forgiving fairways that let a spray-shooter like yours truly scramble around without severe penalty.

EAST COURSE AT THE BROADMOOR

Design: Donald Ross/Robert Trent Jones

Year Open: 1918/1950/1965

7,128 Yards   73.9 Rating   122 Slope

Information: Must be guest of hotel or member of the Broadmoor Golf Club. (719) 634-7711, ext. 5150.

WEST COURSE AT THE BROADMOOR

Design: Donald Ross/Robert Trent Jones

Year Open: 1918/1950/1965

6,937 Yards   73.4 Rating   128 Slope

Information: Must be guest of hotel or member of the Broadmoor Golf Club. (719) 634-7711, ext. 5150.

As you contemplate your approach shot to the fifteenth green on the East Course, recall that it was on this hole—then the eighteenth—in 1959 that a pudgy young college boy from Ohio edged Charles Coody one-up in the finals of the United States Amateur Championship for his first "major" title. The kid's name, which you'd better have guessed by now, was Jack Nicklaus.

The third course, designed by Arnold Palmer and Ed Seay on a mountainside south of the hotel that seems more suitable for goat husbandry, is another thing altogether. I knew I was in for a long day at the office when I started reading this little pamphlet they hand out in the pro shop. Eleven of the holes, I discovered, have white flags in the middle of the fairway to designate strategic preferred landing points. That's because from the tee (a) you can't see the green, (b) you can't see the trouble you might get in beyond the white flag, or (c) both of the above. The views from the South Course are great; you can see Colorado Springs urban sprawling in front of you and beyond it on east to the Kansas border. Frankly, though, when I'm on a golf course I'd rather see the hole I'm playing. All of it.

SOUTH COURSE AT THE BROADMOOR

Design: Arnold Palmer and Ed Seay

Year Open: 1976

6,781 Yards   71.6 Rating   131 Slope

Information: Must be guest of hotel or member of the Broadmoor Golf Club. (719) 634-7711, ext. 5150.

A word of caution: be sure, when you book your Broadmoor vacation, to specify that you want to stay in "Broadmoor Main," not "Broadmoor West" or "Broadmoor South." The other two are perfectly fine, richly appointed, modern buildings, but neither has the character of the house that Spencer Penrose built. If you want the true, traditional Broadmoor experience, remember the Main.

Always take the long way going to and from your room in the Broadmoor. When you enter the lobby, for instance, instead of making a beeline for the elevator, walk back to the escalator and take it up to the second level; go out on the veranda for a look west beyond the lake over the top of Broadmoor West to Cheyenne Mountain beyond; then meander back through any large meeting room or small ballroom you find open, paying close attention to the elaborately detailed ceilings and carved moldings and antique furnishings as you pass, before taking the elevator on up to your room. Then, when you lie down for a snooze before your afternoon round, you can dream about sitting next to Spencer Penrose in the Tavern Room under the Toulouse-Lautrecs, savoring snifters of 1900 Armagnac, smoking fine cigars, and swapping outrageous tales about fortunes won and lost back in the gold rush days.

YOU PAYS YOUR MONEY AND YOU TAKES YOUR CHOICE

When it was Macy's vs. Gimbel's, I always had a preference. In apple vs. cherry, I have a favorite pie. Tastes Great vs. Less Filling, I'll express an opinion. Veronica vs. Betty, I'd only ask one to the prom. Dodgers/Giants, Celtics/Lakers, bent/bermuda—don't worry, I'm not neutral. Ditto Nicklaus vs. Palmer, Nicklaus vs. Trevino, Nicklaus vs. Watson. Heck, I'll even choose between Minneapolis and St. Paul. What I'm trying to say is that I'm not the kind who waits until all the other votes are counted before sticking up his hand. There's nothing I've ever come across in this world that I haven't formed an opinion about—often hasty, frequently uninformed, sometimes (or so my best friends tell me) just flat out wrong, but an opinion nonetheless, and usually a strong one.

THE GREENBRIER White Sulphur Springs, West Virginia 24986. Just off I-64, about 50 miles from The Homestead. Or is it vice versa? Telephone: (800) 624-6070. Accommodations: 650 guest rooms, 51 suites, 69 cottages. Amenities: Name it. Terms: From $145 to $198 per person, double occupancy, MAP. Assorted packages.

★

THE HOMESTEAD Hot Springs, Virginia 24445. On Route 220 just north of I-64 and west of I-81. Telephone: (800) 336-5771. Accommodations: 600 guest rooms. Amenities: You don't get 5-star, 5-diamond, gold medal ratings unless you have everything. Terms: From $140 to $185 per person, double occupancy, MAP. Assorted packages.

★

Except for one thing. Call me chicken, call me irresponsible, call me anything except not ready to putt when it's my turn, but so help me St. Andrews, I cannot—*will* not—choose between The Greenbrier and The Homestead.

How could anybody? Two grand hotels, each with a pedigree longer than a Greg Norman drive, each with three golf courses and all the trimmings—located just fifty miles apart from one another in the Allegheny Mountains on either side of the West Virginia-Virginia border. Sometimes you come up against really hard choices in life; this is one of those times.

Curative Mineral Waters. Both have them. The waters of White Sulphur Springs, West Virginia (The Greenbrier), and of Hot Springs, Virginia (The Homestead), have been healing people for a couple of centuries, or so legend has it. Don't count on either doing anything for your slice, though. For help with that, check with the club pro at Lourdes.

History. Both have it right up the rafters. The first inn was built on the present site of The Homestead in 1776, so the grande dame of Virginia can truly claim to be a daughter of the American Revolution. Much expanded, and now a full-fledged hotel, the establishment took the name "The Homestead" in 1846. It has been owned and operated by a single family—the Ingalls—since 1891. The nineteenth-century version of the inn burned to the ground in 1901, only to reemerge in greater glory the following year. That was when the familiar red-brick structure that still serves as the main wing of today's Homestead was erected.

By comparison, The Greenbrier is something of an upstart, although it played some pretty good catch-up ball. Not until the early 1800s did the first permanent structures appear at what is now The Greenbrier, when two rows of attached cottages were constructed (they're still in use today). But the first grand establishment was the Grand Central Hotel, more affectionately known as "the Old White," which opened in 1858 on a site immediately adjacent to The Greenbrier of today. The Old White had one of the largest and finest ballrooms in the world, and its huge dining room (300 feet long and 140 feet wide) could seat 1,200 guests at one time. After the Civil War, during which it was used as a hospital by both sides, the Old White became the resort of preference for what was left of the Southern aristocracy and, increasingly, for the new Northern plutocracy. The Old White couldn't survive twentieth-century fire safety codes, however, and was demolished in 1922. Twelve years earlier a tall, columned, 250-room non-Georgian structure designed by Frederick J. Sterner had been erected next to the Old White; it is now the center wing of The Greenbrier.

When it comes to history, call it neck and neck.

Size. Bigger is not always better, but for a hotel to be grand it must have some size to it. The Greenbrier has 650 guest rooms, 51 suites, and 69 cottages (no two of which are decorated exactly alike, by the way) and 6,500 acres of gardens, forest trails, and mountain meadows. The Homestead has 600 rooms and 15,000 acres.

In grandness terms, a standoff.

Setting. If one were in the desert and the other by the sea, you could make a choice on the basis of geography. But The Greenbrier and The Homestead share the same mountain range.

Dead heat.

Beauty. In the eye of the beholder. The Greenbrier is white and Georgian, The Homestead is red brick and Georgian.

Your call.

Amenities. It will come as no surprise to learn that both have everything: sports, activities, services, you name it. Now, I do think it's just barely possible that a certain masseuse at one is a tad better than anyone at the other, but I'm not going to go public with my choice until I've done a bit more research.

Awards and Honors. Both are gold medal recipients in *Golf* magazine's biennial designation of the "Best Golf Resorts in America" (there were just twelve gold medalists in 1990). Tie.

Food. Will it be the roast rack of Greenbrier Valley lamb, or the baked lump crabmeat gratiné with The Homestead seafood dressing? You choose; I haven't decided yet.

Service. The Greenbrier has 1,500 employees to serve a maximum 1,200 guests. Employee turnover is less than 5 percent a year. Over 200 of The Greenbrier's employees have worked at the hotel for more than twenty-five years. The Homestead? Virtually a mirror image. Both are the kinds of places where you hear a lot of "Welcome back again this summer, Mr. Jones," one of the hallmarks of service at a grand—and venerable—hotel.

Flip a coin.

Price. Please.

Golf. Of the Greenbrier's three courses, the Lakeside is the oldest (nine holes in 1910, expanded to eighteen in 1962 by Dick Wilson) and the easiest; the Old White (designed by C. B. Macdonald and Seth Raynor in 1914) is the best loved by Greenbrier regulars; and the Greenbrier (built in 1925, redesigned in 1977 by Jack Nicklaus for the 1979 Ryder Cup) is the strongest.

Begun in 1892, the Homestead Course has the oldest first tee in continuous use in America and is a high handicapper's dream. More challenging is the Lower Cascades Course, designed by Robert Trent Jones (1963).

But the best of the six courses at the two hotels is the Cascades at The Homestead, designed in 1923 by William Flynn and ever since the paradigm of mountain courses. Sam Snead, who's played it a few times, writes in a brochure you receive with your scorecard that "I do believe it's the most complete golf course I know of." Scary, too. Explains Brian McCallen in *Golf* magazine: "Holes are routed on the tilted insteps of the Allegheny foothills, with several tees perched 100 feet or more above wooded ravines. Blind, canted fairways have only yellow-and-black checkered directional flags to aim at." (Yes, I know that sounds suspiciously like Broadmoor South, but Cascades is different. Maybe it has to do with the age of the course, but the mountain goat terrain at Cascades seems natural and unforced.)

HOMESTEAD AT THE HOMESTEAD

Design: By committee
Year Open: Piecemeal, beginning in 1892
5,957 Yards   68.2 Rating   115 Slope
Information: (703) 839-5500

LOWER CASCADES AT THE HOMESTEAD

Design: Robert Trent Jones
Year Open: 1963
6,619 Yards   72.2 Rating   127 Slope
Information: (703) 839-5500

CASCADES AT THE HOMESTEAD

Design: William Flynn
Year Open: 1923
6,566 Yards   72.9 Rating   136 Slope
Information: (703) 839-5500

LAKESIDE AT THE GREENBRIER

Design: Dick Wilson redid original 9 holes and designed an additional 9.
Year Open: 1910/1962
6,333 Yards   70.4 Rating   121 Slope
Information: (304) 536-1110

You get the picture, and I say it's a photo finish. The slight edge The Homestead might enjoy because of its Cascades Course is not all that significant in the grand-hotel scheme of

OLD WHITE AT THE GREENBRIER

Design: C. B. Macdonald and Seth Raynor

Year Open: 1914

6,640 Yards   72.7 Rating   128 Slope

Information: (304) 536-1110

GREENBRIER AT THE GREENBRIER

Design: C. B. Macdonald/Jack Nicklaus

Year Open: 1925/1977

6,709 Yards   73.7 Rating   136 Slope

Information: (304) 536-1110

things. So what can you do to break this deadlock? Simple. You do what Solomon would have done: you cut your vacation in half and divide it equally between The Greenbrier and The Homestead.

When to Go

Go to the Arizona Biltmore any time except the middle of summer; go to the Broadmoor, The Greenbrier, or The homestead any time except the dead of winter.

OFF LIMITS

A grand hotel is a self-contained universe. The best way to enjoy it is to give yourself over completely to its many charms and activities. You should only have to leave campus for a little light sight-seeing. Needless to say, the concierge at any of the grand hotels mentioned here will make all necessary arrangements. But why bother? Each of these places has everything, with the notable exception of discount golf balls.

CHAPTER 14

AMERICA'S SUMMER GOLF CAPITAL
(Bet You Can't Guess Where It Is)

FLORIDA? YOU'VE GOT TO BE KIDDING; FLORIDA in the summer is a steam room.

Arizona? No chance; Arizona in the summer is a sauna.

Colorado?

New England?

Hawaii?

Good guesses, but I've already devoted whole chapters to those places, and there are more than enough golf vacation opportunities in the world without having to repeat.

Brrrrzzzz! Time's up. This is a tough one, and back when I used to live in this place I would never have guessed in a million years that "America's Summer Golf Capital" would someday be . . . MICHIGAN!

A little more than a decade ago, the movers and shakers of northern Michigan's ski industry were wringing their hands about what to do to attract people north in the summers, when there's not any snow on the ground even in northern Michigan. They had all this infrastructure—all these hotels, time-share condos, restaurants—but nobody to sleep or eat in them between April and December. A few resorts had put in golf courses, but golf wasn't a big deal in this part of the world.

What to do? Nobody had an answer, the meeting room was getting stuffy, people were squirming in their seats, when suddenly a voice spoke: "If you build them, they will come."

What? Who said that? Build what?

"If you build them, they will come."

So they did. And they did. And that's how the golf boom began in northern Michigan, and why a group of PR people could—with perfectly straight faces—come up with the trademarked, no less) slogan, "America's Summer Golf Capital."

As I said, back in the late sixties and early seventies when I lived in Ann Arbor, about the last thing I would have called northern Michigan was America's Summer Golf Capital. But that was then and this is now, and I can assure you that yes, there really is a heckuva lot of good golf to be played about four hours' north of the Michigan-Indiana border.

The Michigan Tour starts in Gaylord, a speck on the road map that has become the center of a thriving summer trade in birdies and bogies. From there it's west and north toward Boyne Mountain, a skier's paradise turned golf Mecca in the last decade. Then it's down the coast of Grand Traverse Bay until we reach our rendezvous with the Bear.

Ready? Okay, then. Schuss! . . . er, ah, Fore!

GARLAND

Most big-time golf resorts these days are owned and operated as links of a chain. This is neither good nor bad, necessarily; just a fact. Garland is an exception. A forty-year-old resort with sixty-three holes of golf on three thousand acres of forestland about half an hour east of Gaylord in northern Michigan, Garland is still very much a family deal.

Founded in 1951 by German immigrant Herman Otto as a getaway for family, friends, and employees of his company, Garland Manufacturing, a Detroit-based maker of auto parts, Garland was opened to the public in the early sixties. Today Garland is owned by Herman's son and his wife; their son-in-law is the general manager. Over the years, Garland has evolved from little more than a fishing camp with a nine-hole track chopped out of the forest by Herman to a year-round luxury resort with private jet service to and from its own airport.

The main lodge at Garland is the biggest log cabin east of the Mississippi River, according to the department that keeps track of such things, and it's a sight to see. The same sources say that the fifteen-foot-long pine and spruce logs used to build it in 1986 would, if laid from end to end, stretch for 3.2 miles. (Frankly, I don't think it would go a bit over 3.1 miles, but I won't insist on a recount.) Half the resort's 117 rooms are in the main lodge, the other half in smaller log cabins tucked away in the woods close by.

GARLAND Country Road 489, Lewiston, Michigan 49756. About 225 miles north of Detroit. Telephone: (800) 678-4952. <u>Accommodations</u>: 57 guest rooms in main lodge, 60 rooms in log cabin villas. <u>Amenities</u>: Indoor and outdoor pools, tennis courts, fitness center; fishing in trout ponds and streams on 3,000-acre property. <u>Terms</u>: Room only, from $70 to $110 per person; MAP, from $90 to $150 per person. Golf packages available.

The shortest, tightest, and newest of the three Garland eighteens is Reflections, ostensibly named for "the beautiful shadows and images reflected off the water at various points on the course." But water's not even present, much less in play, on ten of Reflection's holes; the real trouble is the trees, which give the spray hitter plenty of opportunities to play wood tag.

Somewhat longer and a whole lot wetter is Swampfire, where water comes into play on eight of the first nine holes— all nine, if you count as "in play" a body of water that will drown a drive that's topped left about fifty yards off the tee. (I sure do.) If you have any balls left by the time you make the turn, you'll no doubt be happy to discover that twelve, thirteen, and fifteen are bone dry.

The Courses at Garland

REFLECTIONS

Design: Ron Otto

Year Open: 1990

6,464 Yards

Information: (517) 786-2211

SWAMPFIRE

Design: Ron Otto

Year Open: 1988

6,868 Yards   72.9 Rating   131 Slope

Information: (517) 786-2211

MONARCH

Design: Ron Otto

Year Open: 1988

7,101 Yards   74.4 Rating   134 Slope

Information: (517) 786-2211

HERMAN'S NINE

Design: Herman Otto/Ron Otto

Year Open: 1951/1990

3,378 Yards   71.2 Rating   122 Slope

Information: (517) 786-2211

★

The oldest, biggest, and best course at Garland is called Monarch, a long walk in the woods at 7,101 yards from the tips. Once rated as Michigan's top public golf course by the *Detroit News*, Monarch is a stiff test right from the gitgo. The first hole, a 451-yard par 4 monster (427/401 from the blues/whites), has water left and right from the tee, with still more between you and the green on your second shot. It's easy—trust me on this one—to start a day on the Monarch with a snowman . . . or worse.

All three eighteens at Garland were designed by owner Ron Otto (Garland is a family deal, remember), a good amateur who plays to a single digit handicap. The courses are kept in splendid condition, and they properly reward the straight hitter. Hit it straight *and* far and you can post a lights-out score at Reflections, keep it respectable at Swampfire, and hold your own at Monarch. Good tests, but playable and of varying degrees of challenge; all golf resorts should offer so much.

Don't leave, by the way, without taking a run around Herman's Nine. This is (more or less) the original nine-holer that Garland's founder hacked out of the forest. For a time part of an eighteen-hole course called Garland West, Herman's Nine returned to its roots when Reflections was built by incorporating the other half of Garland West with a new nine. There's not a drop of water on Herman's Nine, but enough length and shot values to warrant a respectable 122 slope rating. But the best thing about Herman's Nine is that you don't have to take a cart; you can throw your sticks in a sack and walk it. Just the way Herman used to do.

TREETOPS

The second stop on your tour of America's Summer Golf Capital is about twenty-five minutes away in a sylvan paradise called, appropriately enough, Sylvan Resort. Less than a decade ago little more than a low-rent ski area for day-trippers from the Detroit suburbs, Sylvan today is a glitzy year-round resort complete with a restaurant-bar-disco that it boasts is "the most popular night spot in the Gaylord area." (The *whole* Gaylord area? Wow.)

Without dwelling on that particular claim to fame—I sleep at night, so I wasn't able to verify it—let's turn to the real rea-

SYLVAN RESORT 3961 Wilkinson Road, Gaylord, Michigan 49735. Five miles east of Gaylord, which is about 225 miles north of Detroit. Telephone: (800) 444-6711. <u>Accommodations</u>: 173 rooms. <u>Amenities</u>: Indoor and outdoor pools, fitness center, tennis courts. <u>Terms</u>: Double rooms from $84 to $134. Golf packages available.

son why Sylvan merits the traveling golfer's attention: Treetops, one of the newest, toughest, and best by the Maestro himself, Robert Trent Jones.

Built on rolling terrain overlooking the Pigeon River Valley, Treetops richly deserves it name, bestowed on it by Jones when the course was under construction as he and owner-developer Harry Melling stood on what would become the tee of the sixth hole, a dramatic 180-yard par 3 that dives 125 feet to the green below. The vistas are spectacular, particularly in the early fall when changing leaves paint the treetops vivid hues of yellows and reds.

TREETOPS

Design: Robert Trent Jones (with Roger Rulewich)
Year Open: 1987
7,046 Yards   75.8 Rating   146 Slope
Information: (517) 732-6711

Treetops is all about grandness and heroism and bravery. Playing it is like pursuing the Holy Grail: The only fulfillment to be found in the quest itself, because there can never be a conquest, an achievement of one's righteous goal. (Want a translation of what that psycho-babble means? Play the tenth hole, a par 5 that's 608 yards long—uphill. Now you understand.)

Indeed, Treetops is in many ways a summation of Jones's career-long philosophy of golf course design. The greens are immense and strongly contoured . . . the bunkers are plentiful, large, and steep-sided . . . water, where it's in play, is *really* in play . . . the fairways are wide . . . and it's a long, long way from tee to green (7,046 yards from the black championship tees). Asked by Sylvan's owner to build a championship course that would be "the talk of the Gold Coast," Jones created in Treetops a golf course that is as spectacularly beautiful as it is tough. And while there is no mathematical formula for grading beauty, the slope rating for Treetops is 146, the highest of any course in America's Summer Golf Capital.

From where I sit, I guess you have to say Robert Trent Jones followed his instructions pretty well.

BOYNE HIGHLANDS

Michigan's Lower Peninsula is shaped like a hand, sort of. Detroit is located at the base of the thumb, and Grand Rapids (home of golfer Gerry Ford) is located just south of where the little finger joins the hand. (You still with me?) Now, Gaylord, where we just were, is located at the large knuckle of the middle finger, while Boyne Highlands, where we are going next—and this is the point of all this—is located at the inside tip of the ring finger.

(Whew, that was tough, The state's Upper Peninsula is a piece of cake by comparison. Actually, it's more like a piece of glacier with a lot of trees, at least for about nine months of the year. But back to the matter at hand . . .).

BOYNE HIGHLANDS Harbor Springs, Michigan 49740. About four hours northwest of Detroit—hell, it's even north of Petoskey. Telephone: (800) 462-6963. <u>Accommodations</u>: 165 rooms in the Main Inn, 72 deluxe condo units in the adjacent Heather Highlands Inn, and 70 rooms in the nearby Bartley House. <u>Amenities</u>: Indoor and outdoor pools, tennis courts; health and fitness center staffed by physicians and health care technicians, with the capability of providing a complete physical examination, as well as nutrition and exercise counseling; hiking and biking trails through 6,000 wooded acres. <u>Terms</u>: From $130 to $270.

★

Why is it worth traveling all the way up to the tip of Michigan's ring finger? Because Boyne Highlands is one of the top twenty-five golf resorts in the country. That's what *Golf* and *Golf Digest* both say, and they've been saying it for years.

The main reason is Robert Trent Jones's Heather Course, a graceful beauty that cracked *Golf Digest*'s Top 100 American Courses list in 1971, just three years out of the box. It was bumped from the list in the most recent rankings, but that's because of the quality of new courses that have come on line in the last twenty years, not because of any decline in Heather as a course. Far from it. Now fully mature, Heather looks like it might have been laid down shortly after the glaciers left, and it's kept in immaculate condition. Long and stern, without the severe doglegging that in some courses substitutes for design subtlety, Heather is a championship track that's tough and fair without being terrifying.

Unless, that is, you finish the fifteenth hole clinging to a one-stroke lead but sense that your swing is deserting you. If that's the way it is, Bunky, you'd better hope the other guy doesn't press, because here's what you're looking at down the stretch: Number 16, 419 yards, par 4, pond in front of the green; Number 17, 180 yards, par 3, over water to an elevated green ringed by four deep traps; Number 18, 539 yards, par 5, pond in front of the green. Just think . . . or, better still *don't* think, because if you do, you might just end the day double, double, double. Or worse. (Don't ask.)

The Moor Course, designed by William Newcomb, is maybe a tad tougher, but a lot quirkier. Here the doglegs are severe, the short holes are long (par 3s of 222, 218, and 200 yards from the back tees, plus one of 160), and there are more ways to get wet. The final hole, a 580-yard double dogleg par 5 with two major bodies of water to negotiate, is a real doozy.

But the best reason for the traveling golfer who is serious about the game to stop at Boyne Highlands is to play a new course that opened in 1989, the Donald Ross Memorial. It's too early to tell whether this is a great course—at least it's too early for me to tell; I haven't played it—but it is unquestionably a great idea.

Designed by William Newcomb with assistance from respected teaching professional Jim Flick, the Ross Memorial Course consists of close facsimiles of eighteen outstanding holes from some of the great courses Ross designed, including

The Courses at Boyne Highlands

MOOR

Design: William Newcomb
Year Open: 1972
7,179 Yards   74 Rating   131 Slope
Information: (616) 526-2171

HEATHER

Design: Robert Trent Jones
Year Open: 1968
7,218 Yards   73.7 Rating   131 Slope
Information: (616) 526-2171

DONALD ROSS MEMORIAL

Design: William Newcomb (with Jim Flick)
Year Open: 1989
6,840 Yards   73.2 Rating   131 Slope
Information: (616) 526-2171

many not open to the general public (i.e., to you and me). For instance, Number 1 at Ross Memorial is a replica of Number 6 at Seminole in North Palm Beach (minus the palm trees); Number 6 is Number 6 at Scioto in Columbus, Ohio; Number 18 is Number 16 from Oakland Hills South in Birmingham, Michigan; and so on. Of the great Ross courses represented here, only two—the Detroit Golf and Country Club and Royal Dornoch in Scotland—do not appear among *Golf Digest*'s Top 100 American courses. Just to keep the record straight, Royal Dornoch isn't a Ross design per se—Old Tom Morris laid it out when Ross was just a pup. But it is located in Ross's hometown, he did work there as a young greenkeeper, and he had a hand in its redesign in 1922. It's also ranked eleventh in the *World* by *Golf* Magazine. Trust me, details like this are important.

Owner Everett Kircher and his son, Stephen, who assisted in the selection process, deserve a round of applause for sinking a lot of money in a grand idea. With any luck, that grand idea will be seen in a few years as a grand reality.

Call for literature and you learn at once that there is more than one Boyne in northern Michigan. Back down the road the other side of Petoskey, about thirty minutes away, is Boyne Mountain, the older of two resorts run by the same folks. There are two courses at Boyne Mountain: the Alpine, as up and down a track as its name implies, and the Monument, a monster whose slope rating tips the Richter scale at 139. Neither is a match for any of the three at Boyne Highlands in terms of design, although the Monument is the toughest of the five Boyne courses.

The Monument strives for prestige via a PR gimmick: each hole will be named after a golf notable who plays the course (for a fee) and designates, say, the eighteenth as the Sam Snead hole. But dead golfers have also been drafted to give their names to holes to get the idea off the ground, so the fourteenth is the Bobby Jones hole and the fifth is the Walter Hagan hole. Problem is, Sir Walter spelled his name "Hagen." (I don't believe for a minute that nobody there knows the correct spelling, but somebody is asleep at the switch, maybe because nobody really committed to such a patently artificial stunt.

All this suggests taking a pass on Boyne Mountain and staying at Boyne Highlands, and that's what I would recommend except for one thing: Boyne Mountain has what just may be the best golf package in America. Now, I haven't seen them all, but if what Boyne USA (the umbrella for the two operations) offers isn't the tops, it's gotten be doggone close.

Here's what you get for $820 per person, double occupancy, with Boyne's Super Five Golf Week in 1991: five nights' lodging, beginning with Sunday and ending Thursday night; five breakfasts and dinners; five days of unlimited golf (cart included), Monday through Friday, on *all five* Boyne courses; as much golf instruction as you want; club storage and cleaning; unlimited use of practice range, including balls; a scramble tournament with prizes; a gift package with a sleeve of balls, towel, bag tag, course book, and tees; two cocktail parties; tennis lessons and unlimited court time; and use of all Boyne facilities. The only catch with the Super Five is that you stay at Boyne Mountain; the package isn't good for Boyne Highlands.

The Courses at Boyne Mountain

MONUMENT

Design: William Newcomb

Year Open: 1987

7,086 Yards   75 Rating   139 Slope

Information: (616) 549-2441

ALPINE

Design: William Newcomb

Year Open: 1988

7,017 Yards   73.6 Rating   129 Slope

Information: (616) 549-2441

BOYNE MOUNTAIN Boyne Falls, Michigan 49713. Half an hour south of Boyne Highlands. Telephone: (800) 462-6963. Accommodations: 250 units ranging from hotel rooms and suites to villas and condo units. Amenities: Tennis, biking, hiking, swimming, all sorts of outdoor activities. Terms: From $70 to $100, but what you're interested in is the Super Five golf package.

There is a qualitative difference between the two resorts of similar name. Boyne Highlands is newer, better-looking, and more luxurious—plus its three courses are superior to Boyne Mountain's two. But you have access to all five courses with the Super Five Golf Week, although three of them are thirty to forty minutes from your front door. And for that price, with all that's included, a little drive time before and after your daily thirty-six is an acceptable trade-off.

My recommendation: go for the Super Five.

THE LEGEND

TraveLog/Friday: Leave Boyne Highlands late afternoon when it becomes too dark to follow the track of the ball. Drive south to Bellaire, about forty-five minutes away. Check in at Shanty Creek/Schuss Mountain Resort; grab a couple of steaks and a bottle of wine at Ivanhof Charbroil at Schuss Mountain. Take a pass on the "true nightclub entertainment experience" at the Lakeview Lounge and Ivan's Den, making certain to avoid the Schussycats, a group of "talented collegiate singers and dancers" who are billed us, "a popular feature back for the nineteenth year." (Don't you think their parents wish they'd graduate?) Get a good night's sleep.

SHANTY CREEK/SCHUSS MOUNTAIN RESORT Bellaire, Michigan 49615. Halfway between Petoskey and Traverse City, if that's any help. Telephone: (800) 632-7118. <u>Accommodations</u>: 640 guest rooms, including condos and chalets as well as hotel rooms. <u>Amenities</u>: Tennis courts, fitness center, cycling and hiking trails; fishing in nearby trout streams and in Lake Michigan; canoeing, horseback riding; sporting clays range; two indoor and two outdoor pools. <u>Terms</u>: From $105 to $220 per night, double occupancy. Golf packages available.

TraveLog/Saturday: Play the Legend, an Ed Seay-Bob Walker-Arnold Palmer course, one of their best. *Golf Digest* ranks it in the top fifty American resort courses. Exacting but fair, a truly beautiful layout; built into hillside with many changes in elevation. Make decision at end of day whether to stay an extra day and play it again. Maybe squeeze in an extra round (at least nine holes!) at one of two other tracks on property, the Deskin Course or the Schuss Mountain Golf Club. Former is open, trouble-free confidence booster; latter is strong enough to be used for state tournaments, with especially strong finish. But the Legend's the thing—what the hell, stay over and give it another crack.

The Courses at Shanty Creek/Schuss Mountain

LEGEND

Design: Ed Seay, Bob Walker, Arnold Palmer
Year Open: 1985
6,764 Yards   73.5 Rating   135 Slope
Information: (616) 533-6076

DESKIN

Design: Bill Diddle
Year Open: 1965
6,559 Yards   71.7 Rating   120 Slope
Information: (616)   533-6076

SCHUSS MOUNTAIN GOLF CLUB

Design: Warner Bowen/William Newcomb
Year Open: 1972/1977
6,922 Yards   73.3 Rating   124 Slope
Information: (616) 533-6076

★

HIGH POINTE

Throw your sack in the trunk, get over to U.S. 131, and drive south about twelve miles to Kalkaska, where you turn right on Route 772 toward Williamsburg. Start looking for cheap motels, and don't be choosy. If you get as far as Bates, a few miles past Williamsburg, turn back. (Trust me, you *don't* want to stay at a Bates Motel.) All you're looking for is clean sheets, not a luxury resort, because the next few days are going to be spent playing a public course and you want to set the mood. Not just any public course, of course, but a course intended by its designer to be "the best public course in the world."

A pretty high goal? I should say so, considering that the Old Course and Carnoustie are both public, and that the course in question is the first solo undertaking of a designer who turns thirty this year. But the High Pointe Golf Club, about fifteen miles east of Traverse City, is already acknowledged as a pretty special place, even though it only opened for play in 1989; and the way its reputation continues to soar as more golfers get to play it, who knows?

The architect of High Pointe, Tom Doak, is to golf course design what José-María Olazábal is to the game itself. Both are young and immensely talented . . . both have emerged on the golf scene in the last couple of years . . . and both are expected to become superstars. Soon.

One look at Doak's résumé and you figure they ought to retire his number right now. Degree in landscape architecture from Cornell University (Robert Trent Jones's alma mater). Scholarship to spend a year studying golf courses in Scotland, England, and Ireland. Worked with world-renowned golf photographer Brian Morgan. Four-year apprenticeship with Pete Dye. Chief administrator of *Golf*'s biennial rankings of the 100 greatest courses in the world.

Great, but what has he done for us lately?

HIGH POINTE GOLF CLUB

Design: Tom Doak

Year Open: 1989

6,819 Yards   72.8 Rating   128 Slope

Information: (616) 267-9900. Individuals may book tee times up to 30 days in advance. High Pointe is located at 5555 Arnold Road in Williamsburg, Michigan, about 15 miles east of Traverse City, as the dog legs.

At High Pointe, he transformed an old cherry orchard into what one admiring visitor called "the finest old course of the past twenty years." The phrase is apt because the course does look like it's been there a long time. Making minimum use of bulldozers and maximum use of the terrain's natural contours, Doak laid out fairways and built greens exactly where Mother Nature would have put them if she'd been a golf architect. Not surprisingly, given Doak's background, the course has a strong British feel to it. Large areas of natural rough (i.e., long grass, wild shrubs, wildflowers) between tee and fairway were often left untouched. The front nine meanders across open fields, whose emptiness plays optical tricks around the greens much as in British seaside courses. The back nine climbs into forested, hilly terrain where, writes Brian McCallen of *Golf*, "hidden valleys choked with ferns, wild sumac and scrub pines put one in mind of a British heathland course."

But what most contributes to the British flavor of High Pointe is the fescue grass used for the fairways and the greens. Common in Britain, fescue grass requires less water and fewer chemicals, so score one for the environment. Fescue fairways also play a lot firmer and faster, which is great for adding roll to your shots but not so great if they're rolling toward trouble. Fescue greens, on the other hand, play a lot slower than bent or bermuda, and definitely take some getting used to. Aside from Spanish Bay at Pebble Beach, High Pointe is the only course this side of Lands End to use fescue.

How good is High Pointe? It's too early to say with authority. Despite its older-than-forever look, High Pointe is only a couple of years old, and it deserves a chance to mature before people start assigning it a place in golf history. *Golf Digest* did name it the "Best New Public Golf Course of 1989," *Golf* listed it one of the top ten resort or public courses to come on line in 1989, and *Golf* also included High Pointe among its "50 Best Bangs for a Buck in Public Golf." That's enough praise for now.

Pull Some Strings

If you know somebody who knows somebody, or if your club president or pro (if you belong to one) has any clout, try your darnedest to get on Crystal Downs, a private club in Frankfort on the Lake Michigan shore south of Traverse City. Designed by Alister Mackenzie, who also gave us Cypress Point and Augusta National, Crystal Downs is a jewel. Or so I'm told: I don't know anybody who knows anybody, and I've never played there. But Ben Crenshaw has called it the finest golf course in the United States, *Golf Digest* ranks sixteenth in America's top 100, *Golf* says it's the twenty-first best in the world—and that's good enough for me. Oh, and one thing: if you get on, drop me line and I'll caddy for you.

★

As my mother, who played to a 7 in her prime, would almost certainly have said, we don't want it to get the big head.

THE BEAR

Now it's time to rassle the Bear.

Head east toward Traverse City. Keep an eye out on the right for a seventeen-story glass structure that looks like an escapee from a Houston shopping mall. (Is the Galería still missing a building? Maybe it went north with all the Michiganders who were returning home when the Texas boom went bust.) When you see the Tower, as it's properly called, you've arrived at Grand Traverse Village, where they keep the Bear.

Grand Traverse is not just a resort; it's a resort *complex* that's part of a master plan. You've got your hotel, your regular condos, your luxury condos, your homesites with beach frontage, your homesites with golf course frontage, your time-share deals. Down the pike (and up the road a bit) you've got your Country Club of Michigan (members will play on the twenty-seven Pete Dye holes scheduled to be built there) and your Grand Bay Executive Park, where the final element of your "live-work-play" concept kicks in.

And you thought it was just a place to stay while you rassled the Bear.

Skip the hotel, pass on the condo, and spring big bucks for the Tower Grand Traverse Resort. If you had your heart set on a little something in northwoods rustic, you're going to be disappointed. The style here is more along the line of interna-

---

GRAND TRAVERSE RESORT Grand Traverse Village, Michigan 49610. About 6 miles east of Traverse City. Telephone: (800) 748-0303. Accommodations: 730 rooms, suites, and condo units. Amenities: The works, including a private beach (on the eastern arm of Grand Traverse Bay), splendid trout fishing in nearby streams, lake fishing in Grand Traverse Bay, biking through cherry orchards, hot-air ballooning, and listening to pitches from condo and vacation homes salespersons. Terms: Double rooms from $110 (condos) to $195 (Tower). Golf packages available.

★

tional slick, not to mention luxurious as all get-out, right down to the last Jacuzzi spigot. But if you stay in the Tower you don't have to look at it all the time, which will be your punishment if you stay anywhere else. On the positive side, international slick luxurious can be pretty comfortable as styles go, particularly if you've just been mauled by the Bear. It won't take you long to figure out why *Golf* made Grand Traverse a silver medalist in its most recent ranking of the Best Golf Resorts in America.

"Don't ever play all eighteen holes from the back tees," Jack Nicklaus said after playing an inaugural round on the course that he designed and that developer Paul Nine spent $10 million to build. "I can't."

The scary thing is that he meant it.

The Bear is, by general agreement, the hardest course the Bear has ever designed. You and I aren't about to tackle it from the back tees, of course, but even from the regular tees at 6,176 yards (as opposed to 7,065 from the tips) the slope rating is 138. I don't know your game all that well, but for me that's a tough row to hoe.

THE BEAR

Design: Jack Nicklaus

Year Open: 1985

7,065 Yards   75.8 Rating   145 Slope

Information: (616) 938-1620

★

Rolling land, trees, lakes, and streams gave Jack a varied palette to work with, and he obviously let himself go in getting everything onto the canvas. Bulldozers moved as much as the glaciers had in a lot shorter time as Jack put a row of mounds here, another tier on a fairway there, and elevated yet another green over there. Pot bunkers? You betcha, some close to reaching China. Sand? Not as much as the Sahara, but almost. And so on, right on down to a 467-yard finishing hole with the last 100 yards or so over a pond the size of Lake Huron.

Playing the Bear is a good way to end your sojourn in America's Summer Golf Capital. Chances are pretty good that the

Bear's going to come out ahead, but that's okay. You'll be in good company. Chances are also pretty good that you'll remember your rounds there a long, long time.

When to Go

You don't have a lot of choice. Winter comes early and stays late in Michigan's north country, where the golf season is mid-May through mid-October, with a near certainty of some pretty chilly days at the beginning and end of that span. Traverse City's Cherry Festival takes place in mid-July, August has the best weather, and in mid-September you begin to see fall colors. It's a toss-up.

OFF COURSE

There are summer music festivals sprinkled here and there, there's a lot of fishing to be done, there's shopping at tourist traps in towns like Petoskey and Traverse City, and there are trees to be counted. My advice: Take a book, preferably a long one, published by Doubleday.

CHAPTER 15

THE
GOLF COAST
STATE
18,180 Holes and
Counting

FORGET ORANGE JUICE.

Forget the Dolphins.

Forget 'Gators, Disney World, spring training, drug lords, and golden age residential communities where you can turn to dust in dignity.

Forget Crocket and Tubbs.

Forget the Everglades, because goodness knows the locals have.

When it comes to Florida, all you have to remember is this one thing: Florida is the Golf Coast State.

There are 1,010 golf courses in Florida. Actually, there are more now, but there were 1,010 when this book went to press. Problem is, golf courses pop up in Florida faster than mushrooms in the forest after a summer rain. See! There goes another one. . . .

Now, figuring 6,000 yards as an average length from the middle tees, those 1,010 courses add up to 6,060,000 yards of golf that, if laid out as a single hole, would stretch from Miami to Vancouver and play as a par 30,300. The Mississippi would be a lateral hazard, and the Mexican border OB. Chicago would be deep rough on the right, and I guess you'd have to play winter rules in the Rockies anytime after Labor Day. Quite a hole. And the way I've been playing lately, I'd probably hit the green in regulation—30,298—and three-jack for the bogey.

With so many golf courses to choose from, deciding where in Florida to take your golf vacation is very tough, something on the order of hitting a one-iron or getting a tee time at Cypress Point.

You could pull off your head covers and play them all, starting with Arrowwood Country Club and ending at the nineteenth hole of Zellwood Station. At four courses a week, with a little time cushion for travel and rain-outs, you should be able to finish them all in about five years, assuming they slap a moratorium on building new ones until you hole out. True, I don't know your company's vacation policy, so maybe it would work. But to me, this sounds more like a retirement project than a holiday.

On the other hand, you could spend your entire vacation playing Emerald Dunes on Okeechobee Boulevard, just west of the Florida Turnpike in Palm Beach County. I've never been there so I can't vouch for what kind of track it is, but Emerald Dunes became the one thousandth golf course in Florida when it opened in February 1990. It might appeal to golfers with a sense of history.

And speaking of history, you could spend a couple of fun-filled weeks at Rolling Hills Golf Resort in Fort Lauderdale. Rolling Hills may not ring a bell, and it doesn't show up on anybody's Top 100 list, but you'll almost certainly recognize it once you see it as the golf course that starred in the best golf movie ever made, *Caddie Shack* ("Great!"—Siskel), and *Caddy Shack II* ("Sucks!—Ebert)

Or you could just say the hell with it and put off going to Florida until you're sixty-five.

C'mon, now. Don't be discouraged. Wouldn't you much rather go to Florida now and *shoot* 65? I know I would.

To help make that possible for you, I divided Florida into four golf zones: **Pebble East** (Ponte Vedra and environs), **Magic Kingdom** (metropolitan Disney World), **West Coast** (Tampa-St. Pete), and **Greater Miami** (everywhere else). Then in each zone I determined what I believed to be the single best place to set up base camp for a great golf vacation. After that I identified a handful of courses in each zone, in addition to the ones

at the base camp, that a traveling golfer might want to squeeze into a two-week golf orgy. Next I packed all this information neatly into the pages that follow. Finally, to protect myself and my family fom the completely warranted outrage of the dozens of absolutely first-rate golf courses and resorts that I arbitrarily and capriciously omitted, I entered the Witness Protection Program.

I've done my work. The 65 is up to you.

PEBBLE EAST

"I do believe that Ponte Vedra is the Pebble Beach of the East Coast," Dan Jenkins wrote a few years ago in *Golf Digest,* "just as I believe that Jacksonville is Fort Worth with an ocean, which I say with the most flattering look I can get on my face."

Jenkins, in case you've somehow missed reading *Semi-Tough, Baja Oklahoma, Dead Solid Perfect,* and *The Dogged Victims of Inexorable Fate,* was born and raised in Fort Worth. For him to compare another place favorably to his hometown is high praise indeed: "I've taken my sick slice and Texas hook all over the globe, thanks to journalism, and I've never found a city like Jacksonville, which somehow manages to take a rural humor and honesty, stir it in with an international sophistication and dump it on top of a wild, pristine beauty. Ponte Vedra is part of this."

Like Pebble Beach, Jenkins explains, Ponte Vedra has seasons, weather ("There are lots of times when you can play golf by day and burn logs by night. I like that."), a famous layout in (the TPC Stadium Course—"Island green. Bulkheads. Water. Marsh. Home of the Players Championship, which, depending on your point of view, is pro golf's fifth, sixth, or seventh major."), and a number of other nearby courses worth a detour.

As usual in golf matters, Jenkins is right.

Your primary base of operations at Pebble East is the Marriott at Sawgrass, an intimate little affair with 557 guest rooms, suites, and villas; a thirty-five-thousand-square-foot meeting complex with one eight-thousand-square-foot ballroom and another half that size; a seven-story atrium in the lobby, complete with interior and exterior cascading waterfalls; access to two and a half miles of private ocean beach; three pools; 350 acres of freshwater lakes and lagoons and forests of live oaks, magnolias, and palms on forty-five hundred acres of resort property.

A quiet country inn, it's not.

MARRIOTT AT SAWGRASS RESORT 1000 TPC Boulevard, Ponte Vedra Beach, Florida 32082. Just off A1A between Jacksonville and St. Augustine. Telephone: (800) 872-7248. Accommodations: 557 guest rooms, suites, and villas. Amenities: 81 holes of golf, 3 swimming pools, 10 tennis courts, horseback riding, nature and biking trails, access to private ocean beach, fishing, health club. Terms: $145 per person (double occupancy) in high season (mid-February through May, October through mid-November); $99 the rest of the year. Rate includes room, breakfast, and 1 round of golf per day.

But you're here for the golf, right? I thought so. Then you're in the right place.

The Marriott at Sawgrass will tell you in the flashy brochures it sends you that the resort offers ninety-nine holes of golf at "Five Championship Courses." That's technically true, as they do have an arrangement with an area country club for resort guests to play on an "as available" basis, but it's also irrelevant, as the course in question is of no particular distinction. Anyway, who needs it when you can play where the Players play?

"The Players," of course, are the shining stars of the PGA Tour who come together every March to compete to "the Players Championship" and to bitch and moan about the golf course they have to play it on. Designed by Pete Dye and opened for play in 1980, the "TPC at Sawgrass Stadium Course" (its official moniker) is the most maligned, most debated, most tinkered with great course on the Tour. In the last decade the PGA Tour, which owns the TPC Stadium Course, has spent something like $6 million on changes and repairs to the stage on which its premier annual drama is performed. That's a lot of money to put into a track that's so new; and still there's no general agreement on whether it's a really great one or a tricked-up disaster. *Golf* ranks it fifty-fourth in the world, and *Golf Digest* rates it thirty-second in America, and both put it among the top *resort* courses in the country. But many of the touring pros actively despise the TPC Stadium Course, and a few will even say so. And many more annually complain about the condition they find it in when they come to play in March.

Both sets of complaints need to be taken with a grain of salt. The pros don't really like any course that makes them look bad, and the TPC Stadium Course can certainly do that with its curious lumps and depressions in some fairways, the steepness of slopes around certain greens, and the severity of contouring on most of the greens. All that makes it a tough course, but not necessarily an unfair one, and certainly not "a bleeping tricked-up piece of bleep," as one pro put it to me. Keep this in mind: whenever a touring pro describes a golf course as "a fair set of golf," it means he's just shot 66 in a practice round and figures to knock a couple of strokes off that when the gun goes off. When he has to struggle to shoot par, there's something wrong with the course design or its condition—or both.

The pros' complaint about the course's condition is marginally more justifiable, even though the blemishes that send them into paroxysms of hysteria wouldn't be noticeable to you and me. If they want to talk bad conditions, I could show them a few tracks that would curl their Foot-Joys. But the TPC Stadium Course does get a staggering amount of play, and it can get ragged, at least compared with what the pros usually play on. After all, no one who stays at the Marriott at Sawgrass is *not* going to play it. How could any traveling golfer pass up a chance to fire at the most photographed, most imitated, most overrated hole in golf, the 132-yard seventeenth at the TPC Stadium Course—the infamous Dyevil's Island?

You wouldn't know it from the attention that one gets, but there are seventeen other golf holes to be played at the TPC Stadium Course, many of them more interesting (if not as un-nerving) than the island green at the Seventeenth, and alto-gether they add up to a heckuva fine course—one of the top ten in the country that are open to the public.

Guests at the Marriott at Sawgrass can also play the TPC Val-ley Course next door, another Pete Dye design (this time with Jerry Pate on board as co-designer) that plays almost as long as the Stadium Course but a whole bunch easier for the aver-age player. It doesn't get the respect it deserves or the play of its more famous sibling, but it's well worth a day of your va-cation.

TPC STADIUM COURSE

Design: Pete Dye

Year Open: 1980
6,857 Yards   74 Rating   135 Slope

Information: (904) 285-7777, Extension 6694

TPC VALLEY COURSE

Design: Pete Dye/Jerry Pate

Year Open: 1987
6,838 Yards   72.6 Rating   129 Slope

Information: (904) 285-7777, Extension 6694

SAWGRASS COUNTRY CLUB

Design: Ed Seay

Year Open: 1974

East-West:	7,073 Yards	73.7 Rating	138 Slope
West-South:	6,974 Yards	74.3 Rating	136 Slope
South-East:	6,979 Yards	74.6 Rating	139 Slope

Information: (904) 285-7777, Extension 6694

Note: Members and guests of Marriott at Sawgrass only.

OAK BRIDGE GOLF CLUB

Design: Ed Seay

Year Open: 1972

6,355 Yards   71.1 Rating   131 Slope

Information: (904) 285-7777, Extension 6694. Members and guests of Marriott at Sawgrass only.

MARSH LANDING COUNTRY CLUB

Design: Ed Seay

Year Open: 1986

6,841 Yards   72.7 Rating   131 Slope

Note: Members and guests of the Lodge at Ponte Vedra Beach only.

Better still are the twenty-seven holes across A1A at the Sawgrass Country Club, also open to Marriott campers. Designed by Ed Seay, the East-West nines hosted the Tournament Players Championship (as the event was then known) from 1977 to 1981. Sawgrass is a long course—over 7,000 yards from the championship tees in any combination of nines—with a links feel to it. If the players could choose whether to play the Championship Players here or at the Stadium Course west of A1A, the "old Sawgrass" would win hands down.

Nobody likes to do a lot of packing and unpacking on a vacation, but it's time to check out and move down to the beach proper to the Lodge at Ponte Vedra Beach. Please don't think of this as doing hard time. Anytime someone spends $18 million to build a hotel with only sixty-six rooms, you have to figure the result is going to be pretty luxurious. It is. The Lodge at Ponte Vedra Beach is just that. Decked out in unabashed Mediterranean (lots of tiles, lots of terra-cotta, lots of teal and aqua), the Lodge has three swimming pools and an ocean, a top-of-the-line health center, and a fine restaurant to keep body and soul on speaking terms.

All well and good, you're thinking right about now, but not sufficient reason to pull up stakes. Correct. The real reason is Marsh Landing.

THE LODGE AT PONTE VEDRA BEACH 607 Ponte Vedra Boulevard, Ponte Vedra Beach, Florida 32082. About 20 miles southeast of Jacksonville on the beach east of A1A. Telephone: (800) 243-4304. Accommodations: 66 guest rooms, each with at least one private balcony facing the ocean. Amenities: Three pools; fitness center; windsurfing, sailing, and fishing; tennis at ATP Headquarters; beach. Terms: From $155 to $215, double occupancy, during high season (March 1–October 31). Golf package available.

A 1986 design by Ed Seay, Marsh Landing is simply one of the most beautiful courses in the world. It's laid out near the Intracoastal Waterway in marshland that teems with birds and other wildlife. "It's like playing golf through an incredible nature preserve," says Dan Jenkins. "The nine holes at Marsh Landing that finish nearest the clubhouse are simply the prettiest and most intriguing nine in the area." Marsh Landing is also private, and the only nonmembers permitted to play there are guests at the Lodge at Ponte Vedra Beach.

Now you understand why you have to move. You don't want to miss playing the prettiest course at Pebble East.

MAGIC KINGDOM

Not once in the couple of dozen times that I've been to Orlando have I ever been to Orlando. The Orlando airport, yes, but never to Orlando proper, which I'm told is somewhere north of the airport. Peter Andrews, who writes about golf and many other things, has had a similar experience (or lack of experience) in Orlando: "It took me longer than most people to warm up to the Orlando area as a resort location," he wrote in *Golf Digest* a couple of years back, "because for a long time that's all Orlando was—an area. I used to think of it simply as an airport where I rented a car to head for someplace nice as quickly as I could."

I wonder. Is it possible that there is no *there* there, that there is no Orlando north of the airport? Guess I'll never find out, though, because I'll always be heading west and then south from the airport, to the Magic Kingdom.

"Hey-there, Hi-there, Fore-there . . ."

No! Damn it, I promised myself I wouldn't make a single smart-aleck remark about Disney World. I would just talk about the three courses at Disney World and leave the premises quietly. No jokes about Mickey's four-fingered overlapping grip. I was even torn over whether to mention the sand trap in the shape of mouse ears, and finally decided to let you discover it for yourself. No cheap jokes, and I'm sticking to it.

The Palm Course at Disney World is no joking matter. Just shy of 7,000 yards, it's a fine Joe Lee design with plenty of character. (Not to be confused with the "Characters," who tend to turn up at cocktail parties and other grown-up functions in the Disney hotels and make you feel like an idiot. "What am I doing here?!") Good enough to serve as a late season stop on the PGA Tour, Palm has done time on the *Golf Digest* chart of top 100 American courses and is still ranked by *Golf Digest* as one of the country's best twenty-five resort courses. You'll be a believer by the time you finish the sixth hole, a 412-yard par 4 that challenges you to cut off the dogleg-left to have the best line for your second shot to a long green cut on the diagonal — and punishes you for cutting off too much by drowning your ball.

PALM COURSE AT DISNEY WORLD

Design: Joe Lee

Year Open: 1971

6,957 Yards   73 Rating   133 Slope

MAGNOLIA COURSE AT DISNEY WORLD

Design: Joe Lee

Year Open: 1971

7,190 Yards   73.9 Rating   133 Slope

Information (both courses): (407) 824-2270

★

The Magnolia Course, also by Joe Lee, is another good one; *Golf Digest* puts it in the top fifty in its report course category. Magnolia is a bit longer than the Palm, and it carries a higher USGA course rating (73.9 to 73), but I think you'll agree that it plays a tad easier because of its wider fairways. (Nobody else seems to think so, so maybe I was just hitting them straighter the last time I played Magnolia.)

Take a pass on Lake Buena Vista, the third Joe Lee course at Disney World. It's an okay course: shorter, sportier, less water, fewer bunkers than its two more challenging siblings. But there are too many much better courses in the Magic Kingdom neighborhood for you to settle for just okay. Not only that, but the scorecard has a big picture of Mickey *and* Goofy on its cover, each of them decked out in suitable golf attire. Magnolia scorecard has Mickey, Palm has Goofy, and that's bad enough. It's all I can do to haul out my scorecard and write down another big number when there's just one Character grinning up at me. Two is at least one too many.

The only reason to stay at one of the Disney World hotels while you're playing in the Magic Kingdom is if your traveling party includes under-age non-golfers and you've had to use them as an excuse for going there in the first place. If so, my condolences. Walt Disney World gives me the heebie-jeebies. Does anybody know whether Uncle Walt is still lying around in a freezer somewhere, waiting to be thawed out when medical science has made enough progress to make him as good as new again? (He did have that done, didn't he? Am I dreaming all this up?)

The place to pitch your tent while in the Magic Kingdom is at the Grand Cypress Resort, a few miles north of Disney World toward the Orlando airport, and as close as you can get to golf heaven.

Try this one for size: forty-five holes of Jack Nicklaus at his best, including a new eighteen based on a very old model that can actually be played by the likes of you and me . . . a whopping great 750-room Hyatt Regency with all the Hyatt special effects, including a monster lobby atrium and half-acre free-form swimming pool with a dozen waterfalls and three whirlpools . . . another 146 rooms in Mediterranean-style villas scattered unobtrusively around the golf complex . . . one of the best golf schools in the business, complete with its own three-hole teaching course and classroom . . . enough other activities

---

GRAND CYPRESS RESORT 1 North Jacaranda Orlando,
Florida 32819. About 20 minutes from Orlando International Airport. Telephone: (800) 835-7377. <u>Accommoda-
tions</u>: 750 hotel rooms and suites in Hyatt Regency Grand
Cypress and 146 rooms in villas. <u>Amenities</u>: forty-five
holes of Jack Nicklaus-golf, twelve tennis courts, forty-
two stable equestrian center, croquet, hiking and biking
trails, and a huge, free-form pool with fake boulders and
twelve waterfalls. <u>Terms</u>: From $210 to $370 for a hotel
room, double occupancy, in the Hyatt Regency Grand Cypress; from $275 for a club suite to $1,100 for a four-
bedroom villa in the Villas of Grand Cypress.

★

(twelve tennis courts, complete equestrian center, health spa,
even croquet) to keep a sports-minded camper sweating for
weeks.

The headline act is golf, of course, featuring two nines—the
North and the South—that form a course ranked number two
in Florida (by *Golfweek*) and among the top 100 courses in the
country (according to *Golf Digest*). Long from the championship tees (7,024 yards) but much more accessible from the
blues (6,349 yards), the North-South tandem draws its strength
and challenge not from length alone, but from Nicklaus's willingness to move earth (if not heaven) to get what he wanted.
"Flat land doesn't bother me," the Golden Bear says in the
course guide. "I enjoy the challenge. We went down to the water table and created from there."

The process must have given a battalion of bulldozer drivers
the wherewithal to send their kids up north to college, because
what was once a flat-as-a-Florida-pancake orange grove is today a linkscape of dunes, mounds, moguls, terraced fairways,
grass bunkers, sand bunkers, pot bunkers, and Omigod bunkers. When it was new and raw back in 1984, it had a tricked-
up feel to it. Now, with less than a decade to mature, it seems
like it's been there forever. How come the rest of Florida
doesn't look like this?

The East nine, built a few years later, still feels a little like
the earlier nines felt when they were young, so maybe there's

hope. But right now, the East is the only weak link in the entire
Grand Cypress operation, as far as I'm concerned. Unfortunately, given the need to keep all three nines in rotation, you
can't always be sure of playing the two nines you want, particularly when the course is crowded. It's worth juggling your
schedule if necessary to stick with the North-South combo, and
that'll be a lot easier to do now that there's a new kid on the
block.

OLD COURSE AT GRAND CYPRESS

Design: Jack Nicklaus

Year Open: North and South, 1983; East, 1985.

North-South: 7,024 Yards   73.9 Rating   130 Slope

South-East: 6,937 Yards   74.4 Rating   132 Slope

North-East: 6,955 Yards   73.9 Rating   130 Slope

NEW COURSE AT GRAND CYPRESS

Design: Jack Nicklaus

Year Open: 1985
6,773 Yards   72.1 Rating   126 Slope

Information: (407) 239-4700. Ext. 1909. Open to resort
guests only. Tee times may be reserved up to sixty days in
advance.

The New Course at Grand Cypress pays homage to the Old
Course at St. Andrews. There is a "Swilcan Burn" crossing in
front of the first hole, complete with stone bridge. There are
fourteen double greens, all evoking the shape and contours of
their St. Andrews analogues. The Principal's Nose, Deacon
Sime, Hell Bunker, and other venerable Old Course landmarks
both perfectly natural in the Florida sunshine. With only a couple of trees on the entire course, the golfer has to contend with
difficulties in depth perception caused by lack of definition
just as at traditional links. And the fairways roll, dip, and bulge
as if they had been shaped by the retreating sea instead of
modern machinery.

The New Course is no slavish copy of the Old. That wouldn't have been possible even if Nicklaus had wanted it. Rather, it's a loving, forthright tribute to one of Nicklaus's favorite courses in the world, the site of two of his British Open titles.

But the best thing of all about the New Course is that the average golfer will find it a whole lot of fun to play. That's right, fun. Not an exercise in frustration. Not a struggle to stay alive. But fun, because Jack wanted it that way.

Too often, the real estate developer who puts up mega-bucks for the Jack Nicklaus name on a course intended to sell homesites has something else in mind. It's hard to imagine a developer saying to Jack: "Here's a million bucks to cover your fee, over and above construction costs. Now design me a short, sporty little track that's fun but not too much of test." Usually the conversation goes more like this: "See that big, tough, mean course you designed at Desert Mountain Seaside Point? Draw me up one that's bigger, tougher, and meaner."

The New Course at Grand Cypress is not like that. It's a good, high-quality course that's also playable—which makes it a perfect stablemate to the big, tough, mean old course at Grand Cypress. Says Peter Andrews of the New Course: "This is a premier resort golf course that goes to the top of any well-ordered list." That's certainly where it is on mine.

There are other mighty fine golf courses in the Magic Kingdom, the most notable being Arnold Palmer's **Bay Hill Club,** a *Golf Digest* top 100 course and host of a PGA Tour event. To play it, though, you have to be a guest of the **Bay Hill Lodge** (407-876-2429). Up in some honest-to-God hills northwest of Orlando is the **Mission Inn Golf and Tennis Resort** (904-324-3101), a homey, low-key place that's been around for a while. If you're looking for a place to decompress, Mission Inn could be just the ticket. On the southern edge of the Magic Kingdom is the **Grenelefe Resort** (813-422-7511), with three long, challenging layouts by Robert Trent Jones, Ron Garl, and Ed Seay.

Worth playing? You betcha. Worth playing if it means leaving Grand Cypress? That's another matter. If you're a single-digit handicapper, take on Bay Hill. If you're a long hitter who loves nothing better than hammering his tee ball into the next time zone, give the Grenelefe trio of 7,000-yarders a go. And if you've been living in the flat land too long, head for the hills and Mission Inn.

But the best move of all, for my money, is to stay at Grand Cypress for the duration. A day or two at Palm and Magnolia maybe. Ditto an outing to Grenelefe. But spend the rest of your time at Grand Cypress, bouncing between North-South and the New Course.

Resort golf just doesn't come any better.

GULF COAST

Nobody likes snakes. Herpetologists may say they do, but they really don't. Finding snakes interesting and worthy of study is not the same as liking them. Snakes are simply not likable. Show me a kid who has a pet boa constrictor and I'll show you a kid who's going to cause the world a heap of trouble when he grows up. Remember the Garden of Eden? They had a great little nine-hole course back in the woods there until a snake came along and spoiled everything. Try a little associative slang: snake-eyes, snake pit, snakebit, snake oil, snake in the grass. Notice any positive connotations? The bottom line is this: Anybody who slithers up to you and says there's this snake he really likes is speaking—you guessed it—with a forked tongue.

Unless, that is, the person's a golfer and he's talking about Copperhead.

The Copperhead golf course is the star attraction at Innisbrook, a sprawling 1,000-acre golf resort in Tarpon Springs, twenty miles west of Tampa. This is one snake that everybody likes. *Golfweek* magazine has ranked Copperhead the number-one course in Florida for five consecutive years. *Golf Digest* ranks it sixty-ninth among America's top 100 courses. *Golf*

INNISBROOK Post Office Drawer 1088, Tarpon Springs, Florida 34688. About 20 miles northwest of Tampa International Airport on Route 19. Telephone: (800) 456-2000.
Accommodations: 1,000 suites in 28 low-rise lodges.
Amenities: 6 pools, fitness center, 18 tennis courts, Australian Tennis Institute, fishing, cycling, wildlife preserve.
Terms: From $180 for a club suite (i.e., 1 large room) to $216 for a 1-bedroom suite in high season (February/mid-April). Both include kitchen, and balcony or patio.

★

awarded Innisbrook its second straight silver medal for being one of America's top resorts, largely because of Copperhead. And the people who like it the most are people with single-digit handicaps, because this is one tough mother of a course.

At 7,000 yards and change from the championship tees, Copperhead is long enough to test even a big hitter like baseball Hall-of-Famer Mike Schmidt, a Copperhead devotee who broke in with the Philadelphia Phillies the same year the course opened (1972). The Phillies' spring training camp is just

---

COPPERHEAD (27 HOLES) AT INNISBROOK

Courses 1 and 2
Design: Larry Packard
Year Open: 1972
7,031 Yards   73.5 Rating   135 Slope

Courses 2 and 3
Design: Larry Packard
Year Open: 1972/1974
6,836 Yards   72.4 Rating   128 Slope

Courses 1 and 3
Design: Larry Packard
Year Open: 1972/1974
6,981 Yards   71.8 Rating   129 Slope

ISLAND COURSE AT INNISBROOK

Design: Larry Packard
Year Open: 1970
6,999 Yards   72.8 Rating   133 Slope

SANDPIPER AT INNISBROOK

Design: Larry Packard
Year Open: 1971
6,999 Yards   72.8 Rating   117 Slope

Information (all courses): (813) 942-2000

★

down the road in Clearwater, and Copperhead came to be Schmidt's home course-away-from-home for six weeks of the year. As soon as he could afford it, Schmidt started staying at Innisbrook in the spring to be closer to his second great sports love. Veteran superstars get a few extra days off during spring training and often don't accompany the team on bus trips to games across state, so in recent years Schmidt had a lot more time for golf at Copperhead. The result: a seven handicap at a track with a 73.5 course rating and a 135 slope rating, not too shabby for a third baseman.

(I tell you this so you won't suggest a little fifty-dollar Nassau with double presses the next time you run into Michael Jack on the driving range at Innisbrook.)

But there's more to Copperhead than length. There are also eighty-foot elevations (yes, in central Florida), seventy-three sand traps, and more tall cypress and pine trees closer to dog-legs in the fairway than are absolutely necessary for shade. The ten water hazards are there mainly for decoration; unlike at most Florida courses, your biggest fear at Copperhead is not a watery grave. The undulating terrain, which makes you think you're in North Carolina instead of Florida, is what ultimately makes the course's length so tough to handle. Frankly, I'd rather try to handle a real copperhead than some of the sloping lies at Copperhead.

There are three nines at Copperhead. Numbers 1 and 2 compose the championship layout; Number 3, at 3,393 yards from the tips, can be matched with one of the other two to give higher handicappers a happier day in the sun. In addition, there are two other eighteen-hole courses at Innisbrook, one of which, the Island Course, is good enough to join Copper-head on *Golf Digest*'s list of the top fifty resort courses in the country. You don't get to be called "Island" without there being a lot of water close by, so bring an extra sleeve of balls.

Innisbrook is owned and operated by an outfit called Golf Hosts, Inc., which also owns and operates Tamarron, the splendid golf resort in Colorado. Obviously, they know a thing or two about managing golf operations, further evidence of which is the Innisbrook Golf Institute, one of the best golf schools in the country. Trivia buffs take note: Innisbrook was Florida's first successful condominium resort.

Innisbrook has 1,000 handsome suites distributed through 28 low-rise lodges around the large, beautifully landscaped property, so you don't feel like you're jammed into a golf dormitory. The tennis program ranks as high as the golf program, and there are six pools ready to catch any golfer who decides to drown himself after a bad round. And if you want to go native, just walk to the center of the property: the golf courses wrap around a wildlife preserve.

Some people don't like even the idea of Florida golf, because the courses are too flat and there's too much water. For them, Innisbrook just may be the perfect Florida golf resort. And for people who do like Florida, it's even better still.

Just watch out for the Copperhead. It bites.

GREATER MIAMI

. . . and now, the five nominations for Best Performance by a Golf Resort in Greater Miami are . . .

1. *The Boca Raton Resort and Club.* A pink fantasy in Late Alhambra style created by eccentric genius Addison Mizner in the mid-1920s and a Florida architectural landmark ever since . . . 5 stars from Mobil, 5 diamonds from AAA . . . Boca Raton means "Mouth of the Rat" in Spanish . . . a classic 1926 William Flynn course, retooled by Robert Trent Jones (1956) and Joe Lee (1988) . . . another eighteen at nearby Boca Country Club. **Telephone: (800) 327-0101.**

2. *The Breakers.* The Italian Renaissance as produced and directed by Cecil B. DeMille . . . Flemish tapestries! Crystal chandeliers! Medici fountains! . . . a short, flat Donald Ross course with subtle charms on the front lawn . . . additional eighteen holes at Breakers West twenty minutes away . . . center of Palm Beach society and winter home to the rich and snobbish since the 1920s . . . *the* place for debutante and charity balls . . . summer camp for kids ten to fifteen that teaches them swimming, tennis, and basics of investment and personal finance (really) . . . honoree in Grand Hotel Hall of Fame . . . located in Palm Beach. **Telephone: (800) 833-3141.**

3. *The Doral Hotel and Country Club.* Five golf courses, including the Blue Monster, battlefield for the Doral Ryder Open . . . large, sophisticated fitness center and pampering palace, the Doral Saturnia Spa, on premises . . . golf school headed by Jimmy Ballard, once tutor to Curtis

Strange and Hal Sutton . . . located in northwestern Miami. **Telephone: (800) 327-6334.**

4. *PGA National.* Four golf courses on campus, including the Champion, a killer track originally designed by George and Tom Fazio and reworked by Jack Nicklaus . . . water comes into play on seventy of seventy-two holes (seems like even more) . . . fifth course ten minutes away . . . headquarters of Professional Golf Association of America . . . 335-room PGA Sheraton serves as dormitory for golfers who log 160,000 rounds a year at three Fazio courses and one Arnold Palmer-Ed Seay track . . . located in Palm Beach Gardens. **Telephone: (800) 325-3535.**

5. *Turnberry Isle Yacht and Country Club.* Brand new 271-room country club hotel next to two fine Robert Trent Jones courses . . . South Course hosted several LPGA events, 1980 Senior PGA . . . shorter North Course good for building confidence . . . located in North Miami Beach. **Telephone: (800) 327-7028.**

We're running a little short of time tonight, so on behalf of all the nominees I want to thank their developers, their architects, their directors of golf, their superintendents of maintenance, their grounds crews, their respective parents, and my lovely wife, Sharon. And now, the envelope please . . .

Wait a minute. Before I tell you who won, let me tell you how tough it was to decide. Each of the five nominees holds a silver medal awarded by *Golf* magazine to the top golf resorts

---

DORAL HOTEL AND COUNTRY CLUB 4400 NW 87th Avenue, Miami, Florida 33178. About ten minutes northwest of Miami International Airport. <u>Accommodations</u>: 650 rooms and suites. <u>Amenities</u>: Five golf courses (plus a nine-hole executive course), fifteen tennis courts, pool, equestrian center, lake fishing on the property, cycling and jogging trails, and one of the biggest, splashiest spas this side of Nirvana, the Doral Saturnia. <u>Terms</u>: From $245 to $345, double occupancy, in high season (January through April). Golf packages available.

★

---

in the country. Each has a distinct personality. Each obviously offers a lot more than a bed and a tee time. Each is a great place to spend a vacation.

Academy voters eliminated . . . okay, *I* eliminated three of the nominees—Boca Raton, Breakers, and Turnberry Isle—on the grounds of not enough golf. If you're going to be spending a week or more at a place, you're going to want more than two

THE DORAL RAINBOW

Blue Course
Design: Bob von Hagge/Dick Wilson
Year Open: 1961
6,939 Yards   72 Rating

Red Course
Design: Bob von Hagge/Dick Wilson
Year Open: 1961
6,120 Yards   68.5 Rating

White Course
Design: Bob von Hagge
Year Open: 1965
6,208 Yards   69.1 Rating

Gold Course
Design: Bob von Hagge/Bruce Devlin
Year Open: 1968
6,384 Yards   70.5 Rating

Silver Course
Design: Bob von Hagge/Bruce Devlin
Year Open: 1984
6,801 Yards   71.7 Rating

Information: For advance tee times up to 60 days prior to arrival, call (305) 592-2000, Extension 2333 for Blue, Red, White, and Gold Courses; (305) 594-0954 for Silver Course.

Note: Doral courses scheduled to have slopes calculated in 1991.

★

golf courses at your disposal. That left two still in the running:
PGA National and Doral.

Both are golf factories—and I mean that in the best possible
sense. Each has a soup-to-nuts range of other facilities, but the
primary business of both is golf. From the time you first pull
into the parking lot until the time someone puts your clubs in
your trunk when you leave, everything at both places is geared
to getting you onto a golf course as quickly and efficiently as
possible. And both do a great job at it.

And *now,* the envelope please. And the winner is . . . Doral!

What it finally comes down to is that the Blue Monster is a
better course than the Champion. The supporting courses at
PGA National are a shade better than their Doral counterparts,
but when it comes to star attractions I prefer the Doral's. Tough
as it is, the Blue Monster plays fairer than the Champion, even
after the latter's redesign by Nicklaus, which made it a much
better course.

Maybe it all comes down to the final hole at Doral, a 425-
yard par 4 that bends left into a prevailing wind with water all
the way down the left side. The green is slightly elevated with
a sharp slope down to the water and bunkers on both sides.
Most years it plays as the toughest finishing hole on the PGA
Tour, which makes it all the sweeter if you catch a good drive,
long and down the right side, then smooth a middle iron to the
left center below the hole, and read the right-to-left break just
right for a closing birdie.

On the other hand, if you hook into the water off the tee,
then drown a second ball trying to be a hero, next pop it into
the trap on the right, and finally skull it out of the sand across
the green, down the slope, and into the water on the other side,
you can call me up and tell me to go to hell.

And I'll give you the number of PGA National.

When to Go

High season in Florida is mid-January through late April. That's
"high" as in high prices and high numbers of people, so be
prepared. Ocean breezes help alleviate the heat in Pebble East
in the summer, but you know what they say—it ain't the heat,
it's the humidity. And the farther south you go, the worse it

gets. For my money, the period of October through mid-December provides the best combo of good weather and relief from the tourist rush.

OFF COURSE

It's a bit of a joke, really, trying to suggest things for you to do in Florida when you're not playing golf. If there's one thing that Florida has more of than golf courses, it's tourist attractions. Tourism is Florida's biggest industry, bigger even than geriatric care, oranges, and drugs. You won't have any trouble at all finding something to do if it rains.

Everything in the Sunshine State is measured in how far you are from **Walt Disney World.** For example, a promotional brochure for the Lodge at Ponte Vedra Beach, way up in the northeast corner of the state, lists Walt Disney World, EPCOT, and MGM Studios as "Area Attractions"—just 2½ hours away! If you're forced to travel with people under ten years of age, I suppose you have no choice.

Heading south from Pebble East, **St. Augustine** is worth a detour. It's billed as the oldest town in America. Of course, "old" in Florida usually means "pre-air conditioning," but St. Augustine does have a genuinely historical look and feel to it.

Tarpon Springs, where Innisbrook is located, is the Sponge Capital of America. Go down to the docks, have a bowl of fish chowder at one of the dockside joints, and take a half-hour boat trip into the harbor where a diver in full gear will go over the side and come up with a big green, slime-covered sponge.

You can't drive fifty miles in Florida without running into some theme park or other, even if it's only a disgusting reptile farm–gas station–hamburger joint complex somewhere just off the interstate. The best is probably **Sea World** (305-351-0021), about five minutes north of WDW near Orlando.

While you're in the greater WDW metropolitan area, look up the **Tupperware Museum and Factory** (305-847-3111) on U.S. 441, at Tupperware's corporate headquarters. To my dying day I'll regret not visiting once when I spotted it while in the Orlando area. Sorry I'm unable to give more precise directions, but I don't know exactly where it is—some suburb, I think. (So fire me.) But I've got to believe it's worth your finding out.

In the south, be sure and visit the **Everglades** while you still can. Years from now, you can tell your grandchildren what this great, moving sea of grass looked like before our it was destroyed.

Miami is a fascinating place, full of contradictions and surprises. You can stand in line for two hours to eat stone crabs at Joe's in Miami Beach, or you can tucker into a bowl of conch chowder at Joe's on the Miami River. You can drive through Green Village South (a.k.a. Coconut Grove) and into Coral Gables and wonder if you're still in the same time zone. You can gape at the palaces on the Intercoastal and speculate about which were bought with drug money. You can cruise up Collins Avenue and marvel at the greatest concentration of art deco architecture this side of the 1930s. And you can top an evening on the town with a late-night bowl of *moros y cristianos* (black beans and rice) at the Versailles Restaurant (305-444-0240) on Calle Ocho (Eighth Street), the Sunset Boulevard (or Michigan Avenue, or Main Street) of Miami-Havana, USA.

CHAPTER 16

BEACHCOMBING ALONG HURRICANE ALLEY

Unburied Treasures of the Eastern Seaboard

NO GOLF RESORT EVER CAPTURED THE FANCY of the traveling golfer in America faster than Wild Dunes, a luxurious 1,600-acre paradise that opened in 1980 on the Isle of Palms, South Carolina, just fifteen miles from Charleston. In awarding Wild Dunes a gold medal in 1988 for being one of America's top twelve golf resorts, Brian McCallen of *Golf* magazine explained why:

> While most golf courses in the Carolina Low Country are relatively flat, the Links at Wild Dunes has as its back-nine backbone a mile-long, 50-foot-high dune ridge created by a prehistoric hurricane. [The back nine . . .] exhibits great topographical variety, with holes chiseled into the flanks of the dune ridge, holes routed near tidal inlets and marshland, holes strung along the Intercoastal Waterway . . . and a pair of finishing holes that play nip and tuck with the Atlantic.

Then along came Hurricane Hugo and blew it all away. Hugo slammed into Isle of Palms in September 1989 with 135-miles-per-hour winds and 20-foot-high waves. The two oceanside holes on the Links Course were destroyed. Most of the resort's

buildings were flattened. Over a thousand trees were up-
rooted. What the prehistoric hurricane had left on the island,
Hugo sought to reclaim.

The Links Course has been rebuilt, with designer Tom Fazio
directing work (without fee) on the reconstruction of the two
oceanside holes. The companion Harbor Course was completely altered, by common agreement for the better, a classic
case of necessity being the mother of invention. But over a
year later, barely a quarter of the resort's lodging units had
been rebuilt, a new golf and tennis center was not scheduled
to open until the spring of 1991, and there were some specu-
lation that a tightening economy and the immensity of the job
to be done might delay Wild Dunes' complete comeback in-
definitely.

The point of all this is not that the most tragic result of Hurricane Hugo was the wrecking of a gold-medal golf resort. That
would be obscene, given the horrible devastation at Charleston
and elsewhere, not to mention the loss of lives to Hugo.

The point is that the golf resorts perched on the barrier islands from Florida to North Carolina along Hurricane Alley are
mighty vulnerable to Mother Nature. When she decides to re-
arrange some dunes, or aerate the land by ripping out a few
thousand trees, or cut a new channel, or move a barrier island
a few inches west, or blow away some buildings to pay back
greedy land developers for their assaults on the Low Country's
indigenous culture and fragile ecosystems, she damn well
does it.

The moral? Don't take your golf vacation along Hurricane
Alley in hurricane season.

AMELIA ISLAND

Okay, you've been waiting patiently since we struck out on the
New England Tour back in Chapter 1, so here it is . . .

GOLF TIP NUMBER 1

How to Blast Out of the Sand on Amelia Island

1. *Dig both feet down until the sand covers your shoe-
laces; you must have an absolutely solid mooring to
pull off this shot.*

2. *Close the club face of your pitching wedge—not your sand wedge, which you can leave at home—to ensure maximum penetration as your club head moves through the sand.*

3. *Take a full backswing, rotating your hips to the max, and swing down and through as hard as possible, entering the sand about four inches behind the ball. The idea is to take as much sand as you can.*

4. *Make a full turn and follow through so that you're facing the flag, but ignore the flight of the ball. Instead, check the shower of sand for flying pieces of eight.*

Now, before you start complaining about how that tip flies in the face (not to mention the hair) of everything you've ever read about sand play, answer this question: when was the last time you got up and down out of a greenside bunker? Just as I thought—it's not as if you'd mastered all the other tips about sand play you've studied so assiduously over the years. Besides, my tip wasn't about saving par, but about finding buried treasure on Amelia Island.

The first tourists to visit Amelia Island weren't a foursome of Atlanta proctologists looking to polish their single-digit handicaps. The first tourists were notorious hustlers like Red Legs Greaves, Calico Jack, Gasparilla, Blackbeard, and Captain Kidd, guys who always improved their lies, always used a foot mashie in the rough, and always coughed while you putted. To heinous villains like them, tapping down spike marks around the hole in brazen violation of USGA rules was no worse than cutting a throat, which is what they routinely did to anybody who wouldn't let them play through. They were bloodthirsty, rampaging, pillaging pirates, those early visitors, which is why legends persist today of treasure chests stuffed with gold doubloons that they left buried in Amelia Island's shifting sands.

(So what do you think *now* of my golf tip?)

You'd expect, after 20 years of digging to construct 45 holes of terrific golf, 23 tennis courts, 650 units of resort housing in 16 residential clusters, a world-class spa, numerous swimming pools, and 1,500 private homes, the developers of the Amelia Island Plantation ("plantation" is the code word for "development" in this part of the world) would have found *something*. But no, not so much as a brass farthing.

I figure the loot is still there. Big and fancy as the resort is, with every creature comfort attended to and plenty of balm for the soul as well, there are twelve hundred and fifty acres of sand, shrubs, pines, dogwoods, live oaks, marshes, Spanish moss, and lagoons there, mostly of your pristine nature, and I think they just haven't dug in the right spot . . . yet. Why else would *Golf* magazine continue to award Amelia Island a *gold* medal as one of America's top twelve golf resorts?

AMELIA ISLAND PLANTATION Highway A1A South, Amelia Island, Florida 32034. About 35 minutes north of Jacksonville International Airport. Telephone: (800) 874-6878. <u>Accommodations</u>: 650 units, ranging from hotel-style rooms to deluxe 3-bedroom villas. <u>Amenities</u>: Fishing (offshore, surf, lagoons, bass fishing in famed Lofton Creek); 23 tennis courts, top-rated instructional programs; fitness center and spa; horseback riding (on the beach as well as inland); youth program (huge range of activities for kids); and more (paddleboating on lagoons, bicycle paths, hiking through 1,250-acre complex). <u>Terms</u>: From $153 for a non-ocean view double room (hotel-style) to $401 for a deluxe ocean view villa (1 bedroom). The 3-bedroom villa is only $507, so why not bring both sets of parents and save a bundle?

What's that? Well, yes, I suppose it could also have something to do with the resort's two golf courses. As matter of fact, now that you mention it, I'm sure it does.

The original twenty-seven-hole Pete Dye layout, which opened for play in 1975, is a short but treacherous foray through salt marsh, sand dunes, and live oak trees dripping Spanish moss. Dye must be partial to trees, because the fairways are narrower than the gap between Lauren Hutton's two front teeth. The greens are small and tricky ("It breaks toward the water" doesn't help much here because there's water everywhere), and they're well guarded by sand (both bunker and dune formats). None of the three nines tops 3,000 yards from the regular tees, but that doesn't make driving a day at the beach; anyone who sprays the ball is going to be looking at some big numbers at the end of the day. Short-but-straight hitters, on the other hand, will walk away with everybody else's money.

AMELIA LINKS

Design: Pete Dye

Year Open: 1975

Oakmarsh
3,308 Yards   70.5 Rating   130 Slope

Oceanside
2,831 Yards   69.3 Rating   121 Slope

Oysterbay
3,153 Yards   68.8 Rating   121 Slope

Information: (904) 261-6161, extension 5381

⭐

The Dye cast at Amelia Island Plantation is tricky without being tricked up, demanding but not ridiculous. The Ocean-side and Oakmarsh nines earned the course a place in *Golf Digest*'s tabulation of "America's 75 Best Resort Courses," but you can substitute the Oysterbay nine for either of them and not feel like a guest at a B-list party. And you can play them back to back to back and feel like you've earned a second cocktail in the Admiral's Lounge before your Mousseline of Crab and Jumbo Shrimp in the Dune Side Club.

Still hungry for golf the next morning? Make for Tom Fazio's Long Point Club, a younger (1987) but bigger brother to the Dye course. There's a little more of everything at Long Point.

LONG POINT CLUB

Design: Tom Fazio

Year Open: 1987
6,775 Yards   72.5 Rating   127 Slope

Information: (904) 261-6161, extension 5381

⭐

More live oaks, more water, more marsh, more yards—about 700 more from the back tees. The greens are bigger, too, which opens up three-putt opportunities that don't exist on the Dye nines. Like the Dye course, Long Point is beautiful and, because of the marshy nature of the land around it, even more pristine, particularly on the back nine.

Not that there has to be, but there's more to Amelia Island than golf. A four-mile-long stretch of beach, horseback riding, excellent bass fishing in nearby streams and lagoons, bicycling on trails blazed through thick forests, visiting the funky old port of Fernandina Beach up the road, and playing tennis on one of the resort's twenty-three courts should fill your days if you come to your senses and give up golf.

Plus, of course, there's always Captain Kidd's treasure chest to look for. Speaking of which, I have this old map with an "X" marked in the sand trap on the . . . well, to find out *which* hole, you're just going to have to get out there and dig.

ST. SIMONS ISLAND

The grand dame of all the golf islands dotted along Hurricane Alley is St. Simons, located due north of Amelia about forty miles as the dolphin swims. (You can figure nearly twice that by car.) Hilton Head has been in the golf vacation business since 1959, Kiawah since 1976, and Amelia since 1975. But St. Simons first started catering to upper-crust duffers back in 1928, when The Cloister opened its doors on Sea Island.

(An island unto itself because of a skinny little meandering river that cuts it off from St. Simons proper, Sea Island is in every important cultural and historical sense an integral part of the larger whole, evidence of which is the fact that The Cloister's Sea Island Golf Club is located on the southern end of St. Simons. 'Nuff said.)

The original hotel, a small affair with only forty-six rooms, was designed by Addison Mizner, the architect responsible for the fabled Boca Raton Resort Hotel in Florida. The style was "Spanish Mediterranean," which translates as tiled roofs and stucco walls, a choice the Spanish Franciscans who established a mission at St. Simons in 1568 would have blessed. Subsequent additions echo Mizner's original themes. Today, The Cloister's 264 rooms are clustered in 4 smaller buildings and 9 guest houses as well as in the main hotel.

THE CLOISTER Sea Island, Georgia 31561. Halfway between Savannah and Jacksonville, just across the Intercoastal from Brunswick, Georgia. Telephone: (800) SEA-ISLA. (That's the only unclassy thing about The Cloister.) <u>Accommodations</u>: 264 rooms of substantially varying sizes and views. <u>Amenities</u>: Posh. My favorites are the putting green and the pitch-and-putt located on the grounds, the 5 miles of private ocean beach, and the 10,000 acres of development-free forest. <u>Terms</u>: In high season (from March 15 to May 31), from $124 per person for a "regular" room to $346 per person for a "deluxe oceanfront room" (double occupancy); Full American Plan. No credit cards. Checks accepted.

President Calvin Coolidge presided at the opening of The Cloister, possibly the single most energetic act of his presidency. Presidents Dwight Eisenhower and Gerald Ford visited The Cloister while in office, presumably to play golf. President Jimmy Carter was a guest, probably out of loyalty to a Georgia institution. (Given their values and their personal commitment to helping the helpless, though, I don't see Jimmy and Rosalynn being all that comfortable at The Cloister, which probably burned their sheets after their departure rather than risk offending the hostelry's rock-ribbed Republican clientele.)

But certainly the most intriguing entry in the hotel's register is that of a pair of newlyweds—he was a Navy lieutenant, she the daughter of a magazine publisher—who came to The Cloister on their honeymoon. They signed in on January 9, 1945. Their names: Mr. and Mrs. George Bush.

(Come to think of it, he was probably there for the golf; she got the honeymoon.)

The Cloister follows the same blueprint for gracious good living and subdued elegance as the grand hotels visited back in Chapter 13, but with a Southern drawl even more pronounced than either The Greenbrier or The Homestead. Like them, it commands 5 stars and 5 diamonds from the stars and diamonds people (although it does have to make do with a mere silver medal from *Golf* magazine). But The Cloister is even more firmly rooted in another era: it offers Full American Plan only, and it accepts no credit cards. (The hotel will take your check, probably without demanding two forms of ID; or it will send you a bill after your departure. Can you believe it?)

A bastion of Southern comfort and relentless charm, The Cloister positively drips with tradition and gentility, from the croquet games on the lawn to tea in the lounges on chilly winter afternoons to the Friday night plantation supper. Gentlemen will please wear coat and tie to dinner, thank you very much. My, you certainly look lovely tonight, Miss Melanie.

You don't need to wear a coat and tie on the golf course, even though the four separate nines by four different architects that constitute the Sea Island Golf Club were built by four different architects on the site of one of the antebellum South's most famous plantations. (No, not Tara.) The Retreat Plantation in the late eighteenth century perfected "Sea Island cotton," a high-quality long staple varietal whose fame lived long after King Cotton was killed in the Civil War. About all that's left as

SEA ISLAND GOLF CLUB

Design: Walter Travis/Colt & Alison
Year Open: 1927/1929
3,272 Yards   70.8 Rating   121 Slope

Seaside
Design: Colt & Alison
Year Open: 1929
3,333 Yards   71.8 Rating   124 Slope

Retreat
Design: Dick Wilson
Year Open: 1960
3,326 Yards   71.6 Rating   126 Slope

Marshside
Design: Joe Lee
Year Open: 1973
3,192 Yards   70.4 Rating   121 Slope
Information: (912) 638-5518

★

a reminder of those times is the "Avenue of Oaks" that used to lead up to the big house, a corn barn that now houses the golf clubhouse, an old burial ground, and the ruins of Retreat's slave hospital.

You could probably start another civil war at the nineteenth hole by getting Sea Island regulars going over which two of the four nines make the most enjoyable eighteen, but Seaside (1929) and Plantation (1927), the two oldest nines at Sea Island, form the course ranked by *Gold Digest* among the top fifty resort courses in the country. The other two, Retreat (1960) and Marshside (1973), are solid, perfectly maintained courses only a notch less interesting than their older brothers. Seaside is a links course built on the edge of St. Simons Sound; Plantation and Retreat wind back in among the live oaks and Spanish moss; and Marshside squeegees through a salt marsh crisscrossed by tidal inlets.

The best thing about the Sea Island Golf Club overall? No condos. No luxury vacation homes overlooking any tee box, fairway, or green. No nothing except trees and golf. Yes, Virginia, there is a Santa Claus.

The best hole? Probably the seventeenth at Seaside, one of the greatest par 4s in golf. You can play left off the tee, in which case your ball needs to stay aloft 220 yards to carry White Heron Creek, the payoff for doing so being an unobstructed second shot to the green. Or you can play right off the tee, a much safer route, but one that leaves you looking at two huge, mounded bunkers that hide the green. Your call.

Next door, the St. Simons Golf Club has a fine Joe Lee course that's also open to Cloister guests, should you grow tired of the four Sea Island nines. I figure that could happen after three, four weeks.

ST. SIMONS ISLAND GOLF CLUB

Design: Joe Lee

Year Open: 1971

6,490 Yards   71 Rating   120 Slope

Information: (912) 638-5131

And if you like a little less starch in your underwear, you might want to try the King and Prince Beach Resort, a smaller, less formal, but still venerable hotel at the tip of St. Simons. The decor here is Spanish colonial, and the style considerably less grand, but the King and Prince has been doing a good job catering to its middle-crust clientele since opening in 1935.

KING AND PRINCE BEACH RESORT P.O. Box 798, St. Simons Island, Georgia 31552. Just across the Intercostal from Brunswick. Telephone: (800) 342-1212. Accommodations: 125 rooms in hotel, 48 in condo units. Amenities: Beach, indoor/outdoor pools, tennis. Terms: $69 without ocean view, $99 with ocean view. With is better.

★

There is a hitch. Guests at the King and Prince can get a tee time at the Sea Island Golf Club only on an "as available" basis. Practically speaking, this is not a problem except during high season, but there are no guarantees, and no way to know in advance.

The fallback is not a half-bad one, though, as guests of the King and Prince do have playing privileges at the Hampton Club, a private course about ten minutes away. This 6,465-yard Joe Lee track is a beauty with a twist: holes twelve through fifteen are laid out on a series of four small islands in the salt marsh that borders the main body of the course. Make a side bet on who in your foursome drowns the fewest balls.

THE HAMPTON CLUB

Design: Joe Lee
Year Open: 1989
6,465 Yards   71.4 Rating   122 Slope
Information: (912) 634-0265

★

A couple of final, not altogether relevant notes: St. Simons is the place where John and Charles Wesley first began to spread the gospel of Methodism in the colonies in 1736; and it is the

place where Vice President Aaron Burr sought refuge after kill-
ing Alexander Hamilton in a duel—proving once again that
you can run, but you can't hide.

HILTON HEAD

Once upon a time, Hilton Head was the cat's pajamas, the hottest ticket in town, the playground of preference for the newly
rich whose life ambition was to have a vacation home on the
fairway and a magnolia tree in the backyard. So what if you
had to settle for a condo overlooking a parking lot: Hilton Head
was still an exclusive address, one that unleashed flood tides
of envy when you mentioned it casually in the club bar back
home.

Thirty-something years after Sea Pines opened as the proto-
typical modern mega golf-residential-resort development, one
that has been copied up and down the Eastern Seaboard, the
picture is a little different. Today Hilton Head is home to about
20,000 full-time residents, plus nearly twice that many tourists
on a given day. At times the William Hilton Parkway (Highway
278), which runs almost the full length of the foot-shaped island, resembles the Santa Ana Freeway at rush hour, particularly when a big convention hits town. You got your Wal-Mart,
you got your Golden Arches, you got your Days Inn. There are
still plenty of fancy houses spread among the trees, but now
they have to share their once-exclusive paradise with ticky-
tacky time shares. It ain't the same.

All this means that Hilton Head is now accessible to the likes
of me, so I'm not really complaining. What do I care if another
secluded hideaway for the affluent few gets overrun with the
guys from my foursome? But this book is supposedly about
5-star golf vacations, so it's fair to ask why bother including
Hilton Head. The answer is easy: because of the golf.

There are thirty golf courses at Hilton Head and immediate
environs. (Call 803-681-5980 for *Golfer's Guide,* a free hand-
book that describes them all.) Most of the thirty are accessible
(one way or another) to the traveling golfer, several are worth
a detour, and a trio are among the very best courses in the
country. If you don't think that's sufficient reason for visiting
Hilton Head, then maybe you picked up the wrong book by
mistake.

The best place to stay on Hilton Head is the Palmetto Dunes Resort, which in 1990 received a silver medal from *Golf* magazine as one of the country's top golf resorts. Palmetto Dunes has all the usual amenities, from tennis to water sports to decent restaurants, plus it has three golf courses that are better than any other public (i.e., resort) course on the island save one, Harbour Town at Sea Pines.

You could make a good case for staying at Sea Pines, which has two other so-so courses as well as Harbour Town. It's a judgment call, but I'd rather have easy walking access to the Palmetto Dunes trio and drive to Harbour Town than vice versa. Plus at Sea Pines all accommodations are in villas (i.e., condos) and private homes that are spread out all over the "plantation" (i.e., real estate development), and I'm just not a big fan of condos. If you are, the Sea Pines information number is (800) 845-6131.

You have a couple of housing options at Palmetto Dunes, but your best bet is the Hyatt Regency. It's a huge place (505 rooms), but it's been recently renovated and makes up for its lack of intimacy with a whole gang of convenience. I'm a believer in not having to drive to the first tee when I'm on vacation—except, of course, when Hord Hardin calls up Motel-6 and asks me to drop by for a game.

The three courses at Palmetto Dunes are named after their three designers, all of them household names in houses where golfers live.

HYATT REGENCY HILTON HEAD (PALMETTO DUNES) P.O. Box 6167, Hilton Head Island, South Carolina 29938. About 45 minutes from the Savannah Airport. Telephone: (800) 233-1234. <u>Accommodations</u>: 505 rooms, including 31 suites and 2 Regency Club (concierge) floors. <u>Amenities</u>: 3 golf courses; 25 tennis courts; fitness center; beach; three pools; full range of water sports, including water skiing and windsurfing; bicycling on beaches and 25 miles of bicycle paths; horseback riding; bird watching in four nature preserves (not to be confused with birdie watching on the 3 golf courses). <u>Terms</u>: From $125 to $290.

★

The oldest and friendliest is the Robert Trent Jones Course, whose abundance of water is fairly easily avoidable because of the generously wide fairways. ("Fairly easily" means I didn't have to buy a sleeve of balls at the turn.) The Jones is no cakewalk, but neither is it one of his championship tracks. Have fun and score well.

The middle child and the toughest to handle is the George Fazio Course, which opened in 1974 and has been bringing golfers to their knees with its 132 slope rating ever since. Slope rates a course on a number of factors, only one of them length. But at 6,873 yards, it's Fazio's length that gnaws at your handicap, principally because it has only two par 5s. Eight of the par 4s are 400-plus-yards long from the gold (i.e., championship) tees, and six of them are 400-plus from the blues. I don't

---

ROBERT TRENT JONES COURSE AT PALMETTO DUNES

Design: Robert Trent Jones

Year Open: 1969

6,707 Yards   72.3 Rating   123 Slope

Information: (803) 785-1138

ARTHUR HILLS COURSE AT PALMETTO DUNES

Design: Arthur Hills

Year Open: 1986

6,651 Yards   71.4 Rating   127 Slope

Information: (804) 785-1140

GEORGE FAZIO COURSE AT PALMETTO DUNES

Design: George Fazio

Year Open: 1974

6,873 Yards   72.4 Rating   132 Slope

Information: (803) 785-1130

★

know about you, but there's a direct correlation between the number of two- and three-irons and fairway woods I hit and the number of 6s that turn up on my scorecard. By the time I get to the finishing hole, a 462/445/432-yard monster, I'm usually finished. Even so, it's a terrific course, one that deserves its ranking among *Golf Digest*'s top fifty resort courses in the U.S.A.

Almost certain to join it once it ages a bit is the youngest of the three Palmetto Dunes tracks, the Arthur Hills Course. Brian McCallen of *Golf* magazine calls it "a prototype links with New Age touches, like heroic carries over water and thick clumps of love grass on the dunes." The links feel comes from the rolling dunes that Hills was smart enough to leave where he found them. Because he employed the natural terrain so well, Hills didn't need to introduce fairway traps (there are none) or rough (there's very little) to give the course definition, and he counted on the natural fairway undulations to give it teeth. Give the Hills a bullet now and watch it rise on the charts in the next few years.

By the way, anyone meeting love grass up close and personal will understand immediately why Robert Mitchum wrote H-A-T-E on the knuckles of his other hand in *Night of the Hunter*. Hit it in the middle of the stuff and you're better off taking an unplayable than trying to hack it out. Trust me on this one

As much good, wholesome, outdoor fun as the Palmetto Dunes three provide, however, they are not the headline act at Hilton Head. Since 1969, when a forty-year-old named Arnold Palmer won the first-ever Heritage Classic, that honor has gone to the Harbour Town Links.

There are a handful of special stops on the PGA Tour that the pros genuinely love, not just for the money or the prestige of

---

HARBOUR TOWN GOLF LINKS

Design: Pete Dye (with Jack Nicklaus carrying his bag)

Year Open: 1969
6,650 Yards   74 Rating   134 Slope

Information: (803) 671-2446

★

Private—Members Only*
*(But There Are Ways)

Three of the best courses at Hilton Head are private: the Long Cove Club, a 1981 Pete Dye design ranked twenty-first among the country's top 100 courses by *Golf Digest*; the Calibogue Course at the Haig Point Club on nearby Daufuskie Island, a spectacular Rees Jones track that *Golf Digest* ranks twenty-eighth; and a Jack Nicklaus course, the Melrose, also on Daufuskie Island.

The first is worth calling in every favor ever owed you, just for the chance to experience Pete Dye at his pluperfect best. Get letters from your home pro, your club president (if you belong to a club), your pastor, Strom Thurmond, anybody who might carry a little clout in this corner of South Carolina. Long Cove is that fine a course.

Haig Point is an easier nut to crack. All you have to do to play there as a guest is be a bona fide potential buyer of an outrageously overpriced slice of the real estate development that is the reason why the course came into existence in the first place. Recently, though, since our 1980s chickens have started coming home to roost, the real estate market for luxury vacation homes has been a little slow, there are no Silverados waiting in line to shovel the Daufuskie Island developers a little FDIC-guaranteed long green to tide them over until Ronald Reagan gets re-elected.

What's all that got to do with the price of a good cigar? Well, it means that the definition of "bona fide potential buyer" may have gotten a little looser. It's a matter for you and your conscience to work out, but I have a feeling that if you have given even a passing thought to buying a vacation home any time in the next decade or so, the real estate people out on Daufuskie would be just tickled pink to pocket your greens fee for a round (or two) on their very private course.

Call the Haig Point sales office at (800) 992-3635 for information about homesites (they start at $70,000) and about visiting the golf club. Don't tell them I sent you.

★

the event, but for the golf course as well. Riviera, home of the
Los Angeles Open, is one such place. Colonial in Fort Worth is
another. Harbour Town is in the same league.

The pros love Harbour Town so much that Greg Norman,
speaking for all of them, incurred a big fine from the PGA Tour
a few years back for complaining loudly and publicly about
course conditions. (If you can't say something nice, don't say
anything at all is the Tour's official policy.) For a decade or so,
as the Sea Pines empire disintegrated in the face of recession,
mismanagement, and Chapter 11, Harbour Town had been going to pot. Unpruned trees turned tough approach shots into
impossible ones, already small greens eroded to postage-
stamp size, and heavy public usage took a steeper toll as
maintenance budgets were pinched. Fortunately, Norman's
blast worked. New Sea Pine owners, embarrassed by his criti-
cism and fearful of losing the MCI Heritage Classic, embarked
on a costly five-year renovation program designed to bring this
early Pete Dye masterwork to what it once was.

Play this strong, traditional course as it wanders through
moss-covered live oaks and get a crash course on making strategic choices. Understand anew the importance in classical
golf of the middle- and long-iron approach shot, as you try to
hit Harbour Town's small greens. Feel the rush as you come
out of the woods for the grand, demanding finish on seventeen
and eighteen with the Calibogue Sound to the left and the Harbour Town lighthouse dead ahead.

My guess is that along about then you'll be in 100 percent
agreement with Curtis Strange, who says that "Harbour Town
is one of my five favorite courses in the world."

KIAWAH ISLAND

The final island stop on our whirlwind run up Hurricane Alley
considers itself just plain damned lucky to still be there to
greet us. When Hurricane Hugo smashed into the South Carolina coast in 1989 it devastated Charleston and the surrounding area but left Kiawah Island, just about twenty miles to the
south, virtually unscathed. That was a great break for the traveling golfer, because the Kiawah Island Inn is one of the premier golf resorts on the Eastern Seaboard.

Start with the food. You might as well, because check-in
time is not until 4 P.M., and frantically trying to squeeze in a

round before dark doesn't make any sense when there are so many delicious local oysters, shrimp, crab, and clams to be eaten before bedtime. Carolina Low Country cuisine is built around seafood, and nobody does it better than the folks in the kitchen at the **Jasmine Porch.**

KIAWAH ISLAND INN P.O. Box 12357, Charleston, South Carolina 29412. About 20 miles south of Charleston. Telephone: 800-654-2924. <u>Accommodations</u>: 150 rooms in the inn, 260 villas (from 1 to 4 bedrooms). <u>Amenities</u>: 26 tennis courts, 2 pools, beach; full range of activities and programs for kids, 3 to 12. <u>Terms</u>: Inn rooms come in woods view, lagoon, dunes view, ocean view, and deluxe ocean view at $125, $135, $155, $175, and $195, respectively. One-bedroom villas range from $145 to $245, depending (but not exclusively, one hopes) on the view.

The restaurant, located within the Kiawah Island Inn, offers great views out to sea as well as first-class renditions of Low Country classics. It's a great place to spend the late afternoon, sipping a little she-crab soup and waiting for the sunset. And the early evening, working on a steaming seafood pie redolent of fresh herbs. And the late evening, rationalizing that you're on vacation and you'll work off the Carolina mud cake tomorrow. Before you know it, it's time for breakfast. (Be sure to have the shrimp grits; they're a local delicacy.)

But you didn't come all this way to eat, however appealing the idea might seem. You came here to play golf at three courses with three utterly different personalities.

MARSH POINT AT KIAWAH ISLAND

Design: Gary Player
Year Open: 1976
6,203 Yards   71.8 Rating   126 Slope
Information: (803) 768-2121

TURTLE POINT AT KIAWAH ISLAND

Design: Jack Nicklaus
Year Open: 1981
6,919 Yards   73.5 Rating   132 Slope
Information: (803) 768-2121

OSPREY POINT AT KIAWAH ISLAND

Design: Tom Fazio
Year Open: 1988
6,678 Yards   71.8 Rating   127 Slope
Information: (803) 768-2121

★

Marsh Point, designed by Gary Player, is aptly named. Water comes into play on thirteen holes (even more, if you play the way I do). The problem is, you don't see all the water until after you're in it, as many of the hazards are invisible from the tee box. Not fair? I agree. But the second time around, you can score on this stretched-out former executive course because it's only 6,203 yards from the back tees. Now that you know where the water is, all you have to do is hit it where it isn't. (No extra charge for this golf tip.)

Turtle Point, designed by Jack Nicklaus and named one of the top seventy-five resort courses in the country by *Golf Digest*, is long, lean, and mean. Built mostly in a forest, the fair-

ways are so narrow that you think maybe the blade broke on
Jack's saw. (He really could have cut down a few more trees,
particularly on the par 5s where I usually trot out my double-
fast swing to get a little extra mileage.) Then, on the back nine,
you pop out of the woods for two long par 3s and a long par 4
right along the ocean, where the wind treats your tee ball like
a badminton shuttlecock. You'd be a whole lot more confident
about going back into the woods to finish with a couple of pars
if the green of the 429-yard par 4 eighteenth weren't wedged
in behind a pond.

Osprey Point, designed by Tom Fazio, is also carved out of a
forest, but one with four natural lakes that Fazio has managed
to turn into hazards on fifteen holes. (It's a loaves and fishes
deal, as far as I see, with maybe a little bulldozer help here
and there.) Unlike Marsh Point, Osprey Point gives you a good
look at the water you're about to hit into. I've always said that
honesty is the best policy.

The big news on Kiawah, of course, is the big course that
Pete Dye has built for the 1991 Ryder Cup matches. How big?
About 7,200 yards from the championship tees, give or take a
half wedge. That's big. Dye was given two and a half miles of
primo beachfront to work with, and the commitment from
Landmark, the company that owns the resort, that there would
never be any real estate development immediately around the
course. This book went to press before it was opened for play,
but on the basis of preliminary sightings it promises to be a
great course, one worthy of what has become in recent years
a great sporting event.

(It's still an odd choice for the Ryder Cup—a brand-new
course, when so many older, prestigious courses would have
leaped at the honor; not all that easy to get to on causeways
never intended to handle the kind of traffic this year's matches
could draw; and smack dab in the middle of Hurricane Alley
in September, which is when Wild Dunes—just thirty miles
away—was flattened. But that has to do with some mighty peculiar politics inside the PGA of America, and not with where
you spend your vacation.)

This will, I predict, be hailed by everyone who plays it as one
of the great courses of the world. And as tough as it will be for
the pros from the back tee. The Ocean Course's wide landing
avenues will make it playable by ordinary hackers. The ocean
is in view from every hole, ten of the holes play alongside the

beach, and there's not a condo in sight. If you can find a more exhilarating test of golf anywhere in the land, I'd like to join your foursome.

When to Go

Winter days can be chilly, particularly if the ocean winds are up, but with a sweater you'll be just fine. July and August are the wettest months, but most of the moisture comes in late afternoon showers. August and September can be dicey because of tropical storms. Spring is the best time, but a lot of other people think so, too. But who are we kidding? The weather anytime in Hurricane Alley is generally as good as the best weather anywhere else. So go anytime.

OFF COURSE

One thing about the barrier islands that you stop at on your Hurricane Alley tour is that once you're there, it doesn't make a lot of sense to leave in search of fun and games. The one exception is Kiawah, where you should definitely budget a day for visiting **Charleston.** People who knew the city before Hugo will weep at its frightful wounds; people who have never seen it before will marvel at how beautiful it still is. Everywhere else, don't leave camp.

CHAPTER 17

LUCK OF THE IRISH

The Emerald Necklace

ET'S HAVE A LOOK AT IRELAND AND INDIANA.
They are, geographically speaking, roughly the same size and shape; and both there names contain seven letters and start with the same vowel. But other than that, they don't have anything in common. For instance, the most important city in Ireland is Dublin, a fabled and fascinating place, one of the great cities of the world; the most important city in Indiana is Indianapolis, which shines only in comparison with Terre Haute. The average annual rainfall in Ireland is almost twice what it is in Indiana. In seacoast, Ireland enjoys a commanding lead over Indiana, a couple of thousand miles to 0. And at any given time during the day or night in Indiana, it's a full five hours later in Ireland.

But the main difference is that Ireland has over 400 golf courses for its 5 million inhabitants—taking the population of the Republic of Ireland and Northern Ireland together, which is not how everyone there wants to be taken—while Indiana, with half a million more people, has only 333 golf courses. Moreover, the traveling golfer is welcome at all 400-plus Irish courses, while he couldn't get past the parking lot at the 101 Hoosier courses that are "Private—Members Only."

That's why this chapter is about Ireland, not Indiana.

If you didn't know Scotland had invented golf, you'd swear it got its start in Ireland, so seamlessly is the game woven into the fabric of Irish society. In Ireland you're never more than twenty-five miles from a golf course, be it a nine-hole village track or a championship layout. As in Scotland, golfers in Ireland look on golf as an essential part of everyday life. A golf course is not a place to do business, or a place to wear silly clothes you wouldn't be caught dead in anywhere else, or a place to flash your wealth and power by setting up barriers to keep nonmembers out. It's a place where the game's the thing.

Nowhere is this more evident than among the jewels that constitute the Emerald Necklace, the tour of Ireland's great links outlined below. Starting at Dublin, and working counterclockwise three quarters of the way around the Irish shore, the traveling golfer can experience links golf the equal of anything in Scotland. On sandy, treeless land shaped by water and wind as the sea retreated millions of years ago, these courses seem as natural a part of the landscape as the giant dunes and wild grass that define their fairways.

So different from golf courses in America that they seem to be for another game, golf-like but not quite golf as we know it, links take some getting used to. If this is your first experience, you may not like them at first ("Too much wind. Too many dunes and too much rough to negotiate. Too many elevated greens. Too much wind. Courses not as well manicured as at home. Punitive rough. Too many sidehill lies. Too much wind.")

But be forewarned. Links touch some people's souls with a magic wand. Ask Tom Watson. Ask Ben Crenshaw. Once touched, you'll never be the same.

Heavy wind today? Good. Let's play.

1. ROYAL DUBLIN

Located just three miles from downtown Dublin along the north side of Dublin Bay, Royal Dublin is a strong course, challenging enough to host many major events, including Irish Opens won by Seve Ballesteros (1983, 1985) and Bernhard Langer (1984). It plays to 6,828 yards and par 73, which is cut back to 72 for tournaments by turning the tough eighteenth

(dogleg right with OB on same side to discourage corner-cutters) from a short par 5 into a huge par 4. Says Lee Travino: "The finish here, from the thirteenth tee onward, is as tough as you find in golf." Open to visitors except on Saturdays and Wednesday afternoons, (Irish doctors have to play sometime, don't they?) Royal Dublin is a great course.

Set up base camp for the first two stops on the Emerald Necklace tour at the Sutton Castle Hotel just outside Dublin. Once you leave Dublin, though, I strongly suggest you take potluck at the small hotels and bed-and-breakfast places that dot the coastline. Although I do note a couple of grand exceptions later on, in my experience you simply can't go wrong in rural and coastal Ireland by following a simple rule with regard to lodging: the smaller, the better.

SUTTON CASTLE HOTEL Redrock, Sutton County Dublin. About 4 miles from Dublin Airport. Telephone: (01) 322688. <u>Accommodations</u>: 20 rooms. <u>Amenities</u>: Sailing and fishing across the road, and plenty of golf nearby.

★

2. PORTMARNOCK

If the rough isn't knee-high by late July, there's been a drought. Ireland's premier tournament course (thirteen times the site of the Irish Open), Portmarnock is laid out among rolling sand dunes on a peninsula that juts out into Dublin Bay. Don't go by the yardage alone in selecting clubs: for example, figure to hit a driver and a 2-iron on windy days at the 385-yard four-teenth—and that's almost every day. The most memorable hole: the famous fifteenth, a 192-yard par 3 that runs parallel to the beach, thereby subjecting tee shots to offshore winds powerful enough to blow them sideways. Says Ben Crenshaw: "The fifteenth has to be the best par 3 on earth." That, from a man with firsthand knowledge of the seventh at Pebble Beach and the twelfth at Augusta National, is not a load of blarney.

3. COUNTY LOUTH (BALTRAY)

Great Britain's leading golf publication, *Golf World*, calls County Louth (also known as Baltray, for the name of the town where it's located) one of the best-kept secrets of Irish golf. We've heard that one before, but this time it's true. A strong, interesting course that forces you to think as well as swing—the two weakest parts of my game, unfortunately. In addition to great golf, County Louth has fourteen bedrooms for rent at shockingly low rates. Throw in a great Irish breakfast and you have one of the great B&B&G (Bed & Breakfast & Golf) deals this side of golf heaven.

4. ROYAL COUNTY DOWN

Across the border in Northern Ireland, County Down is one of the great ones. Huge sandhills, covered in heather and gorse, dominate the landscape. Every hole nestles in its own valley bordered by giant dunes, while in the background the Moun-tains of Mourne that frame the course march down to the edge of the sea. It is a stunningly beautiful, dramatic setting. Royal County Down was designed by Old Tom Morris way back when, and it remains today one of the four or five greatest courses in the British Isles. Great name, too.

5. ROYAL PORTRUSH

It seems that a giant named Finn McCool once tried to build a causeway to the Hebridean Island of Straffa so that he could bring his lady love, a giantess of surpassing beauty, back to Ireland. The sea swept him and the causeway away, and all

The Emerald Necklace

1. ROYAL DUBLIN GOLF CLUB

North Bull Island, Dollymount
Dublin 3, County Dublin
Republic of Ireland
Telephone: (01) 336346

2. PORTMARNOCK GOLF CLUB

Portmarnock, County Dublin
Republic of Ireland
Telephone: (01) 323082

3. COUNTY LOUTH GOLF CLUB

Baltray, Drogheda
County Louth
Republic of Ireland
Telephone: (041) 22329/22444

4. ROYAL COUNTY DOWN GOLF CLUB

Newcastle, County Down
Northern Ireland
Telephone: (039) 6723314

5. ROYAL PORTRUSH GOLF CLUB

Bushmills Road, Portrush
Country Antrim
Northern Ireland
Telephone: (0265) 822311

6. COUNTY SLIGO GOLF CLUB

Rosses Point, County Sligo
Republic of Ireland
Telephone: (071) 77134

7. LAHINCH GOLF CLUB

Lahinch, County Clare
Republic of Ireland
Telephone: (065) 81003

8. BALLYBUNION GOLF CLUB

Ballybunion, County Kerry
Republic of Ireland
Telephone: (068) 27146

that is left today are gigantic boulders and what appear to be sculpted stone pillars rising from the sea.

And so it came to pass that a spectacular stretch of seashore in the north is known as the Causeway Coast, after the Giant's Causeway. Go. See it yourself. No way those rocks were cut to such uniform shape and measure by water and wind. It had to be a giant. Had to be.

The Royal Portrush Golf Club is located on the coastal road that runs from the Giant's Causeway past the ruins of Dunluce Castle, which lent its name to one of the finest links in the British Isles. The Dunluce Course at Royal Portrush is the only course in Ireland to have hosted a British Open (1951). On the occasion, here's what the great British golf writer Bernard Darwin had to say about Royal Portrush:

> It is truly a magnificent course and Mr. H. S. Holt, who designed it in its present form, has thereby built himself a monument more enduring than brass. The course does not disdain the spectacular, such as the one-shot hole called "Calamity Corner" with its terrifying sandy cliffs and its gadarene descent into unknown depths to the right of the green; for the most part the course does not depend on any such dramatic qualities, but on the combined soundness and subtleness of its architecture. . . . I find it hard to imagine a more admirable test of golf.

There are three other terrific links courses within a few miles of Royal Portrush along the Causeway Coast: Portstewart (Telephone: [0265]-832015), Castlerock (Telephone: [0265]-

848314), and Ballycastle (Telephone: [0265]-762536). If there were an award for the "Best Four Links Courses With Twenty-five Miles of Each Other," this quartet would be a favorite. Then there is the powerful appeal of the little hotels and friendly pubs in the unspoiled fishing villages along this magnificent seashore. Who knows, you just might decide to cancel the rest of your trip, take early retirement, change your name to Seamus, get a part-time job at the Bushmills distillery down the road to cover your greens fees, marry someone named Bridgett, and spend the rest of your life trying to solve the mystery of Finn McCool. Can't say that I'd blame you.

6. ROSSES POINT (COUNTY SLIGO)

Ireland is too small for anywhere in it to be truly remote, but everything's relative; and Sligo, on the west coast, is just about as remote as it gets. While not a best-kept secret (thank goodness!), the links course at Rosses Point doesn't get the respect it deserves because it's so far away from where journalists prefer to hang out and from where package tour operators prefer to operate. What that means to you is unhurried midweek golf on a course with wonderful views across Donegal Bay and plenty of golf character. Intones the voice of British golf, Peter "the Mellifluous" Allis: "I think Rosses Point is a gentle sleeping giant and something people should go and look at. I think they will come away marvelling at its beauty. The great test of any golf course is that it can be a tremendous test for the highest quality player and great fun for the modest competitor, and that is where Rosses Point has got it made."

How Far Is It from Here?

Dublin to Baltray	30 miles
Baltray to Newcastle	70 miles
Newcastle to Portrush	88 miles
Portrush to Sligo	121 miles
Sligo to Lahinch	135 miles
Lahinch to Ballybunion	67 miles

★

HALFWAY HOUSE

It's midway through your trip around the Irish coast, you've been logging two rounds a day, you've developed a taste for draft Guinness, and all's right with the world. Suddenly, out of the blue, someone in your traveling party suggests a change of pace from the excellent but modest small hotels and bed-and-breakfasts you've potlucked into since Dublin, and asks plaintively whether there isn't something a bit, you know, more luxurious and splendid in this beautiful but, you have to admit it yourself, sort of empty corner of Ireland, maybe something with a tennis court or two and a spa and some lovely formal gardens to stroll through.

What do you say, sport? What I say to you is be a hero and knock off a little R&R in baronial splendor at Ashford Castle in County Mayo.

Now, before you say "hold the Mayo," let me tell you about Ashford Castle. Piled along the shores of Lough Corrib near the town of Cong, Ashford Castle is a grand hotel with enough storybook appeal to set your companion's Irish eyes to smiling. Lots of crystal, lots of chandeliers, more heavy silver cutlery beside each plate at dinner than is absolutely necessary, enough tapestries to recarpet the entire club back home. The works. (Makes you feel just a little smug for having the foresight to pack your coat of mail; you'd have felt naked without it.) There's even a little nine-hole course on the grounds to warm you up for more formidable dragons to be dealt with in the neighborhood, including one just down the road in Lahinch.

ASHFORD CASTLE Cong, County Mayo. About 25 miles north of Galway. Telephone: (092) 46003. <u>Accommodations</u>: 80 rooms, give or take a dungeon. <u>Amenities</u>: Suitable for a feudal lord. <u>Of special note</u>: the angling classes and the excellent trout and salmon fishing nearby.

★

7. LAHINCH

How can you tell whether it's going to rain? Easy. If the goats are well out on the course at Lahinch, munching peacefully in the rough, the day will be dry. But if they're bunched up closer to the clubhouse, it doesn't matter how sunny the sky is right now—the rain will come before you complete your round. But even if the goats move *into* the clubhouse, a little rain (or even a lot of it) shouldn't dampen your resolve to play this slightly eccentric genius of a course.

First laid out by Old Tom Morris, Lahinch was retooled in 1928 by Alister Mackenzie, who had this to say when he was finished: "Lahinch will make the finest and most popular course that I, or I believe anyone else, ever constructed." This from the man who had just finished Cypress Point and Crystal Downs, and who would presently begin work with Bobby Jones on Augusta National, and who, as a Scot, was not given to over-statement.

Okay, he exaggerated. But only a bit, because Lahinch is—how many times have I said this already?—a truly great golf course. Its hills, hollows, and mounds make every shot a test of perspective, and the subtle rolls and dips in the superb links turf make every lie a bit different from the last. The par 4s are exceptionally strong, with devilishly placed fairway bunkers and strong rough (the goats should eat faster!) placing a pre-mium on accuracy of the tee and ability to hit your mid and long irons.

There is also a delightful anachronism at Lahinch. Called the "Dell," it's a 156-yard par 3 requiring a blind shot to a green hemmed in on three sides by huge mounds. A white stone on the side of the mound in front of the green provides a target line; the stone is moved every time a new hole is cut. What could be easier? All you have to do is pull out your 156-yard club, take aim, and let 'er rip.

After thirty-six holes on a long summer day at the "St. An-drews of Ireland" (as Lahinch is called), you'll probably be in the mood for a little brown whiskey (Jameson's in this part of the Emerald Isle), a joint of mutton, and a big, comfortable turret room in an honest-to-God castle. Dromoland Castle, about forty minutes away near Shannon, has all that and more, including suits of armor, wood-paneled drawing rooms, and walls creaking in history. Once the county seat of the O'Brien clan, it's now a first-class base camp for traveling golfers looking to taste the wild beauty of southwestern Ireland.

(P.S.: If your name is O'Brien, don't bother asking for a discount. Family ties only go so far.)

DROMOLAND CASTLE Newmarket-on-Fergus, County Clare. About 10 miles north of Shannon Airport. Telephone (061) 71144. <u>Accommodations</u>: 75 rooms. <u>Amenities</u>: Befitting a luxury castle.

---

8. BALLYBUNION

Tom Watson on Ballybunion: "It is a course you will always enjoy and never tire of playing. I know I never will. In short, Ballybunion is a course on which golf architects should live and play before they build golf courses."

Peter Dobereiner on Ballybunion: "I have no hesitation in proclaiming that this course is a masterpiece, the greatest links course in the world, and by a clear margin."

Sounds like a meeting of the minds, only there's one little problem: they aren't talking about the same course. Watson is extolling the virtues of the Old Course at Ballybunion, where he spent a week practicing before three of his five British Open championships. Dobereiner, one of the two or three most respected golf writers in the business, is talking about the New Course, designed by Robert Trent Jones and opened for play in 1982.

"It was the finest piece of linksland that I had ever seen," Jones said of the land he was given to fashion into the New Course, "and perhaps the finest piece of linksland in the world." But his piece was cut from the same cloth used to weave the Old Course, so one assumes the same qualities to be present in both. And correctly so. Huge sand dunes, crashing surf, subtly rippled fairways, elevated greens, wind-formed mounds, sweeping vistas out to sea, powerful winds off the ocean . . . the cast is assembled; let the play begin.

There is a lot more great golf in Ireland, particularly down in its southwest corner. Forty minutes south of Ballybunion, on the majestic cliffside that starred in the film *Ryan's Daughter*,

If It's Thursday, This Must Be Ballybunion

Arranging tee times at Irish golf courses is a snap. All you do is write or call the secretary of the club, indicate the date(s) that you want to play, and provide alternate dates if possible. Indicate "morning" or "afternoon"; don't request a specific time. Some courses may want to know your handicap. Others may have certain restrictions on when visitors can play. But Ireland's golf clubs, decidedly unlike their American counterparts, welcome traveling golfers.

Sometimes, though, being your own booking agent can get complicated. Let's say you have to change one tee time in your itinerary; the domino effect on all your other tee times could be catastrophic, with none of the new times you need being available.

A solution that will cost you some money but save you time and headaches is to buy a package tour. While I cannot speak from personal experience, as I have never taken a package tour myself, I suggest you consider what the following tour operators have to offer (and for how much) as you plan your Irish golf vacation. All three have solid reputations in the field, and their packages should give you a benchmark for making own decision.

InterGolf	Owenoak	PerryGolf
(800) 363-6273	(800) 426-4498	(800) 344-5257

Ed Seay and Arnold Palmer built a new course at Barrow for the Tralee Golf Club (Telephone: [066] 36379) in a breathtaking setting. Further south and inland there is the stunningly beautiful Killarney Golf and Fishing Club (Telephone: [064] 31242), referred to by its fans, with justification, as the "Gleneagles of Ireland." And out on the tip of the Ring of Kerry, just about as far southwest as you can get without putting on your bathing suit, there is the life's ambition of an Irish-American millionaire named Jack Mulcahy, whose immigrant's dream was to go back someday to the Old Country and build the most wonderful links course in the world. He came close at Waterville Golf

Club (Telephone: [0667] 4133/4102), whose par 3s, according to no less an authority than Tom Watson, "must be the greatest in Europe, possibly the world."

If you have unlimited time, by all means keep on teeing it up, at these courses and others, both inland and along the coast, all the way back to Dublin. But if your vacation is finite in length, do yourself a favor and save all those other courses for another trip. Spend any days you have left at Ballybunion, playing what Britain's *Golf World* editors describe simply as "the best 36 holes of links golf anywhere."

If Tom Watson were in your spikes, you better believe that's what he'd do.

When to Go

Thank goodness for the Gulf Stream. Because of it, golf is playable the year round in Ireland. At least it is by the Irish, a hardy lot in general and particularly so when it comes to golf. No Irish golfer worth his pint of Guinness would let mere trifles like a pelting rain and a thirty-mile-an-hour breeze deter him from his regular weekly round. January and February are the wettest months, April through September the sunniest. In any case, make sure your rainsuit is in your bag. Summer showers might be brief, but they're still wet.

OFF COURSE

Ireland is truly the magical place it's cracked up to be. If you take the Emerald Necklace route outlined above, you will be traveling along one of the world's most gorgeous coastlines. Almost any side road you venture down will lead you to a beautiful valley, a perfect farming community, a picturesque fishing village. The **Irish Tourist Board** (757 Third Avenue, New York, NY 10017; [212] 418-0800) and the **Northern Ireland Tourist Board** (53 Castle Street, Belfast BT1 1GH, Northern Ireland) will load you down with brochures, but by the end of your trip you'll be following your impulse of the moment with perfect confidence that you won't be disappointed. Save **Dublin** for the end of your trip or for another vacation; there's a clear and present danger that you will like it so much that you won't want to leave. And that wouldn't do, because there'a a lot of golf to be played.

CHAPTER 18

GOLDEN PEBBLE
The Crown Jewel of American Golf

IMAGINE SHAKESPEARE GETTING *HAMLET* EXactly right in his first draft. Michelangelo polishing off his *David* the first time he ever picked up a chisel. Picasso skipping his Blue Period altogether and going directly to *Les Demoiselles d'Avignon*. Beethoven writing his Ninth Symphony first. Babe Ruth hitting sixty home runs his rookie season.

Inconceivable, right? And yet, after just three weeks of tramping around what Robert Louis Stevenson called "the most felicitous meeting of land and sea in Creation"—the Monterey Peninsula in northern California—a real estate salesman who was a distinguished amateur golfer but who'd never designed a golf course in his life sat down at a drawing board and did the impossible: he knocked off the blueprint for one of the towering masterpieces in the world of golf—Pebble Beach.

How did such a miracle come to pass? The key lies in the term "amateur golfer." Remember that the word "amateur" trickles down from the Latin verb *amare,* which means "to love." A man who loved golf, set loose on a landscape of unparalleled natural beauty. Perhaps it makes sense after all.

Jack Neville was the lover's name, one that is nowhere near as well known among contemporary golfers as it deserves to be. No less than four golf course designers of the first quarter of this century—Donald Ross, Alister Mackenzie, A. W. Tilling-hast, C. B. Macdonald—are household names (at least in households populated by avid golfers), and deservedly so. But Jack Neville, with an assist from another amateur, his friend Douglas Grant, has earned a special place in the pantheon of golf heroes for designing what Herbert Warren Wind, a man not given to hyperbole, believes "may well be the best course in the world."

It's certainly the best course this side of Scotland open to Everyduffer, at least to every duffer with plenty of jack in his lime greens and a dream vacation on his mind. And the icing on the cake (or the olive in the martini, depending on the time of day), is that there's more on the Monterey Peninsula than the singular work of art that Jack Neville created.

Besides Pebble Beach, there are two other first-class tracks, each as different from the other as Hogan is from Snead, also operated by the Pebble Beach Company.* Not that any golfer in his right mind—an oxymoron if ever you've seen one—could conceivably tire of playing Pebble Beach every day for two solid weeks (or two solid lifetimes, for that matter). But if you have a lily, why *not* gild it?

The best place to set up base camp is at one of the two inns owned and operated by the Pebble Beach Company. The Lodge at Pebble Beach is older, more traditional in style; the Inn at Spanish Bay is newer, more modern in look. Both are luxurious, well-appointed, elegant, comfortable, world-class hosteleries that offer all the customary amenities and then some. And both are higher than a cat's back in price. (This is a dream vacation, remember? So whip out your credit cards and dream.)

Now, a close look at the three stars in the Pebble Beach crown—with the best saved for last.

---

*A fourth course, the **Del Monte,** located on a hill north of downtown Monterey about fifteen minutes from the Lodge at Pebble Beach, is also operated by the Pebble Beach Company. Opened in 1897, the Del Monte is the oldest golf course in continuous operation west of the Mississippi. It's a wide-open track, pleasant enough, but not in the same league as its three more distinguished stable mates.

The Lodge at Pebble Beach Pebble Beach, California 93953. Take Pebble Beach exit off Highway 1 just south of Monterey. Telephone: (800) 654-9300. <u>Accommodations</u>: 161 rooms, each with a private patio or balcony and a fireplace. <u>Amenities</u>: 4 restaurants, including one of the great nineteenth holes in the world, the Tap Room; 14 tennis courts, a pool, and a fitness center at the Beach and Tennis Club; an equestrian center. <u>Terms</u>: From $265 for a double room with a garden view to $400 for a "premium ocean view." Plus six suites from $850 to $1,000. Book at least six months in advance, preferably more. Be sure to secure confirmed tee times when you make your reservations.

The Inn at Spanish Bay Pebble Beach, California 93953. Take Pebble Beach exit off Highway 1 just south of Monterey. Telephone: (800) 654-9300. <u>Accommodations</u>: 270 rooms and suites, each with a fireplace. <u>Amenities</u>: Access to everything at the Lodge, plus its own 3 restaurants, pool, 8 tennis courts, and fitness center. The Inn has an edge on the Lodge in hiking, biking, beachcombing, and seal-watching. <u>Terms</u>: From $220 for a double room with a "standard view" to $325 for an "ocean view." Suites from $500 to $1,400. Book at least six months in advance, preferably more. Be sure to secure confirmed tee times when you make your reservations.

★

IN THE SCOTTISH MANNER:
THE LINKS AT SPANISH BAY

An eerie, keening sound, at once plaintive wail and demanding call, filters up through the rolling thunder of wave against rock. As the setting sun slides gently into the ocean, the other-worldly song swells and grows more distinct. Suddenly a human shape emerges from the gloaming. Walking in measured stride over close-cropped meadow and grassy hillock, the solitary figure comes closer, ever closer. Now backlit by the fiery

furnace on the distant horizon, he is sole guardian and proud creator of the enchanting sound that mourns the fading day.

"Hey, Louie, what the hell's going on here? That guy out there on the fairway, is he wearing a dress or something?"

Yes. Sort of. Actually, he's wearing kilts and a tartan, and he's playing the bagpipes, in solemn salutation of the oncoming night.

Where are we, Scotland? Not even close. We're in California, not Carnoustie. On the patio of the Inn at Spanish Bay on the Monterey Peninsula, to be exact. And the piper is piping because the golf course encircling the sleek, ultramodern inn draws its inspiration from the ancient courses in golf's ancestral home.

THE LINKS AT SPANISH BAY

Design: Robert Trent Jones, Jr., Tom Watson, and Frank "Sandy" Tatum

Year Open: 1988
6,820 Yards   74.7 Rating   133 Slope

Information: (408) 654-9300

The first time you go around The Links at Spanish Bay, you'll hate it. Guaranteed. No new course in America has prepared you for what you'll encounter here. Tight, rolling fairways with nary a flat lie, bordered by dunes that eat errant shots. Trees on just four holes. More bunkers than you've had hot dinners, some spotted where your better drives will come to earth. Undulating greens that run slower coming downhill and faster going uphill than you could reasonably expect, the better to confound you. Plus the wind, sometimes howling, usually gusting, always there.

But after your second round, and then a third, Spanish Bay begins to grow on you. It dawns on you that—its spectacular setting aside—this is a subtle golf course. A lot of looks, a lot of options, a need for both muscle and finesse. On no less than five of the ten par 4 holes, the smart strategic golfer will go to an iron for his tee shot. On four of the long holes a Scottish chip-and-run can be employed in addition to the lofted shot that is standard issue on most new American courses. The four par 3s vary in look and length, ranging from 126 to 190 from the blue tees. Water comes into play on only one hole, but there's more than enough sand and wasteland to make masochists happy.

The toughest hole is unquestionably Number 12 (432 yards from the back tees), where you'll need a long boomer off the tee to the middle of a narrow fairway to set up your second shot—and that's when the hole turns mean. Now all you have to do is carry a deep chasm onto a well-trapped, steeply pitched green with an elephant buried in the middle. Have fun.

But the best hole is probably Number 5 (459 yards), a great driving hole that gives you three options off the tee: a heroic space shot that carries the three traps in the middle of the fairway that gobble up anything less than 255 yards; a safe play up the left side, leaving a monster fairway wood to a distant green you can't see because of a giant mound; or a drive hit right over a dune to a thirty-yard-wide strip of fairway that you can't see from the tee because of another huge dune. If you don't select the tee option that is consistent with your game, you'll pay. But if you play smart golf, *and* you execute well, you'll have a chance at glory.

Glory aside, the most fun to be had at Spanish Bay comes at Number 14 (par 5, 571 yards from the tips, 535 from the middle tees), where it's "Me Balboa, you Pacific." That's how you feel standing on the tee, big club in hand, looking out over the broad, inviting fairway that runs down, down, down to the deep blue sea in the distance. What a vista! More important, what a place to come out of your shoes with a mighty smash that puts you in eagle range! Wide fairway, downhill all the way, flat green—what better place to dream of eagles?

As befitting its Scottish antecedents, the Links at Spanish Bay is a course that is experienced best on foot. But the only way they'll let you walk it is with a caddy, so be sure and request one when you book tee times.

Give Spanish Bay a chance to grow on you. Odds are you didn't like your first single malt Scotch all that much, or your first oyster, or even your first . . . (ah, well, scratch that: *some* things *are* pretty swell from the gitgo). Spanish Bay will puzzle you at first, because it's utterly unlike most new American courses. You'll have to play some shots that aren't in your normal arsenal. You'll lose some strokes (not to mention a few balls) in the dunes. And you'll be exasperated by the wind.

Be patient. Spanish Bay has subtle qualities that aren't always readily apparent on first stroke. But when you come to understand its soul, it may well win its way into your heart.

INTO THE WOODS: SPYGLASS HILL

The Crosby—sorry the AT&T-Pebble Beach National Pro-Am—is contested over three courses: Pebble Beach, Poppy Hills (beginning in 1991), and Spyglass Hill. Of this trio, the one the pros always post the highest scores on is Spyglass Hill. I'm sure you'll want to have this in mind as you stand on the first tee, 551 yards away from your first putt of the day. (Make that 600 if you're nuts enough to play from the tips).

SPYGLASS HILL

Design: Robert Trent Jones

Year Open: 1966

6,810 Yards   76.1 Rating   135 Slope

Information: (800) 654-9300

★

The first hole at Spyglass Hill is a brutal introduction to what lies ahead: from the back tees, you head down the hill that gives the course its name, make a left-hand turn into the face of the ocean wind, and then ascend an elevated green encircled by traps. Just in case you were wondering, it's the number-one handicap hole—but it's by no means the toughest!

Sure, if you catch your drive just right and hold it reasonably straight, and the weather's been dry enough to give you a good roll, and there's no wind to speak of when you set up for your second shot, and you pure a fairway wood (or second driver) away from the scrub on the left, and your short iron to the green has enough loft to land gently, and you're close enough on the big, undulating green to get down in two putts, then it's possible to chalk up a routine par. Piece of cake.

Eat it while you can, because on the second hole Spyglass turns ugly. Not physically ugly: that's against the law in this part of California. We're talking ugly in the form of a short (only 350 yards from the back tees) par 4 with a landing area that guarantees an uphill lie for your second shot, a green that is cantilevered over the edge of a dune, and a waste area in front to catch lofted shots knocked backward by the wind off the water.

Then there is Number 4, a severe dogleg-left bordered by an ocean of ice plant, which is to ground cover what Devil's Island is to prisons. But the safer you play it to the right, the more you turn a short par 4 (365 yards) into a long one. And don't pat yourself too hard on the back just because your second shot rolls onto the front edge of the green in regulation: you could still be an NFL punt away from the hole on this fifty-yard-long green. (P.S.: It's only twelve yards wide!)

Remember the forest in *The Wind in the Willows*? A dark, forbidding place, populated by bloodthirsty stoats and weasels, where pitfalls abound, and inky shadows shroud lurking danger? Well, once it turns away from the ocean on the sixth hole and heads back up the hill and into the woods, that's the sort of place Spyglass Hill becomes. Minus the stoats and weasels.

But you do have narrow, tree-lined par 4s, long enough by design but made longer by the softness of fairways protected from the ocean winds. Hillside lies waiting for drives that are off just a fraction. Five water holes. Double-breaks on sloping greens. The woods closing in on all sides. No artifice, no trickery, no gimmicks, but a whole lot more load than even a strong man likes to tote.

Don't get the idea, though, that Spyglass is too mean to live.

Not at all. As it winds through an evergreen forest in a hypnotic weaving of graceful curves, the course captivates with its simple, classic beauty. It's a quiet and peaceful place, a suitable home for the local deer, who wander where they please, oblivious to the most errant shot-making. And the course isn't tricked up at all: the challenge is there in front of you, right in plain sight, stern but fair.

Spyglass Hill ain't a day at the beach—that comes next—but you owe it to yourself to give it your best. Just don't expect your best to be good enough.

THE MAIN EVENT

Playing any course for the first time can do funny things to your mind. You're apprehensive. You're understandably tentative about club selection. You rush your swing, try to hit shots you don't normally attempt, get away from your normal game—and get a lot of practice writing big numbers on your scorecard.

And when the new (to you) course is a certified masterpiece like Pebble Beach, the slope rating for your uneasiness works out to about 150. Couple that with expectations that are off the charts, and you're writing a script for a bad movie called *The Big Letdown*.

You can minimize the chances of that movie ever being made by (a) planning to play Pebble Beach *at least* two times, preferably more, during your vacation; and (b) coming to terms with the stubborn fact that each round will take a long, long time to compete. If your vacation schedule permits only one day on the Monterey Peninsula, and if you get antsy when play slows down to a crawl and the par 3s get backed up, take a pass on Pebble Beach. I've never finished a round there in

---

PEBBLE BEACH GOLF LINKS

Design: Jack Neville (with Douglas Grant)

Year Open: 1919
6,799 Yards   75 Rating   139 Slope

Information: (800) 654-9300

★

less than five hours, and it can take considerably longer. If you're not psychologically prepared for that, it could wreck your head and spoil your day. Forewarned is forearmed.

But who am I kidding? You're not about to pass up a chance to play the certified world treasure that Jack Neville sculpted on the Monterey Peninsula, are you? So here you go—the Golden Pebble, hole by wonderful hole.

Number 1: Par 4, 373. The hardest shot in golf? No question about it: the first one of the day. In my book, a good first hole is one that lets you get out there and on your way with minimal anxiety. By that measure, Pebble Beach's Number 1 is a very good hole indeed. A broad expanse of well-manicured grass on the left takes the OB stakes on the right out of play. Start it way left, take it way right, and call it a power fade. Hey, it used to work plenty well for Lee Trevino! But just because it lets you get out of the chute without humiliating yourself, don't think for a minute that Number 1 is a pushover. Whatever you hit to the small green is going to want to roll off, and there are traps on both sides. Easy par, meet easy bogey.

(Where's the ocean?)

Number 2: Par 5, 502. Fairway wider than Rhode Island, rough shorter than many fairways. Anything over 200 off the tee puts you in good position to carry the giant bunker cutting all the way across the fairway 75 yards from the green. A *really* big drive and you start thinking Big Bird, as in eagle. Ho-hum hole? You wish. This green is even smaller than the first. Come at it from anywhere but dead ahead, and you almost certainly wind up in one of the flanking bunkers. Can you stop a sand shot on a garbage can lid? If not, you'll trickle off into the trap on the other side.

(Yeah, but where's the ocean?)

Number 3: Par 4, 388. At first glance you say to yourself, "What is this, Monterey Muni?" And so it seems. Left is jail, but a huge bailout area to right keeps even your biggest banana in play. Stay in the middle and all you'll need is a short iron to get home. At least that's the way it plays on the tee. But wait till you line up your second shot. Is that a two-club wind in your face? Three? Damn, that green is small! Elevated, too, with traps left and right. And, as you'll discover when you get there, fast. Very fast.

(Ah, but there's the ocean!)

Number 4: Par 4, 327. If you ever trudge around with the pros at the Crosby—sorry, the ATT-Pebble Beach National Pro-Am—you'll notice they all play an iron off the tee and take it down the left side. When you play the fourth, you'll understand why. Any shot hit down the middle takes a sharp right toward the ocean. But there are traps along the left flank, so you can't cheat too far left. And the more you think about it, the harder it is to start your backswing. The real challenge, though, comes with the second shot. The green is skinnier than Mike Reid, with deep bunkers on both sides running its full length. Whatever you do, try to keep your second shot below the hole. Wind up above it and you might as well chalk up three putts and walk on to the next hole.

Number 5: Par 3, 166. A long, dark, narrow hallway, right out of *The Shining*. Giant oaks and pines on the left force you to start the ball farther to the right than you want—where, not coincidentally, a giant trap and its little brother guard an elevated green that slopes sharply from back to front. Walk away with a par and you deserve a pat on the back.

Number 6: Par 5, 516. What you get instead is a back-breaker. At Pebble Beach, say the pros, you better get your birdies on the first five holes, because after that the course gets tough. Or, as Lee Trevino once said (as recorded by George Peper in *Golf Courses of the PGA Tour*), "If you're five over when you get to the sixth hole, it's a good time to commit suicide."

For the pros, a par 5 as short as the sixth hole is almost by definition a birdie hole, with the big hitters coming out of their shoes off the tee to get into position for launching their second shots to the green. Not at Pebble Beach. Nobody—not Norman, not Calcavecchia, not anybody—comes here thinking too much about putting for eagle. It happens now and then, but so do complete eclipses of the sun. That's because the last couple of miles of the sixth hole play uphill. *Way* uphill, as in Mount Everest. For ordinary mortals, it plays longer than Highway 1, complete with ocean on the right. On the way up you encounter so many steep lies you'll wish you had corrective shoes. You can't see the green until you get to the top, just the cliff on the right and the ocean beyond. But you can doggone sure feel the prevailing wind in your face doing its damnedest to blow the ball over one and into the other. Have a nice day.

Number 7: Par 3, 107. The seventh hole at Pebble Beach proves once and for all that Nature, when she puts her mind to it, can spot Art two a side and still win one-up. Okay, so maybe nature isn't responsible for the tee box cut into the side of the cliff, or the six traps guarding the kidney-shaped green. But with the giant Pacific breakers smashing against the rocks, and the wind gusting in from just beyond Maui, your mind doesn't dawdle on the transitory doings of man. You're thinking trancendental thoughts, expanding your consciousness, pondering profound questions—such as, "Wedge or five-iron?"

P.S.: That was no typo. You don't pick the club on seven. The wind does.

Number 8: Par 4, 431. Jack Nicklaus calls it "the most dramatic second shot in golf." But to be in a position to take it, you need to hit a perfect tee shot to a blind landing on a high plateau. There, from the top of a bluff, you look down a hundred feet to the crashing surf and over to another cliff upon which is perched a green that's tiny even by Pebble Beach standards. Savor the moment. Take your time. Go through every tip you've ever read about in golf magazines, from step drill to visualization to pre-shot routine. Give yourself every chance, in other words, to hit the shot of your career.

If you don't hit the green, or even make it across, don't be too hard on yourself. You've just followed in the footsteps of a distinguished host of great golfers who've failed before you. Console yourself with the fact that most of the pars carded on this hole when the pros come to town are made by one-putting.

But if you do carry water, cliff, and traps, and end up putting for a 3, the rush of exhilaration will sweep you off your feet. Just don't do your victory dance too close to the edge: it's a 200-foot drop down to the sand.

Number 9: Par 4, 464. Recovered? You'd better be, because the ninth is the number-one handicap hole on the course. In 1988 it was the toughest hole on the entire PGA Tour. What did you expect, a breather? Anything right out of center runs off the cliff, onto the beach, into the surf, and out to sea; next stop, Japan. Sheer length, a severe left-to-right slope to the fairway, and another small green with a left-side bunker make a bogey look good here. (Particularly compared with the snowman who showed up on my scorecard the last time I was there.)

Number 10: Par 4, 426. In case you didn't get the message, the tenth hole offers more of the same—with a twist. Right of center will take you down to the beach again, but too far left is also trouble, in the form of seventy yards of bunker dotted with three grassy hillocks. Tennis, anyone?

A PEBBLE STRATEGY

1. The first time you play Pebble Beach, tee off in the morning, before the afternoon winds blow in.
2. The second and all future times, play later in the day so you accompany the sun as it heads out to sea. This is California, after all.
3. Reserve your tee times at least six months in advance, preferably longer. The number is (408) 624-3811.
4. Bring money. Greens fees at Pebble Beach are the highest in the country. It won't be long before it costs $200 for a round at the Golden Pebble.
5. Hire a caddie. This is a course that cries out to be walked. Hell, it ought to be a crime *not* to walk Pebble Beach. (Note: Caddies aren't always available, so request one when you reserve your tee time, and call back a week or so before to confirm.)
6. Prepare yourself mentally for a five-and-a-half-hour round . . . or more. Be mellow. Kick back. Enjoy the scenery. You've got nothing better to do, because there *isn't* anything better to do than play Pebble Beach on a golden afternoon.
7. Take a couple of extra balls.

Number 11: Par 4, 384. If Pebble Beach were a great symphony, which at one level of reality it is, then the next six holes would be the *andante* movement.

The eleventh, for instance, is an honest-to-God breather, doglegging back away from the water and toward the hills. The rest of life should be so easy, you say to yourself. Only then the prevailing wind turns your Power Fade into a Rainbow Slice, you end up far right with a blind second shot to the green, and finally you play a little bunker hopscotch to turn what could have been a breather into just plain bad breath.

Number 12: Par 3, 202. The bunker in front isn't as big as the Sahara. On the other hand, it doesn't have any oases.

Number 13: Par 4, 392. As you walk toward the thirteenth green, look up ahead and to the left. There's the cliff overlooking the eighth green. Bask in the afterglow of your recent flirtation with glory, but not so long that you play your second shot too far to the right and turn an easy par hole into a tough double bogey.

Number 14: Par 5, 565. A big drive down the middle into the opening of the dogleg-right provides a glimpse of the green way, *way* down there. Hit everything you have again, because you've *got* to use a lofted club on your third shot to have any chance of holding the green. But even if you do come in high and soft and carry the steep, deep bunker in front, you're still in for a shock. This green has two tiers and more curves than Jamie Lee Curtis. You could get seasick trying to plumb bob.

Number 15: Par 4, 397. If you're like me, hitting out of a chute always triggers a bad case of the heebie-jeebies, even when there's no objective reason for them. On this hole, for instance, the carry from the tee is only about 135 yards across a road and over a ravine, and the fairway beyond is of generous width. Okay, the treetops do pinch in on both sides to create a tunnel effect. But there's nothing, on the face of it, to be overly concerned about. Sure. Tell that to your seven-year-old the next time he hears something go bump in the night.

Your left leg starts quivering the minute you step up to the ball. For a second you're sure that your driver has turned into a bat and that Nolan Ryan is out there pawing the dirt, waiting to dish out a little chin music. Next a little voice whispers, "Don't hook . . . don't slice . . . hit the ball on an absolutely straight line exactly down the middle of the fairway." Naturally, you look up and say out loud, "Who the hell do you think I am? Calvin Peete?" This causes your playing partners to back off and look at you funny. No use trying to explain, so you squeeze the club a little tighter to make sure it doesn't slip on the backswing, which you make sure is faster than normal so that you can generate more club head speed and really powder the ball.

Whoosh! Click! Fore left! Crack!

Oh, well—you still have a shot at a barkie.†

---

†*bar'-kie* (n.) what a golfer gets by making par after hitting a tree; first cousin to sandies and greenies, so money changes hands.

Number 16: Par 4, 402. It's a shame you're not going to be standing beside the green to see exactly what happens to your second shot when it lands. Unless you've really boomed a drive down the left center and have no more than a seven-iron coming in, your second shot will arrive with too steep a trajectory, strip away the landing gear, and skitter off back left and down the hill into purgatory. Or even if you're on the left and try to play a high cut shot to the right half of the green where you want to be, you risk having the wind blow your ball into the ravine that the sixteenth shares with the third hole. And if you push your drive too far right, you're either in a fairway bunker or looking from an angle that gives you only half the green to shoot for—the wrong half.

Number 17: Par 3, 209. Pebble is not a true links, even though the official name is Pebble Beach Golf Links. But the seventeenth has a links feel to it. From the tee, it's hard to get a fix on the green, even though it's the longest on the course, because there are no nearby trees or topographical features to define it. Shaped like an hourglass, it runs 115 feet from eleven o'clock to four o'clock. Usually the pin is somewhere on the left half, but you can't judge how close it is to the six small traps in back or the giant one up front.

In 1988, on the second hole of the playoff between Curtis Strange and Tom Kite for the Nabisco Championships, with its grand prize of $360,000, Strange lashed a four-iron into the teeth of a two-club wind and right at the flag, but scowled in disgust because he thought he'd left it short, possibly in the edge of the trap. Kite thought so, too, so he exchanged his own four for a three—and promptly struck it into the back trap. Kite got up and down, but Strange rolled in a six-foot birdie putt for all the cookies.

But the biggest thing that ever happened at the seventeenth was the little flip chip that Tom Watson willed into the cup for a birdie from five yards off the left side in the 1982 U.S. Open. Tied with Jack Nicklaus, who was already in the clubhouse at 4-under, Tom Watson pulled his tee shot into the deep lettuce off the left side. Even up and down looked dicey, since stopping the ball on the green's downslope from where Watson stood wouldn't have been a lock even if the United States Open Championship weren't riding on the outcome.

Number 18: Par 5, 548. What if Watson's sand wedge had lipped out and he'd had to tap in for a par? That would have sent him on to the eighteenth hole needing a birdie to win. He did make a birdie there to win his only U.S. Open title by two shots. But there's a big difference between a cushion birdie and a gotta-have birdie—especially on a hole like the eighteenth at Pebble Beach, with the U.S. Open on the line, and a Golden Bear lurking around the corner, poised to snatch it away from you.

From the tee, it's as if all the challenges and beauty of golf had been brought together, woven into a spectacular tapestry, and hung before you to admire. Distance, sand, water, trees, rough, OB—you name it, the eighteenth at Pebble Beach has it. And, as it looks like it's been there forever, it comes as something of a shock to learn that the eighteenth started life as a 379-yard par 4. Neville and Grant had the original concept— just right-bend the final hole around the water. But it wasn't until 1928 that the tee was moved back, transforming the eighteenth into the timeless marvel it is today.

While the eighteenth at Pebble Beach may lack the history of the final hole at Augusta, or of the Home Hole at the Old Course in St. Andrews, no finishing hole in golf can touch it for sheer beauty and drama. The long horseshoe bend around the seawall, the giant cypresses in the middle of the fairway daring you to be brave, the treacherous winds blowing in from Carmel Bay, the well-protected green tucked away in the distance at the end of the curve, the surf pounding into the cliff—it's a magnificent hole, as thrilling to play as any in golf.

Whatever your round has been like to this point, a par on the eighteenth at Pebble Beach will make your day, maybe your career, certainly your vacation. I know it made mine.

When to Go

The best times to visit the Monterey Peninsula are from September through November and from March through May. In the middle of the summer, cold air coming off the water meets warm air just inland to create dense early morning fog and overcast days. At least it does so often enough to cause irritating delays in teeing off in the morning, and to make you wonder where the sun went in the afternoon. Do yourself a favor: see Pebble Beach in prime time.

OFF COURSE

Sunset Patrol. About fifteen miles south of Carmel on Highway 1, you'll see a small sign on the right for the **Rocky Point Restaurant.** Get a table by the window, order a Dungeness crab salad and beverage of your choice, and watch the sun set. It's at this point that you first start thinking seriously about moving to California.

Fish Story. Rumor has it that Monterey boasts a top-notch aquarium. I can't vouch for it personally, because every time I've been in the area my sole preoccupation has been birdies. Check it out if you like to look at fish.

Fisherman's Wharf. If you prefer to eat them, Fisherman's Wharf is the place to go. It's chock-a-block with fish restaurants, mostly in the mediocre-to-good range—and none worthy of a ringing endorsement. Your best bet is to follow the crowd, i.e., go on a week night and eat at the one that's the most crowded. Whatever you do, steer clear of one local specialty—squid that has been pounded into a "steak," doused in oil, and grilled. Unless, of course, you are partial to braised inner tube.

Steinbeck Row. John Steinbeck used to live in Monterey, the setting for *Cannery Row.* The real **Cannery Row** has been gussied up to a fair-thee-well, but it's still worth a walkabout.

Shopping. Carmel is a good strolling town, crammed with art galleries and clothing stores. Keep your eyes peeled and you might spot Kim Novak or Doris Day.

Garlic and Artichokes. Up the road a piece to the north, Gilroy is "the Garlic Capital of the World." Buy a garland to make sure your vacation isn't ruined by vampires. Nearby is **Watsonville,** "the Artichoke Capital of the World." There's a restaurant in the middle of town—you can't miss it, unless you don't know what an artichoke looks like—that serves all manner of dishes featuring the mainstay of the local economy: artichoke salad, artichoke soup, deep-fried artichokes, artichoke ice cream, and more. Skip the ice cream.

CHAPTER 19

FROM DRACULA'S CASTLE TO THE KINGDOM OF FIFE
Golf in the Other Scotland

OR EVERY POOR SOUL WHO HAS EVER PURSUED the dimpled pellet, there comes a critical moment. One day you're perfectly content with your regular weekly foursome, complete with two-dollar Nassau and convivial nineteenth hole. The next thing you know your every waking daydream is filled with a single misty image: You . . . teeing it up . . . where it all began. In Scotland.

Probably your first instinct is to shrink back from this vision. If you're like most golfers, negotiating a satisfactory vacation with your life partner and assorted dependents is already tougher than hitting a 2-iron. ("Honey, I've got a great idea! Two weeks in Scotland! You and the kids can eat haggis while I play golf! Whatdya think?")

No thanks. Who needs the grief? Easier to go ahead with the Disney World plans; maybe you can sneak away for nine holes some morning while the family explores the Magic Kingdom. Put Scotland out of your mind. Too hard a sell, even if the family name is McIntosh.

Only thing is, it won't work. Might as well try to talk the but-terfly into giving it another shot as a caterpillar. Birds gotta fly, fish gotta swim, golfers gotta make sure their passports are current. Face it: there's no escape from your Scotland dream, short of melting your irons into plowshares (something we've all considered from time to time). And there's only one cure.

Go.

Convinced? Good. But before you issue mobilization orders to your travel agency, take a close look at your proposed itin-erary. Does it include all the usual stops on the Grand Tour? The Old Course at St. Andrews, Royal Troon, Carnoustie, Glen-eagles, Muirfield, Turnberry, Royal This, Royal That? If it does, put everything on hold and reconsider: there's a better way.

Don't get me wrong: all the stops on Scotland's Grand Tour are utterly, absolutely, unquestionably grand, and you should play them . . . someday. But I believe you'll appreciate them a lot more if you first get acquainted with what golf in Scotland is all about. And the best way to do that is to postpone the Grand Tour, and explore the Scottish game in a more relaxed, less emotionally charged setting. Get a feel for golf in its home-land; then go on to the great championship courses.

The fact is, the most famous courses in Scotland—the ones that top your list, and mine as well—have become larger than life. Shrines. Monuments. Holy places that all True Believers must visit at least once before shuffling off this mortal coil, and preferably between June 15 and September 1. The result: tees backed up by foursomes from Kansas City and Kyoto, Boston and Bonn, bus loads of golfers trying frantically to squeeze eight courses into seven days, or whatever the tour package calls for. If it's Tuesday, this must be Turnberry. Fore!

So if this is your first time, and if you book the Grand Tour in high season, you're setting yourself up for a letdown. Which is why I'm proposing that your first Scottish golf expedition be built around the quieter, less frenetic, but no less wonderful golf to be found elsewhere, off the beaten track, in the Other Scotland.

A WEE GAME OF GOLF

To find out what I'm talking about, throw your clubs into the boot of your rented car at the Edinburgh airport, and drive north across the Firth of Forth into Fife. (Easier done than said.) Pass the turnoff to St. Andrews and keep heading north, to Perth and then Dundee. At Dundee, take the coast road but don't stop off for an afternoon round at Carnoustie. Keep on going up the coast on A-92. Beyond Aberdeen, turn right on A-952 toward Peterhead, a small but bustling and prosperous coastal town thirty-five miles north of Aberdeen. Drive to the center of town and hang a left on Broad Street. At Number 36, two blocks down from city hall, and across from an unmarked obelisk commemorating the repeal of the Corn Laws in 1834, you'll see a butcher shop. Go in, and while you're admiring the veal chops, look for a man with a warm, infectious smile and a shape like Billy Casper. Once you spot him, lean over the counter and say these magic words:

"Might I interest you in a wee game of golf?"

Now, Ian Devenish is a busy man. He owns the butcher shop, a motorcycle repair shop, and has an interest in a couple of other small businesses in town. He and his wife have two lively children and a lot of friends. He's active in civic and business affairs in Peterhead. But chances are good—make that excellent—that Ian will light up the shop with a grin, take off his apron, and ask if you have ever heard of the course at Cruden Bay.

CRUDEN BAY GOLF CLUB

Aulton Road
Cruden Bay, Aberdeenshire AB4 7NN

Telephone: (779) 812285

Probably not, so let me tell you about it.

Around the turn of the century, the Great North of Scotland Railway Company decided to create a seaside Scottish getaway for the upper middle class. They extended a railway link to Cruden Bay, a sleepy fishing village twenty-five miles north of Aberdeen; built a colossal resort hotel in the grand style; and feverishly touted the place as the "Brighton of Aberdeenshire." It worked, at least for three decades of glitzy summer gaiety. But after World War II, the railway closed, the hotel was demolished, and Cruden Bay went back to sleep. Nothing was left as a reminder of its brief moment of glory. Nothing, that is, except a golf course . . . and Dracula's Castle.

The first tee of the Cruden Bay Golf Club—Ian Devenish's home course—sits high on a bluff, with a panoramic view of the course as it runs down, out, and back along the shore. Fairways bend and twist around giant, bush-covered dunes, finding their way to tiny greens nestled into embankments and tucked behind bunkers. Just to the north is the town of Cruden Bay, hunkering down against the wind off the North Sea.

As at most Scottish courses, the holes at Cruden Bay have names, ranging from the mundane ("Claypits") to the lyrical ("Finnyfal"). The 239-yard par-3 fifteenth is called "Blin' Dunt" (rhymes with "Wine Bunt") because you have to give the ball a "Blind Wallop" over a towering dune to reach the unseen green in regulation. (If you make it, the nineteenth hole's on me.) "Whins" is the Scottish name for gorse, the evil, spiny bush that comes into play on the fourteenth if you stray an inch from the fairway and gives the tricky par 4 its name. And "Slains," the name of the first hole, refers to the castle lying in ruins on the cliff in the misty distance.

Dracula's Castle.

"We came in the afternoon, to Slains Castle, built upon the margin of the sea so that the walls of one of the towers seem only a continuation of a perpendicular rock, the foot of which is beaten by the waves." So wrote Samuel Johnson after a visit to Cruden Bay in 1773. "From the windows, the eye wanders over the sea that separates Scotland from Norway, and when the wind beats with violence must enjoy all the terrific grandeur of the tempestuous ocean."

But for Bram Stoker, a regular visitor to Cruden Bay beginning in 1893, four years before *Dracula* was published, Slains Castle and its environs were not merely a vantage point for enjoying the power and glory of nature, but a primary source of inspiration for his exploration of the dark forces of unspeakable evil.

Stoker knew, for instance, that dangerous rocks in the bay known as the Scaurs, had caused many a shipwreck in the waters below Slains Castle, and had also inspired a local legend. Of the Legend of Scaurs he wrote: "When there is a full moon at the Lammas Tide [August 1] and if you have the 'sight,' you can see all the blanched bodies of all the folk who have been savaged by the reef during the past twelve months come out of the sea and make their way to St. Olave's Well so that they can join their spirits in heaven or in hell."

Think about *that* when you tee off on the tenth hole, called "Scaurs" on the scorecard. Or when you stop just beyond the seventeenth tee box to wet your whistle with the delicious, cold water from a little spring, called St. Olaf's Well.

Or when, after finishing your round with Ian, you drive into the village, take a narrow, winding dirt path leading up through thick woods and onto a windswept cliff, and come upon the entrance to Drac . . . eh, *Slains* Castle.

The walls form an empty shell, open to the heavens. No doors hinder passage from room to room, or prevent descent of steeply pitched stone stairsteps into the castle's lower depths. (No, I damned well *didn't* go down them. And neither will you.) The towers and the parapets nearest the sea still stand, a sheer drop of 200 feet between them and the rocks down below. No matter how warm the day, a shiver will run through your spine. I guarantee it.

"We used to play on these walls when we were kids," says Ian. "Can you believe it?"

No, I can't. I also can't believe we're still here; the sun is due to set in ten minutes, and I'll be damned if I'm going to be hanging around here in the dark. A lot can happen in Dracula's Castle after dark, and none of it is pretty. Maybe the thing to do is visit the castle first, while there's still plenty of light, then play golf.)

The Cruden Bay course is a classic links, with plenty of variety and character. At 6,370 yards, the overall length doesn't seem nearly so scary as the castle on the hill. But there are only two par 5s, which leaves a lot of heavy lifting for the par 4s, five of which are over 400 yards long. Add a little wind and weather, and this friendly little course will turn and bite you on the ass.

Ian, the butcher from Peterhead, has just posted a solid 85 to win two pounds, and is now sitting with a pint of bitter in the nondescript clubhouse bar of the Cruden Bay Golf Club, looking out over his favorite piece of real estate on earth. Outside, the wind howls.

"It really is a magical place, is it not?" he asks, only it's not a question. "A truly magical place."

*   *   *

Magical, yes. But unique? Even uncommon? No, not at all, not in the Other Kingdom.

In an area about the size of Oklahoma (minus its panhandle), dozens and dozens of golf courses whose flavor, charm, and character are every bit as distinctive as Cruden Bay can be found from firth to shining firth. Because there are so many of them, and they are so close together, you can play a round in the morning at one course, a round in another in the afternoon, and have a nice, leisurely pub lunch in between.

You should have no difficulty getting a tee time at any of the courses listed below, but it's always a good idea to write to the club secretary well ahead of your planned arrival. Weekends can be tough, because there's a golf boom underway in Great Britain, as well. (If you absolutely must do some sight-seeing to maintain domestic tranquility, schedule it for Saturday and Sunday mornings.)

Say in your letter that you want a morning or an afternoon time, rather than a specific hour; and indicate whether you would like to have a caddy. (Some of the smaller courses don't maintain a ready supply of caddies, and have to make special arrangements.) Include the name of your club, if you belong to one; and your handicap, if it's below twenty.

(If it's above twenty, keep it to yourself. Sometimes club secretaries get the funny idea that people like you and me are going to tear up their courses and slow down play just because we're lousy golfers. My standard answer: I don't play well, but I do play fast.)

Occasionally, I've indicated a nearby hotel, inn, or bed-and-breakfast that would serve nicely as a base camp. But don't hesitate for a moment about simply picking a bed-and-breakfast at random. I can't think of a better value in the world than a nice, clean room in a Scottish B&B and a big, hearty, Scottish breakfast—all for about twelve to fifteen pounds (approximately twenty-four dollars) per person. Unless, of course, it's the greens fee structure in the Other Scotland, where you'll be hard-pressed to spend more than twenty-five dollars for a weekday round.

HIGHLAND FLING

If you think of him as the Little Tramp, it's hard to imagine Charlie Chaplin playing golf. But take away the derby and the cane and the floppy shoes, and replace them with the spiffy

plus-fours and silk shirts more appropriate to the stature of the most powerful film star of his era, and the picture of Charles Chaplin, Esq., on the links comes in to clearer focus.

During the 1920s this picture was on exhibition every summer in the sleepy little town of Nairn, two hours north and west of Peterhead on the Moray Firth, and sixteen miles northeast of Inverness. Chaplin frequently brought his family to Nairn on holidays during the period of his greatest popularity, and he played regularly at the Nairn Golf Club. From all reports, he had a good, compact swing, but very little patience—and without patience, even a sweet swinger is going to post some high numbers at Nairn.

Flat and lacking in drama, Nairn appears at first glance to be little more than a nice walk on the beach. But its small, fast, wonderfully well-maintained greens dispel that notion in a hurry. And if you can't play the Scottish bump-and-run shot, then it's going to take you an extra stroke a hole to find out just how fast those greens are. Add a tricky wind coming in off the water, and you have a spirited but subtle challenge on your hands.

Perhaps that's what Old Tom Morris and James Braid, each of whom had a hand in designing Nairn, had in mind.

(There are two other courses in Nairn: a nine-hole course, Newtown; and Nairn Dunbar. When you stop to ask directions, as you most certainly will, be sure to specify the Nairn Golf Club. The other two are Parkay; the Nairn Golf Club is butter.)

A couple of firths away in Tain, thirty-five winding miles north of Inverness, straight tee shots are the order of the day.

Highland Fling

NAIRN GOLF CLUB

Seabank Road
Nairn, Inverness-shire IV12 4HB
Telephone: (667) 53208

TAIN GOLF CLUB

Tain
Ross and Cromarty
Telephone: (862) 2314

ROYAL DORNOCH GOLF CLUB

Golf Road
Dornoch, Sutherland IV25 3LW
Telephone: (862) 810219

GOLSPIE GOLF CLUB

Ferry Road
Golspie, Sutherland
Telephone: (408) 33266

BRORA GOLF CLUB

Golf Road
Brora, Sutherland KW9 6QS
Telephone: (408) 21417

INVERNESS GOLF CLUB

Culcabrook Road
Inverness IV2 3XQ
Telephone: (463) 233422

Unless, of course, you want to play Br'er Rabbit in the brier patch. Errant drives will send you deep into Tain's heather (called "whins" in this part of Scotland), and after a couple of holes we're talking rabbit stew.

It would be easy to bypass the Tain Golf Club, tucked away along the southern shores of the Dornoch Firth. After all, if you're this far north, chances are you're making a beeline for Royal Dornoch, the region's preeminent holy place to golf pilgrims. It would be easy, but it would be a mistake.

When you play Tain, by the way, be sure to schedule your round so that you'll have time to visit the distillery that brews Glenmoranche, one of Scotland's great single malt whiskies (and little known on these shores). In fact, it's not a bad idea to check neighborhood listings for whiskey distilleries *every* time you book a tee time in Scotland. I didn't become a Scotch drinker until my first visit to Scotland—and after my first introduction to single malt whiskies at the Blair Atholl distillery following a so-so round at Pitlochry, a pesky mountain course north of Perth. My game that day wasn't memorable; the whiskey was.

On a clear day you can just see Royal Dornoch, five miles away across the Dornoch Firth, from points on the back nine at Tain. So near, and yet so far—as you'll discover when you make the twenty-five-mile trek on roads that seem to get narrower with every turn. But like the road to heaven, the road to Royal Dornoch is well worth the journey.

A couple of years ago Ben Crenshaw wrote in *Golf* magazine that "playing a round at Royal Dornoch on a fine day with a breeze is to approach the soul of golf." That pretty much sums it up, although anyone who has ever played there can't help but want to say more.

The course begins on a low, sandy cliff with a commanding view of the sea, then descends a level onto a wind-sculpted ledge that bends and dips along the shoreline. Whereas Nairn is virtually flat, Royal Dornoch is all roll and bulge, swale and depression, with flat areas reserved for only the most carefully struck drives. Twice you ascend major dunes, at the top of which what had been a gentle breeze more often than not turns into a true North Sea wind. Forests of heather border some fairways; others are guarded by waving dune grass.

If the elevated and crowned greens seem vaguely familiar, it may be because you've played a lot of Donald Ross courses back in the U.S.A. After apprenticing under Old Tom Morris at St. Andrews, Ross returned to his native Dornoch, where he was greenskeeper and club professional. When he left to come to America in 1896, his baggage included an admiration for the greens Morris had constructed on Dornoch's natural hillocks when laying out the course a decade earlier. We can be thankful Ross was a careful packer.

The Royal Golf Hotel has an ideal setting just off the first tee, but I prefer the **Trevose Guest House,** a solid, traditional B&B located on the central square in the center of town. For one thing, it's right across the street from the **Dornoch Castle Hotel,** an elegant establishment whose small bar, wedged into one of the towers of the seventeenth-century castle, contains a truly amazing selection of single malt whiskies. But the main reason for staying at Trevose is that Mrs. Jane Mackenzie, head pro at the Guest House, makes sure you get solid value for your money: a clean comfortable room, a simple but delicious three-course meal, and an excellent breakfast for about thirty dollars per person.

TREVOSE GUEST HOUSE

The Square
Dornoch, Sutherland
Telephone: (862) 810269

There are other courses worth a look near Dornoch: the Golspie Golf Club in Golspie, just up the road; a nine-hole course at Brora, just a little further up the road; and the Inverness Golf Club, an hour or so back down the road. But my guess is that once you get to Dornoch, you'll want to stay. And stay. And stay. . . .

After all, when you're this close to the soul of golf, why would you want to go anywhere else?

You pack up and move on for the simple reason that there are so many more great places to play golf in Scotland. For instance, you might want to make a western loop and play three great links courses west of Glasgow: Western Gailes, on the Firth of Clyde, ranked by *Golf* magazine editor George

Western Loop

WESTERN GAILES GOLF CLUB

Gailes by Irvine
Ayrshire KA11 5AE
Telephone: (294) 311649

MACHRIE GOLF CLUB

Port Ellen
Isle of Islay
Telephone: (496) 2310

THE MACHRIHANISH GOLF CLUB

Machrihanish, Campbeltown
Argyll
Telephone: (586) 81213

★

East Lothian

DUNBAR GOLD CLUB

East Links
Dunbar, East Lothian EH42 1LP
Telephone: (368) 62317

NORTH BERWICK GOLF CLUB

New Club House, Beach Road
North Berwick, East Lothian EH39 4BB
Telephone: (620) 2135

GULLANE GOLF CLUB

East Lothian EH31 2BB
Telephone: (620) 842255

★

Peper among his top three personal favorites in Scotland; Machrie, a splendidly isolated jewel on the Isle of Islay; and Machrihanish, a wild, windswept layout on a peninsula that bears the full brunt of the Atlantic's gales.

Or you might want to make your way east of Edinburgh to the rich storehouse of golf treasures in East Lothian: Dunbar Golf Club, with its lightning fast greens, ten miles from Muirfield; the public course at North Berwick; and the three courses at Gullane, whose lush turf moved the great British golf writer Bernard Darwin to new rhapsodic heights over three quarters of a century ago. (See his classic, *The Golf Courses of the British Isles,* first published in 1910.)

And you surely, absolutely, will want to journey into the very heartland of golf in the Other Scotland . . . into the tiny peninsula across the Firth of Forth from Edinburgh . . . into the shadow of St. Andrews itself . . . into the land called Fife.

THE KINGDOM OF FIFE

If you've read Michael Murphy's great book *Golf in the Kingdom,* then you'll know why I recommend that a golfer's first golf vacation in Scotland be built around the "lesser" courses, around the courses of the Other Scotland. And if you haven't read *Golf in the Kingdom,* put this book down right now and go remedy that oversight immediately. Murphy's book is simply the most original, most thought-provoking, most brilliant exploration of the inner game of golf—and of what makes it the greatest of all games—that has ever been written.

Going to Fife to play golf and skipping St. Andrews may sound utterly perverse, and frankly I don't expect many takers. But even if you do play the Old Course on your first trip to Scotland, be sure to allow plenty of time for the other courses in Fife as well.

To do so, set up base camp at Rufflets, a pleasant country hotel just outside of St. Andrews on the Strathkinness Low Road. Great name, huh? Jack Nicklaus stays at Rufflets when the British Open is in town because it offers him a modicum of peace and quiet, compared with posher digs in St. Andrews proper. I figure, if it's good enough for Jack, it's good enough for me. Just look at what staying there has done for *his* game.

RUFFLETS COUNTRY HOUSE HOTEL Strathkinness Low
Road, St. Andrews, Fife KY16 9TX <u>Telephone</u>: (0334)
72594

★

What's so special about Fife? Well, for one thing, they've been playing golf there a long, long time.

"Several gentlemen in and about the Town of Craill who were fond of the diversion of Golf agreed to form themselves into a society which should be known as the Craill Golfing Society—the Society was accordingly instituted upon 23rd day of February 1786."

And so was formed, three years before the Constitution of the United States, the seventh-oldest golf club in Scotland. Not one that you've likely heard of, to be sure. But one whose history can be reconstructed from a richly detailed record, quite remarkably complete, of the society's activities over the past two centuries: monthly matches and a grand dinner at the Golf Inn, whose landlord was one of the society's original eleven members; fines, typically in the form of buying rum punch for everyone, for failure to wear the society's scarlet jacket with yellow buttons; land disputes between golfers and tenant farmers over grazing rights; the construction of a new eight-hole links course in the 1850s on a farm known as Balcomie; praise for the course from no less than Old Tom Morris ("There is no better in Scotland . . ."), who would go on to lay out an additional nine holes; special assessments for the building of a clubhouse. It's all there, including a decision in 1874 "that iron cases be got for the eight holes on the links to prevent the holes from being destroyed"—the first known reference in golf history to metal cups in holes.

Flash forward to the present and you'll find, running up and down a bluff and along a tiny strip of isolated coastline, a modest, unpretentious beauty of a course. Nothing spectacular, certainly not a championship layout, but nowhere near as easy as it appears. The course is always in good shape, with firm, true links turf and surprisingly fast greens, but not obsessively manicured, the way American courses tend to be.

What the Balcomie Course at Crail has to offer is a perfect

example of the Scottish way: take the land as you find it, add only what is essential. If that means five par 3s on the back side, with only two short part 5s (500 and 480 yards), adding up to only 5,720 yards from the medal tees (only 5,202 from the front), then so be it.

The Kingdom of Fife

CRAIL GOLFING SOCIETY

Balcomie Clubhouse
Crail, Fife KY10 3XN
Telephone: (333) 50686

GOLF HOUSE CLUB, ELIE

Elie, Fife KY9 1AS
Telephone: (333) 330331

LUNDIN GOLF CLUB

Golf Road
Lundin Links, Fife KY8 6BA
Telephone: (333) 320202

LADYBANK GOLF CLUB

Annsmuir
Ladybank, Fife KY 7 7RA
Telephone: (337) 30814

SCOTSCRAIG GOLF CLUB

Golf Road
Tayport, Fife DD6 9DZ
Telephone: (382) 552515

★

Ten winding miles away, the village of Elie is wedged between rolling fields and the sea, its original raison d'être solidly rooted in both. As with other villages and towns in Fife, Elie's sole trump card is its simplicity. No grand castles or churches, no smart restaurants, no tourist attractions per se. Nothing at all fancy. A place to refurbish your spirit, not to kick up your heels.

The same goes for its golf course. Longer than Crail at 6,235 yards, the Golf House Club at Elie has only two par 3s and no par 5s. (It got its name in the mid-1870s when four members of the Earlsferry and Elie Golf Club put together a project to build the current clubhouse.) The course starts in town, on a hill behind a high stone wall on the main street, then runs out to the shore, where it gives you a classic links experience: wide, undulating fairways; hard, true turf; small, fast greens. And the wind. In Scotland, you can never forget the wind.

Quirks? Try this: a pre-World War II submarine periscope mounted in the starter's shack that allows him to peer over a ridge about seventy-five yards from the first tee and determine whether it's safe for the next foursome to play away. Or this: a 219-yard par 3 from an elevated tee that lets you see over the town, across the Firth of Forth, all the way to Muirfield.

Elie is a private club, which in Scotland means that the public is welcome. All you have to do is ask properly. (Try that at Burning Twisted Gnarled Tree Country Club in Anytown, U.S.A., and see how far it gets you.) Day guests are also welcome in the clubhouse, thank you very much. In Scotland, you won't find most of the barriers that we've seen fit to build around golf.

And so it is everywhere in Fife. From Lundin on its southern shore to the Lundin links on Fife's southern coast to Ladybank in the rolling pastureland of the interior to Scotscraig near the River Tay in the north, the game is far too integral a part of the social fabric for it to be made inaccessible. It's the same wonderful, complex, simple, ageless, exasperating game on both sides of the Atlantic. But in Scotland, it's no big deal. It's just a part of life.

You may not learn that lesson if your first trip to Scotland is the Grand Tour. Not that you won't have the experience of playing some of the world's great courses. It's just that sometimes a great course's fame can blow the whole experience out of proportion and become a burden. Let's say you've wrangled your way onto Muirfield, the hardest of all the Scottish courses to secure a tee time on, and you have a single do-or-die day to make it worthwhile. I don't know about you, but my first-tee jitters are bad enough already. I don't need the extra burden of

knowing that with every lousy shot I'm blowing a lifetime opportunity.

In the Other Scotland, you won't have to carry a bagful of
impossible expectations along with your rain suit. You may
well have to carry your golf bag, or at least pull it on a "trolley."
Motorized golf carts are an oxymoron in Scotland, where people have the strange notion that the game should include a
little exercise. But by playing the courses of the Other Scotland, you'll do more than build up your stamina. You'll develop
a deeper understanding of the simple, unadorned beauty of
the greatest game of all, the way it's still played in its ancestral
home.

And when you've finished with your pilgrimage, you should
go home and immediately start planning your second trip.

This time: the Grand Tour.

WHEN TO GO

Even during the middle of the summer you shouldn't have too
much trouble getting weekday tee times in the Other Scotland,
so aim for July–August. September is almost as good in terms
of weather and a whole lot better in terms of crowds.

OFF COURSE

Castles. Strong ale. Battlefields. Quaint villages. The cultural
riches of Edinburgh. Roast lamb. Woolen goods. Beautiful
countryside. Salmon fishing. The Loch Ness Monster. Who
could ask for anything more?

Unless you are a crotchety xenophobe who hates everything,
you won't have any problem finding plenty to do after you've
finished your day's round(s). The **British Tourist Authority,** 40
West Fifty-seventh Street, New York, NY 10019 (212-581-4700),
is a positive font of pamphlets, and a good place to start when
planning your trip.

In general, the northwestern part of Scotland has the best
scenery, while the east has the best golf courses. But beauty is
in the eye of the beholder, whether it's a long par 5 or a
heather-covered mountainside, and you're not likely to come
up short of golf *or* scenery anywhere you go.

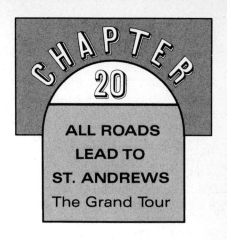

CHAPTER 20

ALL ROADS
LEAD TO
ST. ANDREWS
The Grand Tour

YOUNG NINETEENTH-CENTURY ENGLISHMEN OF serious mien, suitable means, and elevated social status typically undertook, on completion of their studies at Oxford or Cambridge, a Grand Tour of the Continent. While there was a certain amount of unhurried moving about from one capital to another, the usual destination was the warmer climes of southern Europe, more specifically southern France and Italy. The usual duration was a year, more or less. The unstated purposes of the Grand Tour were, among other things, for the young m'lords to learn the local language (albeit with intentionally bad British accents), to get a little color in their cheeks, to visit dutifully and inspect minutely a long checklist of bona fide architectural treasures, to observe from a discreet distance the curious mores of the hot-blooded races, to read a bit of poetry, to eat good food for the first time in their lives, and to sow a few wild oats. They congregated in Nice and Florence and Rome and Venice, where they wrote long letters home, had tea together, and pined for the drawing rooms of Belgravia. For some few it was a time of serious self-explora-

279

tion and dedicated study of another culture. For most it was a long, languorous, well-financed holiday.

The only thing missing was golf.

The Grand Tour of a modern-day traveling golfer from America compares quite favorably with the nineteenth-century version. It's shorter, you won't learn another language (although you'll hear yours spoken in a wonderfully different way), you're not likely to get a tan, the food won't be as good, and the wild oats are up to you. But you will view some spectacular architecture (landscape division), you can drink as much tea as you like, and there will be plenty of self-exploration. Plus there will be great golf.

The golf courses that will be the primary components of your Grand Tour should, I strongly believe, have certain things in common. They should be in Scotland, the Home of Golf. They should be links, because the game originated on linksland. They should be venerable. They should be positively dripping with tradition and history. And they should have hosted at least one British Open.

These stiff criteria for the traveling golfer's Grand Tour eliminate the great links of Ireland (visited in Chapter 17), the links of Scotland that have not hosted a British Open (some of which are described in Chapter 19), the links in England that have (Royal Birkdale, for example), and the great Scottish moorlands courses at Gleneagles. Too bad, or, as the British say, "Tough darts."

I assume your Grand Tour will last something less than a year—more on the order of two weeks. And I also assume you'd like to play each of the courses on your Grand Tour at least twice, to give yourself a better chance of understanding their distinct personalities. That means keeping the list of stops to six, maximum, which just so happens to be the number of courses that fit the original criteria stated above.

The six courses on the Grand Tour are Ailsa at Turnberry, Prestwick, and Royal Troon in the west of Scotland and Muirfield, Carnoustie, and (of course) the Old Course at St. Andrews in the east. One is a hotel/resort course, two are public, and three are private—but all, in the Scottish tradition, can be played under certain conditions by the traveling golfer who is respectful of the game. The courses in each set of three are close enough together to break your Grand Tour neatly into two distinct parts. You could, if you choose, change lodging only once.

The Grand Tour is not something to be undertaken lightly or too early in a golf career. I don't mean to go stuffy on you this late in the match, but I do believe a person should have played golf for a number of years, developed a certain level of proficiency, and studied the game's history at least a bit before teeing off at the Old Course. How snobbish am I on the subject? Try this: I think you should have a handicap of eighteen or better (you'll have to on some courses, if they choose to enforce their own rules for visitors); and I think you should have read Bernard Darwin, Herbert Warren Wind, Michael Murphy, and Dan Jenkins on golf in Scotland before taking your Grand Tour. So send me to snob prison.

To organize your Grand Tour properly will take considerable time—at least nine months, probably more—if you do it yourself. You will need to write or call each of the six courses on the Tour and reserve tee times. You could get lucky and have everything click the first time around, but chances are you will spend some fair amount of time juggling dates and available times until you fix your schedule. You start, predictably enough, with the course on which you ideally want to finish: St. Andrews.

(As I noted when discussing Ireland in Chapter 17, a golf tour package might cost you a few more bucks but will certainly save you a lot of time and headaches. They're advertised all the time in the golf magazines. Three operators with good reputations are PerryGolf (800-344-5257), InterGolf (800-363-6273), and Owenoak (800-426-4498). Check them out. At the very least their packages will serve as a standard for comparison.)

The St. Andrews Links include the Eden (opened in 1913), the Jubilee (1897), the New Course (quite old, actually; it opened in 1894), and the Old Course (no one knows for sure, but 1457 is the earliest historical reference; naturally it's changed a bit over the years). There is also a nine-hole course, known affectionately and accurately as the "Wretched and Recent," that I mention at all only for the sake of completeness.

All the courses at St. Andrews are owned by the city and are open to the public. The Old Course is always closed on Sundays, as well as during the third week in August when the Royal and Ancient Golf Club holds its annual meetings. Because of the tremendous demand to play the Old Course, certain restrictions and procedures have been set down by the Links Management Committee. Here are the most pertinent rules, from an official Links Management Committee publication:

1. *Reserved Times*

   Applications for reserved times should be made to the Secretary, who will advise if the date is available and the amount of the reservation fee. This procedure should be completed not less than eight weeks in advance of the date of play.[**Note: Better make that eight months.**] Reservations are not granted on Saturdays or on Thursday afternoons, and the course is closed on Sundays.

2. *The Daily Ballot*

   For unreserved times, play is determined by a daily Ballot (at no charge) between the months of April and October. To enter the Ballot, two names must be given to the Starter for each starting time, by 1415 hours on the golfing day previous to that on which it is desired to play. [**Note: A certain percentage of all tee times are left free for the daily Ballot, but no one outside the Links Management Committee seems to know what the formula is for determining the percentage, which varies over the course of the main April to October playing season.**]

3. *Single Players*

   Single players are not permitted to reserve a starting time or to enter the Ballot. Nevertheless, if there is a gap in play, the Starter is permitted to allow a single player to play off. It frequently occurs that single players join an existing 2 or 3 ball game on the tee, but this must be arranged by the individuals concerned.

4. *Caddie Carts*

   Caddie carts or golf trolleys are not permitted.

5. *Employment of Caddies*

   Although not employed by the Committee, all caddies must be registered and players desiring a caddie should arrange this through the Caddie Master.

Although the most recently published rules state that no letter of introduction is needed to play the Old Course, you may be required to submit an official USGA handicap card. In the summer of 1990, for instance, the Links Management Committee started enforcing a maximum twenty-four handicap rule that had long been on the books. The idea is to make sure that golfers on the Old Course have sufficient playing ability to keep up the pace of play and to keep from ruining the day for foursomes behind them. It's a good rule.

Unfortunately, play has recently been cut back at the Old Course, although demand continues to rise. Five years ago, tee times commenced at 6 A.M. in high summer and continued into the late afternoon at seven-minute intervals. Starting in the summer of 1990, the first tee time is at 8 A.M. and the interval has been extended to ten minutes. The net effect is a 35 percent reduction in available tee times compared with five years ago. This drastic action was taken to protect the course, which had become seriously worn down from overuse. No golfer who respects what the Old Course represents to the game can fault the Links Management Committee for taking this step. But it does make it harder.

Yet surprisingly enough, an individual golfer who simply shows up in St. Andrews has an excellent chance of getting on the Old Course, much better than that of two or more golfers in a group who enter the Ballot. The individual won't be able to participate in the Ballot for a reserved time, but he can apply to the Starter each day to be fitted in to a threesome or a twosome. It'll be up to him to make the arrangements, but golfers at the Old Course are generally on their best behavior, so it shouldn't be a problem.

At Royal Troon, Prestwick, and Muirfield you must write well in advance to request a tee time, and you should submit as well a letter of introduction from your club and a copy of your official USGA handicap card. The lower your handicap, the more well known your club is, the better your chance of getting a tee time. Turnberry requires a handicap card from non-guests of the resort for play on the Ailsa Course. Carnoustie is a public course and does not require a letter of introduction or handicap card.

Once you get your tee times lined up, everything else will fall into place. I make a number of specific recommendations on places to stay in the pages that follow, but you could spend every night of the Grand Tour at an average Scottish bed-and-breakfast and have just as grand an experience—perhaps even better, as you might well meet more people like yourself, only with British accents. Traveling British golfers, by and large, leave the fancy hotels to foreigners.

After all, the game's the thing.

TURNBERRY

Turnberry Hotel
Attention: Golf Course Reservations
Maidens Road
Turnberry
Ayrshire KA26 9LT
Telephone: (655) 31000
Note: Preferred times and lower greens fees for guests of
the hotel.

PRESTWICK GOLF CLUB

The Secretary
2 Links Road
Prestwick
Ayrshire KA9 1QG
Telephone: (292) 77404
Note: No visitors on weekends.

ROYAL TROON GOLF CLUB

The Secretary
Craigend Road
Troon
Ayrshire KA10 6EP
Telephone: (292) 311555
Note: No visitors on weekends. Women visitors permitted
on Mondays, Wednesdays, and Fridays only.

MUIRFIELD

The Secretary
The Honourable Company of Edinburgh Golfers
Muirfield, Gullane
East Lothian EH31 2EG
Telephone: (620) 842123
Note: You'll need a letter of introduction from your club
and a handicap of no more than 18. Open to visitors on
Tuesdays, Thursdays, and Friday mornings only.

CARNOUSTIE CHAMPIONSHIP LINKS

Links Paradise
Carnoustie
Angus DD10 8SW
Telephone: (241) 53789

THE OLD COURSE AT ST. ANDREWS

The Secretary
Links Management Committee of St. Andrews
Golf Place
St. Andrews
Fife KY16 9JA
Telephone: (334) 75757

★

TURNBERRY

The RAF saved London during the Battle of Britain, but it destroyed golf at Turnberry.

That was a pretty fair trade-off, all things considered, but it wasn't until 1951 that the two courses at the world's first golf resort were reopened after having been transformed into an airbase, complete with eighteen-inch-thick concrete runways and assorted hangars scattered about the fairways. For a while its reopening had been touch and go, but in the end the breathtaking beauty of the site virtually mandated that golf be played there.

Of all the great Scottish links, the Ailsa Course at Turnberry commands what is unquestionably the most dramatic and spectacularly beautiful site. Across the water to the northwest are the high peaks of the Island of Arran, which lends its name to Turnberry's second course, a solid, gorse-lined track laid out inside Ailsa. To the east, the rolling fields and meadows of Carrick are as green as Ireland. And to the southwest, eleven miles from shore, looms the huge granite outcrop known as Ailsa Craig.

There's a saying in these parts that "If you cannot see Ailsa Craig, it's raining; if you can see Ailsa Craig, it's about to rain." They don't have a saying about the wind that I know of, but they need one. Of all the links on the rota of British Open venues, Turnberry is probably the most affected by weather, and that's saying a lot.

Remember the 1990 British Senior Open, the one Deane Beman almost won? It was on tape at some weird hour on ESPN, and it probably drew a smaller TV audience than their fishing show. But it was really great watching the likes of Player (the eventual winner), Palmer, and, yes, Beman trying to stand up in 35-miles-per-hour winds, smothering 120-yard drives into the rough, not reaching the par 4s, standing helplessly as approach shots were blown off the green. Those guys were playing the way *we* play! Or the way we play when there's no wind.

Turnberry's greatest golf moment? Die-hard members of the Greg Norman fan club might say it came at the British Open in 1986, when the Shark won his first—and to date his only—major. For everybody else, it was in 1977 at the first British Open ever played at the Ailsa Course, when Tom Watson shot 68-70-66-65 to beat Jack Nicklaus, who shot 68-70-66-66. It was only the greatest one-on-one duel in golf history.

Turnberry's Ailsa, quite the youngster as Scottish links go, still trails its peers in tradition and lore, although Watson-Nicklaus in the 1977 Open did make up a lot of ground in that department in one weekend. But with its substantial edge in sheer natural beauty, Turnberry definitely deserves a place in your rota. It's not a bad place to start your Grand Tour.

WHERE TO STAY

Turnberry, Troon, and Prestwick are so close together you could easily set up camp in one spot and play them all. From the Marine Hotel overlooking the eighteenth hole at Royal Troon, for example, it's just five miles south to Prestwick and another twenty or so down the coast to Turnberry. You could stay at the Marine, a big, luxurious, recently renovated seaside hotel; or for about half the price (and considerably fewer amenities) you could stay at the Piersland House Hotel, a nearby nineteenth-century manor house with fifteen pleasant rooms and a comfortable, low-key feel to it. Or if you're a fan of the great Scottish poet Robert Burns you could stay at one of three fine establishments in Ayr, his old stomping grounds: the Caledonian, the Pickwick, or the Savoy Park. But this is the traveling golfer's version of the Grand Tour, remember, so do yourself a favor and begin at the Turnberry Hotel.

TURNBERRY, HOTEL

Maidens Road
Turnberry
Ayrshire KA26 9LT
Telephone: (655) 31000

MARINE HOTEL

Crosbie Road
Troon
Ayrshire KA10 6HF
Telephone: (292) 312727

PIERSLAND HOUSE HOTEL

Craigend Road
Troon
Ayrshire KA10 6HD
Telephone: (292) 31227

CALEDONIAN HOTEL

Ayr
Ayrshire
Telephone: (292) 269331

PICKWICK HOTEL

Ayr
Ayshire
Telephone: (292) 260111

SAVOY PARK HOTEL

Ayr
Ayrshire
Telephone: (292) 266112

★

The Turnberry is a living, breathing testimonial to the finely honed appreciation of luxurious excess in the Edwardian Age. Perched high on a cliff overlooking its two golf courses and the seas beyond them, it was built at the turn of the century by the Glasgow & South-West Railway Company primarily to attract golfers up from the south on holiday. The huge marble bathrooms and the grand public rooms testify to an age gone by, while the health spa helps ease the pains of the one we're in. To top it off, the splendid dining room looks out over the sea and serves excellent food that is more than worthy of the view, and accompanies it with one of the most extensive and excellent wine lists this side of Robert Parker's next book. (P.S.: Don't tip the kilted bagpiper; it only encourages him.)

PRESTWICK

There hasn't been a British Open title contested at Prestwick since 1925, and there'll never be another. Time has passed it by. Today's touring pros would tear it apart like a pitch-and-putt. They'd never build a course like it today. Home to the first dozen British Opens in a row (1860–72) and a dozen more over the years, Prestwick is an anachronism, a throwback, a relic, a has-been.

And whatever you do, make sure you play it.

Never mind the commuter trains roaring along the east boundary of the course as you tee off on the first hole. Or the railway ties facing the Cardinal bunker on the third hole, the very same pieces of lumber that inspired Pete Dye. Or the huge sandy mounds called the Himalayas between you and the green on the fifth, a blind par 3 where you don't know whether you're on the green or in the pot bunkers surrounding it until you've climbed to the top. Or the many other oddities of this little swatch of history that hosted the first British Open the year before the American Civil War broke out.

Apropos of blind shots, here's what Pete Dye had to say a couple of years back in *Golf* magazine:

> Before I visited Prestwick, or any of the great Scottish courses, I was expounding to a group that included the great Tommy Armour about blind shots to fairways and greens. I said blind shots have no place on a great golf course. Mr. Armour looked at me. "Laddie boy," he said, "it shows how little you know about the game of golf, as a blind hole is only blind once to a golfer with a memory."

Armour went on to explain, Dye writes, that the anxiety created by a shot to a blind target is part of what makes a golf
course great. Prestwick, for that and many other reasons having to do with the soul of the Scottish game, is a great course,
one that any golfer with a memory will come to treasure.

ROYAL TROON

The 1989 British Open, the one Mark Calcavecchia snatched
out of Greg Norman's mitts on the fourth playoff hole, showed
Americans watching the championship on TV a very different
Royal Troon from the great links that appears on everybody's
Top 100 list of the world's great courses. No wind. No rain. And,
most extraordinary of all, no rough. A year-long killer drought
in western Scotland had nullified one of Royal Troon's historic
defenses, tall dune grass off the fairways thick enough to en-
snare small dogs.

But even at its most defenseless, Royal Troon gave a good
show, didn't it? Tom Watson turning back the clock in the first
three rounds . . . Norman making one of his characteristic
final-round charges in a major . . . and Calcavecchia hitting the
five-iron of his life on the fourth playoff hole to set up an eight-
foot birdie putt. Much ado was made out of Norman's play on
the last two playoff holes, in which he bogied seventeen after
hitting to the edge of the green and drove into a fairway bunker
320 yards away down the right side on eighteen. You heard all
the second-guessing: he should have putted from off the green
on seventeen, he should have hit a three-wood on eighteen,
once in the trap he should have played safely out, and so on.

But keep in mind that on that last day of the 1989 British
Open there were exactly five birdies made on eighteen—and
Calcavecchia, who played it twice, made two of them. Don't
think of the 1989 British Open at Royal Troon as yet another
major that Greg Norman lost; think of it as the first major that
Mark Calcavecchia won.

There was a lot of grumbling from many of the younger
American pros seeing Troon for the first time in 1989, a lot of
complaining that the greens and the fairways were too hard.
But it's a great course nonetheless, one chock full of history.
Known as Old Troon before receiving the Royal designation on
the occasion of its centennial in 1978, Troon by any name is
strong enough to humble the proud and punish the errant. In
1982, for example, it turned a young American golfer named

Bobby Clampett inside out. Clampett, who earlier had posted a 66 that still stands as the course record (shared with Sandy Lyle and Tom Purtzer), had almost lapped the field when he came to the sixth hole, a 577-yard par 5 that's longer than January when the wind's in your face. By the time he was finished, Clampett had taken eight strokes—and was finished. Has anybody heard much from Bobby Clampett since then?

Playing at Old Royal Troon won't shatter your career, but it will give you an appreciation of how demanding a simple-looking links can be, especially if there's a little wind, maybe a drop or two of rain, and the rough has grown thicker than a porcupine's hair.

You'll carry home with you memories of an easy, ego-building start . . . undulating fairways pocked with bunkers . . . a plethora of sand hills and heather and gorse . . . and the toughness of the incoming nine, from the Railway hole (the eleventh), where Jack Nicklaus once took a 10 in Open play, to the wicked Crosbie (the fifteenth), a 445-yard par 4 with more bumps than Gypsy Rose Lee on a narrow fairway pinched 200 yards out by fairway bunkers left and right. But what you'll remember most is the Postage Stamp.

At 123 yards, the eighth hole is the shortest on the course, and possibly the shortest on any course ever to host a major championship. Short but not sweet. Set into the side of a looming sandhill, the green is protected by deep, straight-faced bunkers in the front and on both sides. The bunkers are so deep that if you get into one, there's a better than even chance that your blast out will end up in the one on the other side. And so it goes, and goes. Many are the golfers over the years who have finished this hole with a ball in their pocket. Arnold Palmer didn't have that luxury in the 1973 British Open; he had to keep on hacking until he got to 7. Club selection depends on the wind; anything from pitching wedge to middle iron. Oh, and one more thing: Be sure to hit it straight. The green at Postage Stamp is relatively flat and quite long, but only about eight paces wide. That, in case you were wondering, is how the hole got its name.

MUIRFIELD

After you've licked the Postage Stamp one last time, toss your clubs in the boot and head east toward Edinburgh. Next stop:

Muirfield. It'll take a little less than three hours—or four, if you're as skittish as I am about driving on the left-hand side of the road. (By the way, when renting cars in the British Isles be sure and specify automatic drive. If you're right-handed and get a car with a stick shift, you'd better be prepared to become ambidextrous on the spot.)

Your destination is the Greywalls Hotel, an Edwardian establishment to which you must apply for a reservation at least nine months in advance to have a prayer of getting in.

GREYWALLS HOTEL

Muirfield
Gullane
East Lothian   EH31 2EG
Telephone: (620) 842144

Designed in British country style at the turn of the century by the noted architect Sir Edward Lutyens, Greywalls sports a walled garden designed by the every-bit-as-famous Gertrude Jekyll (no relation to the doctor). Greywalls has twenty-three rooms, small for a hotel but not shabby for a private home, which it once was. Sir Walter Scott fans will want a room at the front, for the views south to the Lammermuir Hills. Monty Python loyalists may prefer a room at the back, so they can go around making jokes about the Firth of Forth and the Fields of Fife, which they'll be able to see looking north. (Not the fields, really, but it sounds better than Hills of Fife, which is what you do see.) But as swell as the views, garden, comfortable rooms, and excellent service at Greywalls all are, the real reason for staying here is that it may help you get a tee time at the home course of the Honourable Company of Edinburgh Golfers, the world's oldest golf club.

The Hon Coy, as it's commonly referred to (though not to its face, and certainly not by colonists), was established in 1744, which makes it ten years more ancient than the Royal and Ancient. Since its founding, the Hon Coy has been synonymous with the socio-economic elite of Scotland. Its members decided over two centuries ago to cede jurisdiction in matters pertaining to golf governance to their junior colleagues of the

R&A, and to retain for themselves and their successors the governance of all other aspects of Scottish life. So far, it's worked out fine.

To play Muirfield, you must write well in advance. Be sure to give a number of alternative dates, if possible, because there's always this or that club match going on. Weekends are out. So are abject duffers (no handicaps above eighteen permitted), so don't mention yours if it's more than that or offer to show them any proof unless they ask. Do include a letter from your club president, if you belong to a club. And be prepared for a rebuff. In part because of the enormous number of requests, and in part because of its many club tournaments, Muirfield is the toughest private course in Scotland to get on.

That's where Greywalls comes in. Hang the views, garden, comfortable rooms, and service; what you're paying the big pounds for is a special arrangement the hotel has with the club that permits a limited number of its guests to play the course at certain times. *Now* you get the picture. It's called covering all bases, or would be if this were a book about baseball travel.

(If you manage to wrangle a tee time at Muirfield on your own and decide you want to save a king's ransom by staying at more modest digs, try the Open Arms Hotel (great name!) in nearby Dirleton or the Mallard (great duck jokes!) in even nearer-by Gullane.)

OPEN ARMS HOTEL

Main Street
Dirleton
East Lothian   EH39 5EG
Telephone: (620) 85241

MALLARD

East Links Road
Gullane
East Lothian   EH31 6PR
Telephone: (620) 843288

★

All your machinations will be well worth it. Frank Hannigan, former senior executive director of the USGA and now a columnist for *Golf* magazine, has this to say of the Hon Coy's home track: "Muirfield has everything desirable in golf—a fascinating mixture of holes, history, wind, stunning scenery and a great lunch."

The holes, history, wind, and scenery come in a fascinating package, one with the front nine unwrapping clockwise around the perimeter of the course, and the back nine running counterclockwise inside it. This gives whatever weather is around, and there's usually a lot, the opportunity to prey on you from all angles during the course of the round. Downwind on one hole becomes "In your face!" on another, with all sorts of sideswipes in between. The turf is held to be the best found on any links in the world, the bunkers as fiendishly placed as they come. No hills, no water, just rolling, rippling linksland. But unlike some of the older links, there's not a single blind shot at Muirfield.

"You can see where you are going and you get what you hit," says Jack Nicklaus, who believes Muirfield to be the fairest, best test of all the championship courses in the British Isles. He likes it so much he even named his Ohio home course Muirfield Village. "There's not a weak hole on the course," echoes Tom Watson. "That's something you could not say of the others."

That's good enough for me. I figure between them those two guys have seen enough to know.

EDINBURGH

If you take the Grand Tour seriously, you're not going to have a lot of time for casual tourism. You'll be eating, sleeping, and thinking golf in the odd minutes when you're not actually playing it. Call it full-stop immersion. Call it nuts. But call it what it is—an intense, focused period of time devoted utterly and absolutely to the game of golf in its ancestral home. If you're worried about how you're going to fill your days, then maybe you ought to think about one of those See-Europe-in-14-Days packages and postpone the Grand Tour until your mind is clear. The Grand Tour is about golf . . . period.

Except, of course, for the couple of days that you spend in Edinburgh.

One of the great capitals of European culture, Edinburgh is a must for the first-time traveler to Scotland, and a treasured friend to the veteran traveler who has come to appreciate its powerful charms. Noted as a center of literature, scholarship, and music for half a millennium, it is also an architectural and visual treasure.

After taking the guided tour of the Palace of Holyroodhouse, where Mary Queen of Scots once reigned, walk up the Royal Mile past St. Giles Cathedral and on to Edinburgh Castle. (This is not a good point to remember that you meant to read some Sir Walter Scott before leaving on vacation, so get started now.) After inspecting the Scottish royal jewels, cross through Princess Street Gardens down to the National Gallery of Scotland. It closes at 5:00, a perfect time for a pint of good Scottish ale, or maybe even two.

If it's summer, you'll have plenty of daylight left to wander through the narrow, cobblestoned streets and ponder the medieval gables and spires in the old part of town. Or, if a vacation isn't complete without some serious shopping, you can gasp at what the exchange rate has done to the purchasing power of the dollar in Burberry's and Scotch House, two fine stores opposite Waverly Station.

For three weeks in August the Edinburgh Festival transforms the town into a beehive of music, dance, and drama. The range and quality of the cultural offerings at this glorious international gathering are simply breathtaking. The British Tourist Authority (212-581-4700) will provide complete Festival schedule and ticket information. If you're there in August, don't miss it.

Among the better hotels are the Caledonian, an Edwardian grand dame at Princess Street and Lothian Road (225-2433); the Carlton Highland on North Bridge (556-7277); and the King James Thistle at 107 Leith Street (556-0111). Call the City of Edinburgh's tourist office near Wavery Station (557-1700) if you pop into town on the spur of the moment (say, when it's pouring cats and dogs at Muirfield). They'll find you a room at a good bed and breakfast if all the hotels are full.

Edinburgh is great for just walking around. It's not so large or complicated that you'll get lost or exhausted, and the variety and richness of its neighborhoods will enthrall you. In my view, this is what all cities ought to be like.

ST. ANDREWS

After playing Muirfield, head back toward Edinburgh. If you've decided to devote a day of your golf vacation to tourism, take it now. Edinburgh is a great city, rich in history and culture, as well as golf courses. Otherwise, loop around Edinburgh and take the Forth Bridge into Fife. Next stop: St. Andrews.

But not to play golf, not just yet. First you need to set up base camp and, if you have the luxury of time, give yourself a few days before you play to get the feel of the place. Back home it's perfectly acceptable to zoom into the parking lot three minutes before your tee time, make sure your shoes are tied, take a single practice swing, and give the ball a ride. Before you start launching your snap hooks and banana slices onto the hallowed fields of St. Andrews, you owe it to yourself to absorb some of the place's soul.

That means finding a place to stay in town. Rufflets, a few miles outside of St. Andrews, is a wonderful country hotel, and if you're an old St. Andrews veteran, it may be the lodging of preference. But for first-timers, I believe it's important to stay in the heart of the "Auld Grey Toon" so that it can rub off on you.

Looking down imperiously on the eighteenth fairway of the Old Course is Rusacks, a nineteenth-century hotel with a distinguished lineage and a fine, though somewhat stuffy, dining room. Recently renovated, Rusacks once catered to the carriage trade; it now houses the merely rich. Two rather more casual establishments, also located within a few paces of the

Old Course, are the Links Hotel and Scores Hotel. It comes down to a matter of mood and pocketbook.

There is even a case to be made for staying at the Old Course Golf and Country Club, namely that by staying there you would be spared having to look at it. A big, clunky modern structure

LINKS HOTEL

Golf Place
St. Andrews
Fife   KY16 9SP
Telephone: (334) 72059

SCORES HOTEL

The Scores
St. Andrews
Fife   KY16 9DS
Telephone: (334) 72451

RUSACKS HOTEL

Pilmour Links
St. Andrews
Fife   KY16 9QJ
Telephone: (334) 74321

RUFFLETS HOTEL

Strathkinnes Low Road
St. Andrews
Fife   KY16 9TX
Telephone: (334) 72594

OLD COURSE GOLF AND COUNTRY CLUB

Old Station Road
St. Andrews
Fife   KY16 9SP
Telephone: (334) 74371

★

plopped down alongside the fairway of the Road Hole, the Old Course Golf and Country Club—a misnomer if ever there was one—is as devoid of personality as St. Andrews is distinctive. But it does have the three things that any good piece of real estate must have: location, location, and location.

Believe it or not, St. Andrews has a few things going for it besides golf. It was once a great cathedral town, and it became a major battleground in the religious wars of the sixteenth and seventeenth centuries. Grand ruins and numerous historical markers testify to man's willingness to kill and destroy in the name of God. It is also a venerable university town, which gives it a life and vitality beyond golf.

But you're here for one purpose. And while it has something to do with religion, and a lot to do with higher learning, it's really about getting your mind ready to play the Old Course.

So you walk the streets where the greats of golf have walked, shop in Old Tom Morris's golf shop, browse through rare volumes about golf in local bookstores, eavesdrop on golf conversations at lunch in the Niblick Restaurant, hoist pints of honest ale in the old railroad stationmaster's house alongside the seventeenth fairway, now a pub frequented by caddies. You walk along Granny Clark's Wynd, a footpath that crosses the eighteenth and first fairways, and then on to the Himalayas, an eighteen-hole putting green whose bumps and dips warrant its name, hard by the second tee of the Old Course. You stroll onto the course itself in the evening after play has finished for the day, out to the 800-year-old footbridge over Swilcan Burn, look back at the Royal and Ancient clubhouse illuminated in moonlight, and let it all sweep over you.

It's almost time.

When to Go

All the stops on the Grand Tour of Scotland are going to be wall-to-wall in the prime summer months. Spring is a little better but a lot wetter. Your best bet is September through early October. You won't be able to play until 10:30 at night, the way you can in these climes in late June, but the relative tranquillity is well worth it.

★

CARNOUSTIE

But before you play the Old Course, play Carnoustie.

Do it because, as the editors of the English magazine *Golf World* have said, "It is a matter of some dissent among golfers as to which course is the best in Britain, but many devotees of the game believe Carnoustie to be the gem in the British golfing crown."

Do it for the experience of hitting a driver on a par 3 hole, as you'll surely have to do on the 248-yard sixteenth ("only" 215 from the regular tees) on a day when the wind is up.

Do it in honor of the "Wee Ice Mon," Ben Hogan, who captured Scotland's golfing heart with his courageous victory here in the 1953 British Open championship.

Do it because you'll never, ever see anything like Carnoustie back home.

Carnoustie is not pretty. Although it has trees, unlike most Scottish and Irish links, it feels barren and severe. In a guide to the championship courses of Scotland (published in the U.K. but not the U.S.A.), Sandy Lyle (with British writer Bob Ferrier doing the heavy lifting) calls Carnoustie "stern, forbidding, a Presbyterian test."

If ever you had second thoughts about plunking down a few pounds to hire a caddie, they are immediately dispelled on the tee box of the 395-yard first hole (377 yards from where you'll be standing) as you stare out onto a grass-covered moonscape of bumps, hollows, scrub bushes, sand bunkers, a clump of scraggly trees off to the left—and look in vain for the green you're supposed to drive toward. Your caddie gently points to a tall white pole that he says is standing directly behind the green. You take his word for it and bang away, then stride out onto a tract of land that looks like it would be more suitable for tank maneuvers than golf.

After playing it a few times, you realize that Carnoustie is, preeminently, a test of your ability to think on a golf course. A ridge or trap (or both) well short of a green that makes the flag behind it appear closer than it is. Masses of heather and gorse in front of a tee that mask the beginning of a fairway and make the carry seem longer than it is. An unseen hollow in front of a green that turns a short into a very short shot. Complex? You betcha. And also long. Carnoustie is 6,611 yards from the regular tees, 6,936 from the medal tees, and 7,200 (gulp!) from the tips of the championship tees. Every hole has a line—your caddie knows it if you don't—but every line has subtle variations, depending on what the wind will let you do.

Yes, Carnoustie is a test, and a darned hard one. By comparison, the SATs were a snap.

Carnoustie is also a test of courage, although perhaps you won't be called on to demonstrate as much as Ben Hogan displayed in 1953 at the sixth hole.

A 529-yard par 5, the sixth hole at Carnoustie has two big traps right in the middle of the fairway and an out-of-bounds fence that starts a few feet off the tee box and runs all the way down the left side of the hole. The hole plays into the wind, so driving the center traps is next to impossible, even for the biggest hitters. The safest route is down the right side, but the farther right you go the more the second shot has to be angled back diagonally across the fairway toward the OB fence in order to set up a clear shot to a green that's protected front-right by sand, rough, and water. Taking the drive down the left side makes for a far easier second shot, but it's also far, far riskier because of the fence hugging the fairway on the left. The gap between the center bunkers and the OB left is just too narrow, no wider than an alley. Driving down that alley, particularly when there's any kind of wind up, is suicidal.

Maybe, but on the final day of the 1953 championship that alley led Ben Hogan straight to immortality.

Keep in mind that Hogan had been an inveterate hooker through the early part of his career; he didn't become a top player until he conquered his tendency to hit everything left. But the hook was always there, lurking, and when his game did suffer a breakdown now and then (yes, it happened on rare occasions to Hogan, too), his old nemesis always resurfaced.

So what did he do at the sixth hole at Carnoustie with the British Open title on the line? He started his drive left of the OB fence and fades it back into the narrow alley between the fence and the center traps. Twice. (They played thirty-six holes the final day back then.) Both times it set up direct second shots to the green from the left, and both times he birdied what is perhaps the greatest par 5 in the world to win the British Open.

When you play Carnoustie, take a second at the sixth tee to look down the fence line and try to imagine what Hogan must have felt like standing there in the same spot. Ask your caddie about it. That day four decades ago made such an impression on Scottish golfers that even the youngest caddies know the story by heart. ("They say his second drive landed on the mark made by his first," my caddie told me.) Try to imagine taking that shot, twice, under those conditions, and you will know this one thing for sure: it took some kind of balls.

No wonder they still call it Hogan's Alley.

BACK TO THE HOME OF GOLF

Take the long way home.

After crossing back into Fife from Dundee, pick a local road heading due south and follow it to the coast of the Firth of Forth. Then turn left and follow the coast road east through the tiny seaside villages of Elie, St. Monance, Pittenweem, Anstruther, and Crail. This route will bring you back into St. Andrews from the east on a narrow country road that looks down on the Auld Grey Toon below. Time it so that you arrive in the later afternoon, but before dusk.

Wherever you're staying, make a beeline to the Old Course Golf and Country Club and go up to the bar on the top floor. Order a drink and watch dusk settle in over the Old Course spread out below. Make a mental note to take the club back low and slow. Light dinner and early to bed.

Tomorrow's the day.

THE OLD COURSE

What's the big deal?

You will—I guarantee it—be disappointed the first time you play the Old Course.

Everyone is.

The main reason, of course, is that nothing could possibly live up to the expectations you'll bring with you to the first tee. The oldest, most famous golf course in the world. The Royal and Ancient clubhouse immediately behind you. The Home of Golf. The dream of all golfers come true. Bobby Jones, Sammy Snead, Tony Lema, and Jack Nicklaus in the foursome just ahead of you.

That's a heavy bag to tote.

You'll also play terribly. Everyone does the first time at the Old Course. (Almost everyone, that is. Mark Calcavecchia shot 68-67-69 in his first three rounds of competitive play at the Old Course during the 1989 Dunhill Cup matches. He should have saved some of those shots for the 1990 British Open at St. Andrews, when he didn't make the cut.)

The main reason you'll score poorly on your first round at the Old Course is that much of the time you won't have a clue where you're supposed to hit the ball. From the second through the seventh, and then from the twelfth through the sixteenth, you could stand on the tee for an hour and not figure out the best line. What you'll see is an expanse of bumps, mounds, dunes, ridges, bushes, sand, and grass. But not a lot that looks much like a fairway.

"Where's the golf course?" asked former U.S. Amateur champion Chris Patton on his first trip to St. Andrews in 1990. At the time he was standing beside the Royal and Ancient clubhouse looking out over a big, well-mown lawn bisected by a footpath, and he wasn't kidding. Now you know, Chris—and you also know that beyond that big lawn, which is the fairway shared by the first and eighteenth holes, the golf course gets even harder to find. (Patton, too, missed the 1990 British Open cut.)

Robert Trent Jones on the Old Course*

The first few rounds a golfer plays on the Old Course are not likely to alter his first estimate that it is vastly overrated. He will be puzzled to understand the rhapsodies that have been composed about the perfect strategic positioning of its trapping, the subtle undulations of its huge double greens, the endless tumbling of its fairways, which seldom give him a chance to play a shot from a level stance. Then as he plays on, it begins to soak in through his pores that whenever he plays a fine shot it is rewarded; whenever he doesn't play the right shot he is penalized in proportion, and whenever he thinks out his round hole for hole, he scores well. This is the essence of strategic architecture; to encourage initiative, reward a well-played, daring stroke more than a cautious one, and yet to insist that there must be planning and honest self-appraisal behind the daring.

*Quoted in *Golf in Scotland and Ireland* (London: Sackville Books).

★

As you have no doubt deduced by now, a caddie is absolutely essential at the Old Course if you want to preserve your sanity and have any fun at all. Trust him. If he says hit it left when right looks best to you, do your best to hit it left. If he says six when you're thinking eight, take the six and put a good swing on it. He'll introduce you to bunkers named Cheape's, Cartgate, Students, and Coffins on the way out, and to others named Strath, the Beardies, Sutherland, and the Principal's Nose on the way in. Quite likely, you'll develop a personal relationship with some of them, but fewer if you listen to his warnings. Your caddie will try to keep you out of Hell and the Valley of Sin and point the way to the Elysian Fields. He will show you the line on 100-foot putts, congratulate you on a good shot even if all it means is saving bogey, and do everything in his power to keep your nerves steady when a shot goes crooked. Being a Scot, your caddie probably won't say all that much; but when he does talk, you listen.

Even with the help of a good caddie, you'll play that first round at the Old Course in a fog. My first time it wasn't until about the fifteenth hole that it dawned on me that most of the holes on the Old Course (fourteen, to be exact) share double greens. You'll barely take notice of how close Swilcan Burn is to the first green the first time you cross it . . . Hole o'Cross (Out) and Hole o'Cross (In) will blur together . . . you won't have any sense of where the bend is in the shepherd's staff until you look at a map of the course later.

One thing you will certainly remember clearly is the Road Hole, because it's simply the toughest, most distinctive, most historic par 4 in the history of golf. It's where the correct line for your drive is over a facsimile of an old railway shed about seventy-five yards in front of the tee. It's where Nick Faldo laid up four times in the 1990 British Open rather than risk hitting onto the road behind the green or into the Road bunker that eats into the front left of the green. It's where Tom Watson lost a chance to win a sixth British Open by doing the former. It's where Japanese pro Tommy Nakajima took four shots to extricate himself after doing the latter—and gave the cruelly steep bunker its second name, the Sands of Nakajima.

You will also remember crossing the bridge on the Home Hole, striding up the fairway toward the Royal and Ancient, and walking in front of Old Tom Morris's shop and onto the eighteenth green of the most famous course in the world, where Jack Nicklaus, in a totally uncharacteristic show of emotion after knocking in a putt to win the 1970 British Open by a stroke, threw his putter high into the air and damned near brained Doug Sanders.

Sometime later, in a few days or a few months, the fog will lift, and the rest of the Old Course will come back to you, a hole here, a hole there. Like an amnesia victim, you'll reconstruct your round, bit by bit, until finally your memory of it will be strong and true enough to start planning what you will do differently the next time you play it.

Bobby Jones gets the last word on the Old Course. The first time he played it was in the 1921 British Open, when he picked up his ball in disgust at the eleventh hole after taking five shots and still not reaching the cup on one of the world's greatest par 3s. Nine years later, he won the British Amateur at the Old Course on the way to completing the most extraordinary achievement in the history of golf, the Grand Slam: the Amateur and Open Championships of America and Great Britain in one season. I guess that qualifies him as an expert:

> The more I studied the Old Course, the more I loved it; and the more I loved it, the more I studied it. So that I came to feel that it was, for me, the most favorable meeting ground possible for an important contest. I felt that my knowledge of the course enabled me to play it with patience and restraint until she might exact her toll from my adversary who might treat her with less respect and understanding.

ABOUT THE AUTHOR

A NATIVE TEXAN, GLEN WAGGONER WAS PERFECT-ing *his banana slice at Stevens Park Municipal Golf Course in Dallas at about the same time that Lee Trevino, across town at Tenison Park Municipal Golf Course, was fine-tuning his power fade. The author was graduated from Southern Methodist University, paving the way for Payne Stewart just thirteen years later. Before embarking on his career as a college professor, Waggoner lived for two years in Spain but never met Seve Ballesteros, who was then starting out in golf as a caddy. The author spent five years at the University of Michigan and twelve years at Columbia University during which time he never touched a golf club. The layoff didn't help, because when he returned to the game after leaving the academic world in 1984 to become an editor and writer at* Esquire *magazine, the slice was still there. He has written about golf, travel, cooking, and fashion for* Esquire *and various other magazines. He has coedited (with Robert Sklar) five editions of* Rotisserie League Baseball *and is one of the founding fathers of the game. He is also a coauthor of two other books—* Esquire Etiquette *(with Kathleen Moloney); and* Baseball by the Rules *(with Kathleen Moloney and Hugh Howard). For the past two decades, he and his wife, Sharon, have lived on the Upper West Side of Manhattan, the only community of one million-plus inhabitants in America without a single golf course.*